Dangerous Weather

DROUGHTS

Revised Edition

Michael Allaby

ILLUSTRATIONS by Richard Garratt

✔®

Facts On File, Inc.

For Ailsa
—M.A.

To my late wife, Jen, who gave me inspiration
and support for almost 30 years
—R.G.

Droughts, Revised Edition

Copyright © 2003, 1998 by Michael Allaby

Facts On File, Inc.
132 West 31st Street
New York NY 10001

Library of Congress Cataloging-in-Publication Data

Allaby, Michael.
   Droughts/Michael Allaby; illustrated by Richard Garratt.—Rev. ed.
     p. cm.
   Includes bibliographical references and index.
   ISBN 0-8160-4793-6 (acid-free paper)
   1. Droughts. I. Garratt, Richard. II. Title.
QC929.24 .A45 2003
551.57′73—dc21   2002013035

Facts On File books are available at special discounts when purchased in bulk quantities for businesses, associations, institutions, or sales promotions. Please call our Special Sales Department in New York at (212) 967-8800 or (800) 322-8755.

You can find Facts On File on the World Wide Web at
http://www.factsonfile.com

Text design by Erika K. Arroyo
Cover design by Nora Wertz
Illustrations by Richard Garratt

Printed in the United States of America

VB Hermitage 10 9 8 7 6 5 4 3 2 1

This book is printed on acid-free paper.

Contents

Preface

What is a drought?

Ten years had passed since the old Ethiopian regime was overthrown and the marxist government installed. They were 10 years of conflict, due mainly to the desire for independence in Eritrea and Tigre, two of the country's provinces. In other parts of the country, guerrilla groups were fighting government forces. War with neighboring Somalia over the disputed province of Ogaden had continued intermittently for eight years and showed little sign of ending. As always, the wars had driven villagers from their homes and farmers had abandoned their fields. Communications had been disrupted. Trucks carrying food and other essential supplies might or might not set out, and if they did, there was no guarantee they would reach their destinations.

The situation was bad, but another factor made it very much worse. Drought had been afflicting much of the continent for four years. The fields the farmers abandoned were empty. The ground was parched, the soil either baked hard or reduced to powder. There was no rain, so there were no crops.

This was a remote corner of the world. Neighboring countries were concerned, and the United Nations was doing its best to help, but ordinary people in America and Europe knew nothing until a BBC television crew on their way to a job elsewhere broke their journey and were appalled at what they saw. The story they told, and the pictures with which they illustrated it, flashed around the world. The year was 1984, the country Ethiopia, and the pictures showed the condition of refugees who had walked across the devastated landscape for days or weeks to reach a camp where there might be food. They were weakened by starvation and sickness. Children were dying. Nearly 8 million people were affected in Ethiopia, and about 1 million died. Drought returned in 1991 and again in 2000. By the end of 2000, the charities distributing aid estimated that three-quarters of the crops had been lost, and 90 percent of the cattle had died.

That is what drought can do.

The Sahel drought

By May, the land across a belt in Africa along the southern edge of the Sahara is parched. Those plants that survive are brown and withered after the long, dry winter months. Then, in June, the rains return. They are monsoon rains (see page 147), heavy and prolonged. Soon rivers flow through what had been dried beds. Everywhere seeds hidden in the soil during the dry season germinate. Shrubs and trees produce leaves. The landscape turns green. Nomadic peoples drive their herds and flocks toward the burgeoning pasture, and farmers sow their crops. It is a farming year that must end in later October. That is when the monsoon rains falter and cease, and the dry season returns. This belt stretches across all or part of Senegal, Mauritania, Mali, Burkina Faso, Niger, Nigeria, Chad, and Sudan. It is called the Sahel.

For a few years in the 1960s, the monsoon rains were heavier than usual and prospects for the Sahel farmers seemed promising. Then, in 1968 and 1969, the rains were light and in 1970 they did not come at all. That year no rain fell, and rain did not fall again until 1973. Even then the rain was sparse. There was no rain in 1974 and another light monsoon in 1975. Since then, the monsoons have been erratic, good in some years and poor in others.

This was the Sahel drought, a period of five years, from 1968 to 1973, during which rainfall was very low or, during the worst years of 1972 and most of 1973, no rain fell at all. By the time it was over, perhaps as many as 200,000 people and 4 million cattle had died.

American drought

It is not only Africa that suffers from droughts. In 2001 at least 50,000 people in El Salvador faced the prospect of hunger, because drought had destroyed their corn, bean, and other crops. The drought affected about 1.5 million people in Central America, but it was in El Salvador that its effect was most severe.

While the eastern United States endured blizzards early in 1996, in Kansas, Oklahoma, and Texas, farmers were being forced to sell cattle for a fraction of their usual value because they could not feed them. The winter wheat crop failed for lack of rain and there was very little grass. Between October 1995 and May 1996, 3.7 inches of rain fell in San Antonio, Texas. The average rainfall for those eight months is 15.8 inches. The drought was so severe it brought fears of a return to the conditions of the Dust Bowl years (see the section "The Dust Bowl," page 136).

Defining drought

Drought is not a word with a precise definition. Three weeks without rain can be enough to trigger a drought emergency in Britain. In other countries no one talks of a drought until several rainless months have passed. A drought is simply a period during which rainfall is markedly lower than the average for that time of year in that place, and consequently water is in such short supply that domestic and industrial users, farmers, and wildlife are affected.

The most obvious effect arises from the lack of water itself. Plants wilt, animals die from thirst, and crops fail. There is a secondary effect, however, which brings more immediate dangers. When vegetation has withered and dried out, the merest spark may be enough to set it ablaze as a forest, bush, or grass fire that can spread rapidly. Early in 1996 the dry conditions led to forest fires in New Mexico, Arizona, and Colorado, and there was even fire in Alaska, fueled by moss on the forest floor and fanned by winds gusting to 25 MPH (40 km/h). There was so much smoke in Anchorage that officials issued an air quality alert.

Wildfires are terrifying—and common at the end of a long, dry summer. In August and September 2001 fires raged through forests and grasslands in California, Idaho, Montana, Nevada, Oregon, Utah, Washington, and Wyoming. Some were big. The fire near Weimar, California, covered 2,000 acres (810 ha) and one to the west of Yosemite National Park covered 11,500 acres (4,650 ha)

The firefighters do their best to contain the fires, but in the end it is usually the onset of autumn rains that extinguishes them. People adjust to the climate where they live, even when they face a seasonal risk of fire. They experience difficulties only when the weather departs from its usual pattern. Ordinary weather may be good or bad, but it is always tolerable for those used to it. It is extreme weather that brings hardship and danger. Drought is one kind of extreme weather, and it can and does happen anywhere.

Introduction

Several years have passed since the first edition of this book was published. Much has happened during those years and the decision to update the book for a second edition gives me a welcome opportunity to report at least some of them. In doing so, I have substantially altered, expanded, and in some places rewritten the original text.

There have been more droughts, of course. The 2002 drought in the United States was especially severe, but there is a drought in some part of the world almost every year. Drought is never far away and no matter how the climates of the world may change in years to come, there is little chance that they will disappear. Indeed, they could become worse. Severe though some of the droughts of recent years have been, they were mild compared with droughts in previous centuries, and droughts that last for decades could happen again.

Climate research has also intensified in recent years. Concern over the possibility that we may be altering the global climate has stimulated funding agencies to increase the resources available for evaluating the likelihood of global warming and its consequences. If we are to understand the extent of this threat—if it is a threat—scientists need to learn much more about the ways the Sun, atmosphere, and oceans interact to produce our day-to-day weather. New discoveries are now being made at an unprecedented rate and, although there is still a long way to go before the global climate is fully understood, we are learning more about it almost every day. This new edition takes account of the most recent relevant findings.

Updating the text has also given me an opportunity to expand it in order to provide more detailed explanations. I have added several new chapters. Some concern the geography of deserts ("Where the deserts are" and "West Coast deserts"). "Climate cycles and oscillations" describes the ways climates change for entirely natural reasons—reasons that have nothing to do with our emissions of greenhouse gases. I have also added two chapters about life in deserts ("Life near the poles" and "Peoples of the desert").

I have retained the use of sidebars to display detailed explanations or interesting items of information without interrupting the main flow of the text. This edition contains many more sidebars than there were in the first edition. These explain concepts from atmospheric science, such as adiabatic cooling and warming, potential temperature, lapse rates, and the intertropical convergence and equatorial trough, and also biological processes. The "biological" boxes include items on the camel and how it is able to thrive in the desert, how plants and animals cope with severe cold, what happens to an animal during hibernation, the different paths of photosynthesis, and osmosis.

Measurements are given in familiar units, such as pounds, feet, miles, and degrees Fahrenheit, throughout the book, but in each case I have added the metric or scientific equivalent. All scientists now use standard international units of measurement. These may be unfamiliar, so I have added them, with their conversions, as an appendix.

The first edition contained no suggestions for further reading. These have been added in this edition. You will find all the sources of further information at the end of the book. The sources include a number of books that you may find useful, but a much larger number of web addresses. If you have access to a computer, these will allow you to learn more about droughts and about climate generally, quickly and free of charge.

We have decided to omit the photographs from the first edition and instead to increase the number of diagrams and maps. These provide more useful information than photographs of such subjects as dust storms, withered plants, and dead cattle. My friend and colleague Richard Garratt has drawn all of the illustrations. As always, I am deeply grateful to him for his skill in translating my crude drawings into such accomplished artwork.

I am grateful, too, to Frank K. Darmstadt, my editor at Facts On File, for his hard work, cheerful encouragement, and patience.

If this "new, improved" edition of *Droughts* encourages you to pursue your study of the weather further, it will have achieved its aim and fulfilled my highest hopes for it. I hope you enjoy reading the book as much as I have enjoyed writing it for you.

— Michael Allaby
Tighnabruaich
Argyll, Scotland
www.michaelallaby.com

WHEN THE RAINS FAIL

Where the deserts are

Droughts can happen anywhere, but this simple statement tells us nothing about what constitutes a drought. It can mean anything from a couple of weeks without rain to several years. At Arica, in northern Chile, an average of 0.03 inch (0.75 mm) of rain fell every year over a period of 59 years. The town of Iquique, to the south of Arica, once went four years with no rain at all. In July of the fifth year there was a shower in which 0.6 inch (15 mm) of rain fell. At In Salah, in central Algeria, on average there is one shower—often a heavy one—every 10 years. The average rainfall there is 0.6 inch (15.2 mm) a year. The map of North Africa shows where In Salah is located.

In Salah is in the Sahara, which is the biggest desert in the world. Arica and Iquique are in the Atacama Desert, which is much smaller than the Sahara but even drier. There are parts of the Atacama where decades pass without even a light shower of rain. Not surprisingly, these places have no names because no one has ever lived there. There are no plants of any kind. The map shows the location of the Atacama Desert, and of the towns of Arica and Iquique.

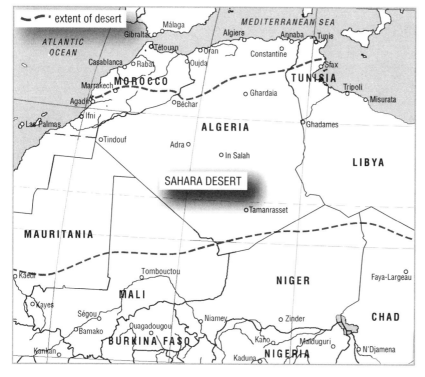

The Sahara, northern Africa.

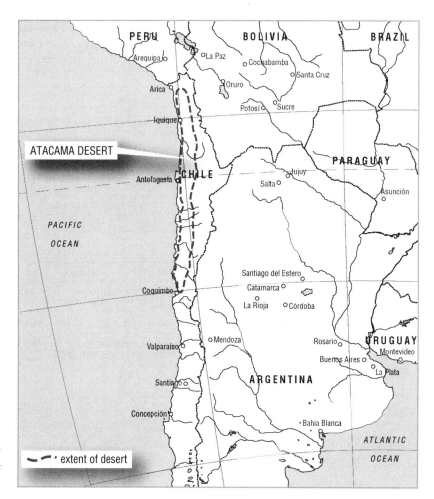

Atacama Desert, which lies along the coast of Chile.

There is a striking difference between the Sahara and the Atacama Desert. The Sahara borders the Mediterranean Sea and the North Atlantic Ocean, but it is a huge area, most of which is a long way from the sea. The Atacama, on the other hand, comprises a narrow coastal strip bordering the South Pacific Ocean. The Namib Desert, in Namibia, southwestern Africa, is a desert similar to the Atacama and almost as dry. The Sahara is a subtropical desert, its climate resulting from the way air circulates between the equator and the Tropics. The Atacama and Namib are West Coast deserts, produced by a different climatic regime.

Deserts where you shiver

When we hear the word *desert*, the picture that springs to mind is of vast expanses of sand dunes and a pitiless Sun blazing from a clear blue sky. We think of unbearable heat and raging thirst with no water within miles.

The interior of the Sahara is like that, and so is the Atacama. The image we carry in our minds is derived from these and other hot deserts. Those are the deserts that are featured in many adventure stories and movies, although it is only during the middle part of the day that the deserts are so hot. Once the Sun has set, the ground rapidly loses the heat it absorbed by day, and nights can be very cold. The box on page 8 explains why.

In July, which is the hottest month, the average temperature at In Salah is 98°F (37°C) and in December, the coldest month, it is 57°F (14°C). Kashi is a town in the Xinjiang Uygur Autonomous Region of China, where the average annual rainfall is 2.5 inches (63.5 mm), spread fairly evenly through the year, the wettest months receiving about 0.3 inch (7.6 mm). Kashi lies inside a desert, but not a hot desert like the Sahara. The average temperature in the hottest month, July, is 78°F (25.6°C), although it has been known to reach almost 90°F (32°C). January is the coldest month, with an average temperature of 21°F (–6°C), but a minimum of 12°F (–11°C). As the map shows, Kashi lies in the Takla Makan Desert.

The Takla Makan is a different kind of desert. It looks much the same as the Sahara, with vast areas of shifting sand dunes where no plants can grow, and in the center it is at least as dry, but it is much colder. Kashi is about 4,300 feet (1,310 m) above sea level in the foothills of the mountains, where it receives a little rain from air that has crossed the mountains. The Tarim Basin at the center of the desert is much lower. Air entering the basin has lost any moisture it might once have held. In some years it does not rain at all.

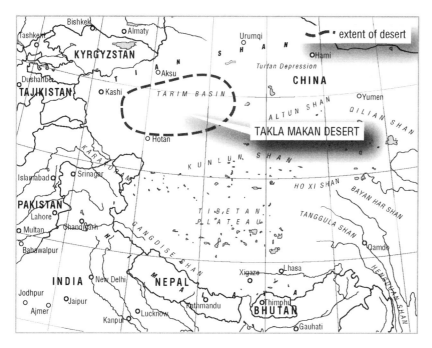

Takla Makan Desert.
located in western China.

Lying to the east of the Takla Makan, the Gobi Desert is better known. It is also less severe. The central part of the desert receives up to two inches (50 mm) of rain a year and most of it supports sparse vegetation. It is only the southeastern part that receives hardly any rain at all. Despite this, there are no towns in the Gobi Desert. Ulan Bator (or Ulaanbaatar), which is shown on the map, is the capital of Mongolia. It is a thriving city, but it does not lie inside the desert.

South America has a desert comparable to the Gobi, though not so dry. The Patagonian Desert, covering the whole of Argentina to the east of the Andes and south of latitude 39° S, is the largest desert in either North or South America. Its area is about 300,000 square miles (777,000 km²). The average rainfall is less than five inches (127 mm) a year.

The Takla Makan, Gobi, Patagonian, and other deserts like them are isolated from the oceans. The Takla Makan is in the center of Eurasia and surrounded by high mountains. Tibet lies to its south and the Himalayas are on the southern side of the Tibetan Plateau. Air approaching the Patagonian Desert must cross the Andes, losing its moisture as it does so. These are continental deserts.

Deserts full of water

Gobi Desert, which occupies a plateau surrounded by mountains.

It can come as a surprise to learn that some deserts are cold and it may be an even greater surprise to learn that the driest desert on Earth is covered by water to an average depth of 6,900 feet (2,100 m). The water is frozen,

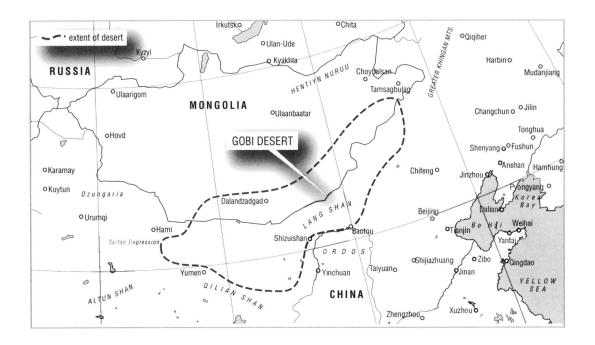

of course, and it never melts, so gradually, over millions of years, the ice grows steadily thicker, even though the amount added to it every year is extremely small. Near the South Pole, at the center of the ice sheet covering most of eastern Antarctica, an average of slightly more than 0.1 inch (2.5 mm) of precipitation falls in a year. Almost all of it falls in February, although a little—less than 0.05 inch (1.3 mm)—falls in January, October, and December.

It falls as snow, of course, and the depth is given after the snow has been melted. This is necessary because different types of snow trap varying quantities of air, so some form much thicker layers than others. Melting the snow makes it possible to compare them. One-tenth of an inch of water is probably equivalent to approximately one inch (25 mm) of fresh snow.

Antarctica is the coldest of all the continents and the South Pole is the coldest part of Antarctica. In the middle of summer (December in the Southern Hemisphere) the average temperature is between –15°F (–26°C) and –21°F (–29°C), although it has been known to rise as high as 8°F (–13°C). The difference is not between daytime and nighttime temperatures, because there is no night during the Antarctic summer. Temperatures in Antarctica reach their lowest soon after the autumn equinox, then remain fairly constant through the winter. This is called a *coreless winter*, and Antarctica is the only place on Earth where it happens. The winter temperature (when the Sun never rises above the horizon) ranges between –69°C (–56°C) and a distinctly chilly –81°F (–63°C), but can fall as low as –117°F (–83°C).

Like Antarctica, Greenland (also called Kalaallit Nunaat) also has a dry climate. Mountain chains run down the eastern and western coasts. Behind them, the center of the country is a high plateau covered by an ice sheet with an average thickness of 5,000 feet (1,525 m). At the center of the ice sheet, the average temperature is about 13°F) (–10.6°C) in summer and –53°F (–47°C) in winter. The annual precipitation over the ice sheet averages about 0.3 inch (8 mm) a year—equivalent to about 3 inches (76 mm) of snow. This makes the climate of Greenland only slightly moister than that of central Antarctica. Both are drier than In Salah and much drier than the Takla Makan Desert. It is hardly surprising that no one lives permanently in central Greenland; all the towns are on the coast.

There are deserts at the poles, deserts in the center of continents, deserts along the western coasts of continents, and deserts in the subtropics. Deserts are very widespread. They cover one-fifth of the land surface of the world, although only 8 percent of the surface is so dry that no plants can grow. The map on page 7 shows where these deserts are located.

What makes a desert?

Deserts are places that receive very little rain or snow, although the air in West Coast deserts is often very moist and fogs are common there. Some deserts are hot, some cool, and some extremely cold.

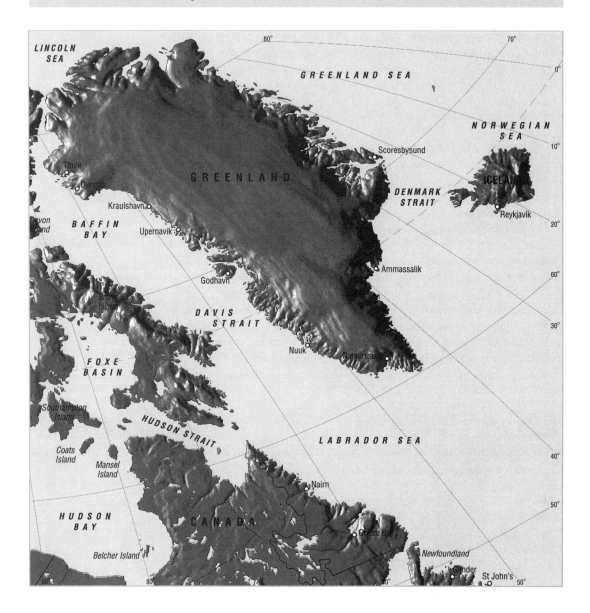

Greenland. the center of which is uninhabited.

What matters is not so much the amount of precipitation (rain, snow, hail, and any other water that reaches the ground from the sky) that a place receives, but the amount of moisture that penetrates the soil and comes within the reach of plant roots. Plants will thrive where the soil is moist. Such a place is not a desert. Water will penetrate the soil if the rate at which it falls exceeds the rate at which it evaporates from the surface.

Obviously, the actual rate of evaporation depends on the amount of precipitation. Water cannot evaporate from the ground unless it fell to the ground first. Consequently, any measure of actual evaporation is meaningless in a region with a dry climate.

The alternative is to measure the *potential evaporation*, which is the amount of water that *would* evaporate from the surface if the supply of water was unlimited and the surface was permanently wet. This can be measured very simply using an evaporation pan, which is a container with an open top and marks down the side to calibrate its depth, rather like some swimming pools. The drawing shows what it is like. When it is filled with water precisely to one of the marks, the water surface is exposed to the air. Some time later the water level in the pan is noted. The fall in the level indicates the amount of water that has evaporated. How often the pan is checked depends on the rate of evaporation—the faster the water evaporates, the more frequently the level needs to be checked. If necessary, more water is added from time to time and the addition recorded. A rain or snow gauge is set somewhere nearby. It is used over a long period, ideally of many years, to determine the average amount of precipitation that falls in each month and, from that, the average annual precipitation. You can measure the potential evaporation near your own home.

If the amount of water that evaporates from an open surface in the course of a year is greater than the average annual precipitation, the ground will be dry, because water will evaporate as fast as it falls. The area is then a desert, but the amount of precipitation and rate of evaporation

The world's deserts are found in the subtropics, in the interior of continents, along the western coasts of continents, and over the polar ice caps.

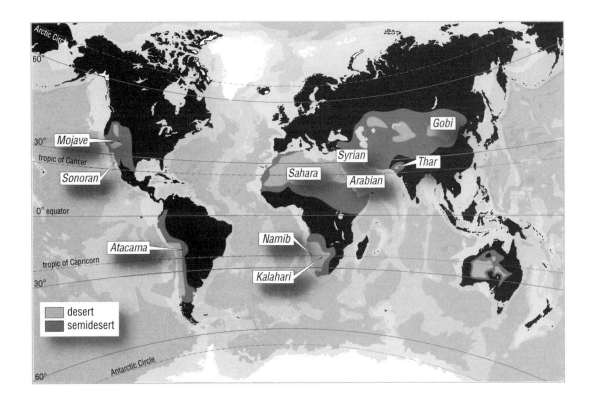

Specific heat capacity and blackbodies

When a substance is heated, it absorbs heat energy and its temperature rises. The amount of heat it must absorb in order to raise its temperature by one degree varies from one substance to another, however. The ratio of the heat applied to a substance to the extent of the rise in its temperature is called the *specific heat capacity* for that substance. It is measured in calories per gram per degree Celsius (cal g^{-1} °C^{-1}) or in the scientific units of joules per kilogram per kelvin (J kg^{-1} K^{-1}; 1K = 1°C = 1.8°F). Specific heat capacity varies slightly according to the temperature, so when quoting the specific heat capacity of a substance it is customary to specify the temperature or temperature range to which this refers.

Pure water has a specific heat capacity of 1 cal g^{-1} °C^{-1} (4,180 J kg^{-1} K^{-1}) at 59°F (15°C). This means that at 59°F (15°C) one gram of water must absorb one calorie of heat in order for its temperature to rise by one degree Celsius (or 0.56 cal to raise its temperature by 1°F). Seawater at 17°C (62.6°F) has a specific heat capacity of 0.94 cal g^{-1} °C^{-1} (3,930 J kg^{-1} K^{-1}).

The desert surface consists of granite rock and sand. At temperatures between 68°F (20°C) and 212°F (100°C), the specific heat capacity of granite is 0.19–0.20 cal g^{-1} °C^{-1} (800–840 J kg^{-1} K^{-1}). Within the same temperature range, the specific heat capacity of sand is 0.20 cal g^{-1} °C^{-1} (800 J kg^{-1} K^{-1}). These values are typical for most types of rock.

Water has a specific heat capacity about five times that of rock. This means water must absorb five times more heat than rock to produce a similar rise in temperature. It is why water warms up so much more slowly than sand and rock. Visit the beach on a really hot day in summer and by lunchtime the sand will be so hot you have to run across it to avoid hurting your bare feet, but when

needed to produce a desert vary from place to place. Less water evaporates from a polar ice sheet than from rocks in the Sahara, because the temperature is lower. Consequently, for an ice sheet to have a desert climate, it must receive less precipitation than would be needed to produce a desert nearer the equator.

There is a precipitation limit, however, below which a desert is likely to form anywhere, regardless of the temperature. Anywhere that receives less than 10 inches (250 mm) of precipitation a year is probably a desert.

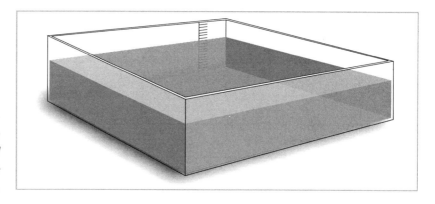

Evaporation pan. Measurements of the fall in the water level are used to calculate the rate of evaporation.

you splash into the water, it is refreshingly cool. The reason for this is the difference in the specific heat capacities of water and sand.

In the desert, the rock and sand, with a low specific heat capacity, heats up rapidly. By the middle of the day it is extremely hot. Specific heat capacity works both ways, though. Substances that heat quickly also cool down again quickly. The molecular configuration that confers a rapid response to absorbed heat also ensures the heat cannot be long retained once the external supply shuts down.

The ground radiates its heat into the sky. If there were clouds, they would absorb much of this heat and re-radiate it, effectively trapping heat and keeping the air warm. But the desert sky is cloudless and the desert behaves much like a blackbody. A blackbody is any object that absorbs all the radiation falling on it, then re-radiates the whole of the absorbed energy, but at a longer wavelength. There is no such thing as a perfect blackbody (some energy is inevitably lost), but the Sun and Earth come close. The wavelength of the radiation from a blackbody is inversely proportional to the temperature: the higher the temperature, the shorter the wavelength.

During the day, the desert rock and sand absorb heat from the Sun. Their temperature rises and they re-radiate their energy into the sky, but at the same time they continue to absorb solar radiation. The balance between the energy they absorb and the energy they radiate allows the surface temperature to rise to a peak in the early afternoon, after which it remains steady. Then, as the Sun sinks toward the horizon, the balance starts to shift. Radiation from the surface remains constant, but less solar energy is absorbed. The surface starts to cool, but slowly. Once the Sun sinks below the horizon and darkness falls, there is no more sunshine for the desert to absorb, but neither is there anything to halt its blackbody radiation, which continues. The surface temperature then plummets. Desert nights are cold. Sometimes they are very cold indeed.

Subtropical deserts

Deserts are dry. Wadi Halfa has a typical desert climate. It is a town on the shores of Lake Nasser, in northern Sudan, and is important because it lies at the end of a railroad and is the place where goods heading north are transferred to ships that carry them down the Nile into Egypt. Wadi Halfa ordinarily receives less than 0.1 inch (2.5 mm) of rain a year. It once went 19 years with no rain at all.

This is not to say it never rains in the desert. Sometimes it does, and when it rains it often rains heavily. A single storm can drop two inches (50 mm) or more of rain on a place that has seen no rain for years. After one of these desert showers, torrential rivers flow through what had been dried beds, called *wadis* (sometimes spelled *ouadi*). There can be widespread floods. At Tamanrasset, Algeria, for example, the average annual rainfall is 1.8 inches (46 mm), but on January 15, 1922, it was hit by a storm with bitterly cold rain that continued through the following day and did not abate until January 17. An eyewitness said water was rushing through the wadi at the speed of a galloping horse. It washed away the huts and gardens of the local inhabitants, who had taken shelter in two abandoned forts. Then the water weakened the outer wall of one of the forts. It collapsed, burying 22 people, of whom eight were killed.

In December 1930 Siwa, Egypt, received 1.5 inches (38 mm) of rain over two days. Ordinarily, Siwa has 0.4 inch (10 mm) of rain a year and 0.1 inch (2.5 mm) in December. The water caused considerable damage to the mud-brick houses in the town.

Mecca (Makkah), in Saudi Arabia, also experiences occasional heavy rainstorms that in the past have sent water streaming down into the valley where the Holy Mosque is situated. An extensive system of storm drains has now been installed to protect the area.

Desert rain is not always so tempestuous. It can be light, and very occasionally it falls as drizzle.

Why does the desert flood?

The Holy Mosque at Mecca (Makkah) is at the bottom of a valley. It was at risk of flooding from water draining down the surrounding hillsides. Yemen, at the southern tip of the Arabian Peninsula, also experiences sudden flooding. It is a mountainous country and rainfall in the mountains is quite high—up to 16 inches (406 mm) a year in the foothills and more than 40 inches (1,016 mm) on the western slopes. Rivers draining the mountains supply water to the coastal plain, where the rainfall is less than two inches (50 mm) a year. Heavy rain in the mountains, caused when air approaching over the sea is forced to rise, can send water cascading into an adjacent desert and flooding large areas. In Yemen there is also a plateau on the eastern side of the country. The average rainfall there is less than four inches (100 mm) a year, but the very rare rainstorms can cause devastating floods. The map shows the location of Yemen.

Sudden floods are not confined to the Sahara or the Arabian Desert. They also happen in America. From July through September there are almost nightly storms over the Sonoran Desert of Arizona. The storms do not always bring rain, but when they do it is torrential. The Colorado and Mojave Deserts in southeastern California can also flood. They receive an average 2–10 inches (50–250 mm) of rain a year, although a whole year may pass with no rain at all. Winter rain is generally gentle and widespread, but in summer the rain falls during violent thunderstorms.

Storms occur when moist air moves into the desert and is forced to rise. El Niño events, which weaken the trade winds or even reverse their direction, can allow moist air to penetrate deserts in the trade-wind belts. Even without the help of El Niño, a relaxation in the prevailing distribution of pressure can allow moist air to enter. It is then warmed by contact with the hot desert surface and rises by convection. Ordinarily it cannot penetrate the temperature inversion that covers the desert (see box on page 12), but if it does, huge storm clouds form as the rising air cools adiabatically (see the box "Adiabatic cooling and warming") and its water vapor condenses. The resulting storm is violent but usually short-lived, and such events are extremely rare.

They cause flooding because there is almost no vegetation to trap the moving water, and over large areas the desert surface consists of bare rock, or there is impermeable rock a short distance below the surface. The water flows across the surface unchecked, raging down hillsides in torrents.

Water soaks into the ground where it can, and it evaporates rapidly in the desert heat. Before long the land is parched once more. Clouds may appear in the sky, but they drift across it and disappear without producing rain. On average, clouds cover 10 percent of the sky over the Sahara in winter and 4 percent in summer.

Why doesn't it rain more?

Air accumulates moisture as it moves over the ocean. When it crosses the coast of a continent it is forced to rise, and if a range of mountains lies approximately at right angles to its path, it is forced to rise steeply and rapidly. As it rises, the air cools adiabatically (see the box on page 13) and its water vapor condenses. There is cloud and rain on the windward side of the mountains. On the far (lee) side, the air subsides. It has now lost much of its moisture and as it descends it warms adiabatically. This lowers its relative humidity still further (see the box on page 14). Consequently, the climate on the lee side of the mountains is very dry. The area lies in a *rain shadow*, and a desert may form there. The diagram shows how this happens. The Mojave Desert in North America and the Patagonian Desert in South America are rain-shadow deserts.

Yemen has mountains and coastal plains.

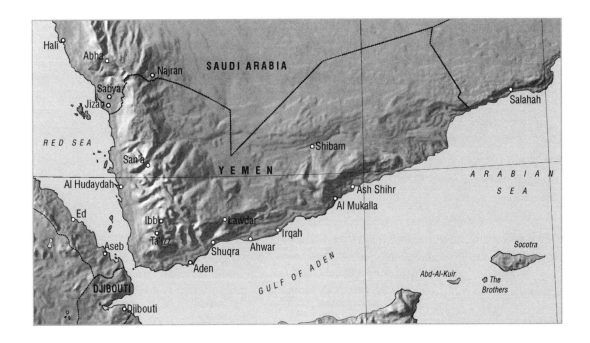

Temperature inversions

Ordinarily temperature decreases with height, but sometimes there is a layer above ground level where the air is warmer than the air below. This is an inversion.

There are three principal ways an inversion can develop.

On clear, still nights the ground cools rapidly by radiating away its warmth. Air next to the ground is chilled by contact, but this cooling extends only a few hundred feet above the surface. Above the surface layer of cool air, there is a layer of air that has not been chilled and is warmer. In the morning, the sun warms the ground, the low-level air is also warmed, and the inversion breaks down.

Frontal inversions form where warm, stable air moves above a layer of cooler air at a weather front. The warm air lies like a blanket above the cool air.

An inversion can also form near the center of an anticyclone, where air is subsiding. As it sinks, the air warms by compression. If the air near the ground is moving, with gusts and eddies of wind, the subsiding air cannot sink through it, so it lies above the turbulent layer. This is the type of inversion that is usually present in the subtropical deserts.

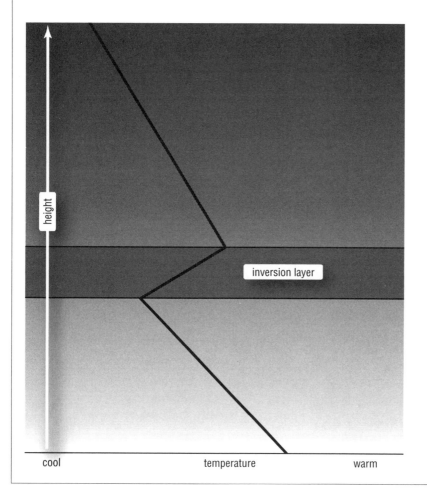

height

inversion layer

cool   temperature   warm

Temperature inversion. A layer of warm air lies above cooler air. Air that is warmed at the surface and rises by convection cannot pass through the inversion layer, where the air is less dense.

Adiabatic cooling and warming

Air is compressed by the weight of air above it. Imagine a balloon partly inflated with air and made from a substance that totally insulates the air inside. No matter what the temperature outside the balloon, the temperature of the air inside remains the same.

Imagine the balloon is released into the atmosphere. The air inside is squeezed between the weight of air above it, all the way to the top of the atmosphere, and the denser air below it.

Suppose the air inside the balloon is less dense than the air above it. The balloon will rise. As it rises, the distance to the top of the atmosphere becomes smaller, so there is less air above to weigh down on the air in the balloon. At the same time, as it moves through air that is less dense, it experiences less pressure from below. This causes the air in the balloon to expand.

When air (or any gas) expands, its molecules move farther apart. The amount of air remains the same, but it occupies a bigger volume. As they move apart, the molecules must "push" other molecules out of their way. This uses energy, so as the air expands its molecules lose energy. Because they have less energy they move more slowly.

When a moving molecule strikes something, some of its energy of motion (kinetic energy) is transferred to whatever it strikes and part of that energy is converted into heat. This raises the temperature of the struck object by an amount related to the number of molecules striking it and their speed.

In expanding air, the molecules are moving farther apart, so a smaller number of them strike an object each second. They are also traveling more slowly, so they strike with less force. This means the temperature of the air decreases. As it expands, air cools.

If the air in the balloon is denser than the air below, it will descend. The pressure on it will increase, its volume will decrease, and its molecules will acquire more energy. Its temperature will increase.

This warming and cooling has nothing to do with the temperature of the air surrounding the balloon. It is called *adiabatic* warming and cooling, from the Greek word *adiabatos*, meaning "impassable."

Adiabatic cooling and warming—the effect of air pressure on rising and sinking air. A "parcel" or "bubble" of air is squeezed between the weight of air above and the denser air below. As it rises into a region of less dense air, it expands, making its temperature fall. As it sinks into denser air, it contracts, making its temperature increase.

Subtropical deserts, such as the Sahara, Arabian, Syrian, and Australian Deserts, form in a different way. They are as dry as they are because the air over them is subsiding on the descending side of the tropical Hadley cells (see the box in the section, "Air movements and the transport of heat"). They are also hot, partly because they lie in low latitudes, but also because the air itself is hot. As it descends, the air warms adiabatically (see the box above).

Subsiding air increases the surface pressure, forming an area of high pressure, or *anticyclone*. There is permanent anticyclone in the subtropics

Humidity

The amount of water vapor air can hold varies according to the temperature. Warm air can hold more than cold air. The amount of water vapor present in the air is called the *humidity* of the air. This is measured in several ways.

The *absolute humidity* is the mass of water vapor present in a unit volume of air, measured in grams per cubic meter (1 g m^{-3} = 0.046 ounces per cubic yard). Changes in the temperature and pressure alter the volume of air, however, and this changes the amount of water vapor in a unit volume without actually adding or removing any moisture. The concept of absolute humidity takes no account of this and so it is not very useful and is seldom used.

Mixing ratio is more useful. This is a measure of the amount of water vapor in a unit volume of dry air—air with the water vapor removed. *Specific humidity* is similar to mixing ratio, but measures the amount of water vapor in a unit volume of air including the moisture. Both are reported in grams per cubic meter. Since the amount of water vapor is always very small, seldom accounting for more than 7 percent of the mass of the air, specific humidity and mixing ratio are almost the same thing.

The most familiar term is *relative humidity*. This is the measurement you read from hygrometers, either directly or after referring to tables—and it is the one you hear in weather forecasts. Relative humidity (RH) is the amount of water vapor in the air expressed as a percentage of the amount needed to saturate the air at that temperature. When the air is saturated the RH is 100 percent (the "percent" is often omitted).

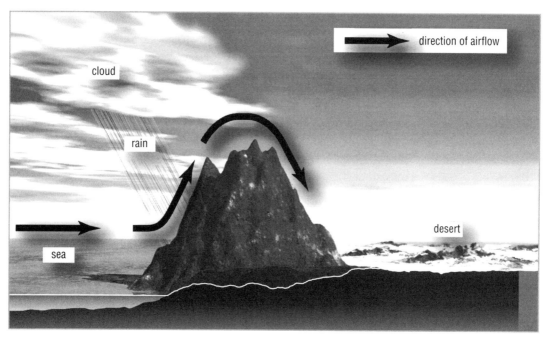

Rain shadow desert. Moist air rises to cross the mountains and loses its moisture. This produces a desert on the lee side of the mountains.

of both hemispheres. In the Northern Hemisphere air flows counter-clockwise around an anticyclone (and counterclockwise in the Southern Hemisphere). The wind flows approximately parallel to the isobars (map lines linking places where the pressure is the same), but close to the surface, friction between the wind and the surface slows the wind a little and causes it to blow across the isobars. Over land the wind crosses the isobars at an angle of about 45° (over the sea, where friction is less, it crosses at about 30°). The diagram shows that the consequence of this movement is to carry air away from the center of the anticyclone. In middle latitudes, where weather systems are constantly changing, this removal of air quickly reduces the pressure. The anticyclone weakens and disappears. In the subtropics, however, the anticyclone is constantly being fed by air subsiding as part of the Hadley-cell circulation. The anticyclones cannot weaken and the general movement of air is away from the center.

This persistent outflow prevents air from entering the area—the desert—at a low level. Moist air approaching from the ocean is deflected by the prevailing winds. Not only does the subsidence of the Hadley-cell circulation produce the subtropical deserts, it also ensures their continuing aridity.

How dry is dry?

Although the subtropical anticyclones are permanent features of the general circulation of the atmosphere (see the box on page 37 in the section "Air movements and the transport of heat"), the subtropical deserts were not always so dry.

At times in the past the climates of the world have been warmer than they are today. The equatorial belt, or intertropical convergence zone (ITCZ), where the trade winds of both hemispheres meet, was wider then than it is now. The ITCZ follows the Sun, moving north in June and south in September. In those days it moved farther, with the result that rain fell on what is now the Sahara in every month of the year. There were forests, lakes, and farms. The northern Sahara was a major grain-producing region, supplying Rome. It became the desert we see today less than 2,000 years ago.

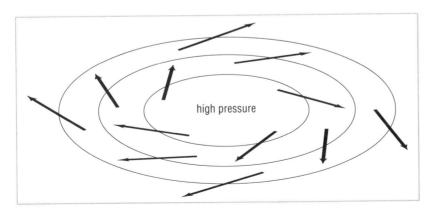

Airflow around an anticyclone. Friction against the surface makes the wind flow across the isobars.

The first of the world's great empires flourished during a time of wetter climate, and its failure and collapse has been linked to a drought that lasted for more than a century and turned the farmlands into desert. The empire covered an area called Akkad, and a number of Sumerian city-states and its capital lay on the banks of either the Tigris or Euphrates Rivers (its precise location is not known). Deserts can appear and disappear.

In order for a desert to form, it is not enough for the annual rainfall to be low. The amount of rain (or snow) that falls must be less than the amount that would evaporate from the surface if the surface were kept permanently sodden (see the section "Where the deserts are" on page 1).

Temperature is important, of course. It is more difficult for a desert to form in a cold climate than in a hot one. Divide the amount of rainfall in a particular area by the average temperature and the resulting figure indicates whether or not that area is a desert.

If the average annual rainfall is close to the minimum below which a desert may form, its seasonal distribution is important. Temperatures are higher in summer than in winter, so evaporation is higher in summer and more rain is needed to prevent a desert from forming.

There is a formula for calculating whether an area is a desert. Rainfall distribution is allowed for by adjusting the formula. If most rain falls in winter, the formula is $r \div t$. If it falls mainly in summer, use $r \div (t + 14)$. If the rainfall is distributed evenly throughout the year use $r \div (t + 7)$, where r is the rainfall in centimeters (to convert inches to centimeters multiply by 0.394) and t is the average temperature in degrees Celsius (to convert °F to °C: $°C = (°F - 32) \times 5 \div 9$). If the answer is less than 1, the area is desert. At In Salah, Algeria, for example, the average annual rainfall is 1.7 cm, falling mainly in winter, and the average temperature is 25.4°C. Applying the formula, $r \div t = 1.7 \div 25.4 = 0.07$, In Salah lies in a desert, in this case the Sahara. Phoenix, Arizona, has 19 cm of rain a year, distributed fairly evenly through the year, and the average temperature is 21.25°C. Applying $r \div (t + 7)$ gives $19 \div (21.25 + 7) = 0.7$. Phoenix lies in a desert, but its desert climate is less extreme than that of In Salah. You could use weather data for your own area (ask for them at the public library) to find out whether you live in a desert. (You could also look out the window, but this way is more fun.)

Oases

Even in a desert, there is water in some places. The Sahara is famous for its oases—lakes in the middle of the desert. Because there is water at the surface, oases support plants and animals. People live around them and farmers cultivate the land.

Oases are supplied by water that moves below ground (see the section "Water below ground" on page 108). There are two principal ways they can form, illustrated in the diagram.

Even in a desert, when it rains heavily some of the water soaks into the ground before it can evaporate. It sinks through the sand and loose gravel

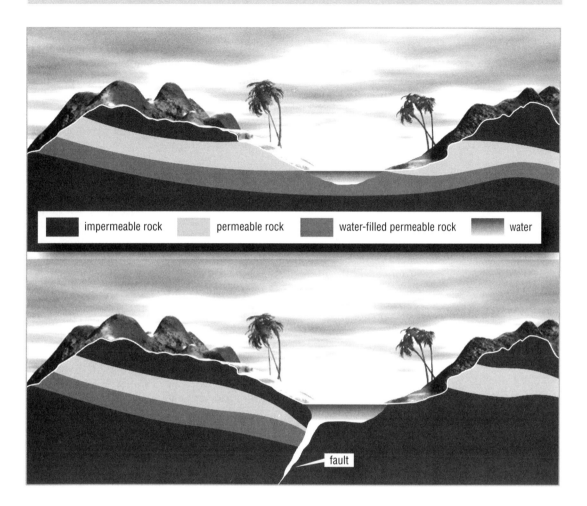

impermeable rock   permeable rock   water-filled permeable rock   water

fault

that covers the desert surface until it reaches a layer of permeable rock, into which it soaks, above a layer of solid rock it cannot penetrate. There it accumulates as groundwater, flowing very slowly downhill through the porous material.

Water may also enter from outside the desert. If the desert is in the rain shadow of mountains, for example, rain falling on the exposed side of the mountains may flow through them as groundwater, into the adjacent desert. Imagine the groundwater flowing over a large area, as a sheet of water possibly hundreds of miles wide, but deep below ground level.

Now suppose that in a certain place the wind has blown away surface sand and gravel. Over many years, the wind has hollowed out the land, forming a deep depression. If this depression is deeper than the surface of the groundwater, water will flow through it and the depression will become a lake. Water will evaporate from the surface, of course, but it is constantly replenished from the groundwater, which also keeps the lake water fresh and wholesome, because on the downhill side of the lake the

Oases. The figures show the two ways an oasis can form.

water continues its journey through the porous rock. The lake is permanent and the land around it is an oasis. This is the situation illustrated in the upper drawing on page 17.

The lower drawing shows a different way an oasis can form. Here, groundwater flows through the porous rock as before, trapped above a layer of impermeable rock, but this time there is a fault in the rock layers. Movements of Earth's crust have fractured the rocks and lifted those on the right (or lowered those on the left) of the drawing. Now the porous layer on the left ends where it meets impermeable rock. The water can flow no farther, so it accumulates and its level rises until it meets the continuation of the porous layer on the right. Between the two, the water level rises to the surface and, once again, a permanent lake forms, as the center of an oasis.

Unfortunately, oases are few and far between, and deserts are hostile places. There is very little water and temperatures fluctuate between extremes. Despite their climate, however, they support a surprisingly large amount of life.

West Coast deserts

Subtropical deserts are dry because it seldom rains, but this does not necessarily mean the air is dry. There are some deserts where the air is very moist for much of the time, yet, apparently paradoxically, these are among the driest of all deserts. At Walvis Bay, Namibia, for example, the relative humidity (see the box on humidity in the section "Subtropical deserts") early in the morning is often higher than 90 percent and by 2 P.M., when the temperature reaches its maximum, the relative humidity is still above 60 percent and often above 70 percent. Yet in March, the wettest month of the year, only 0.3 inch (8 mm) of rain falls, and in an average year there are seven months when no rain falls at all. Walvis Bay lies on the coast, at the northern end of the Namib Desert.

Contrast its climate with that of In Salah, in central Algeria, deep inside the Sahara and far from the coast. There the early-morning relative humidity exceeds 60 percent in winter, but in summer, at 7 A.M., the humidity is below 40 percent and in July it is often below 30 percent. By early afternoon the humidity has dropped to below 30 percent and in July and August to below 20 percent. This is extremely dry. For comparison, the average relative humidity at midday in the air over New York City ranges from 53 percent in April to 61 percent in September and December.

There is no mystery about why the air is moist over a coastal town—its proximity to the ocean explains that. The mystery is why, despite the high humidity, rain is such a rare phenomenon along certain coasts.

These arid coasts are found on the western side of North America, South America, and Africa. They comprise part of the Sonoran Desert in

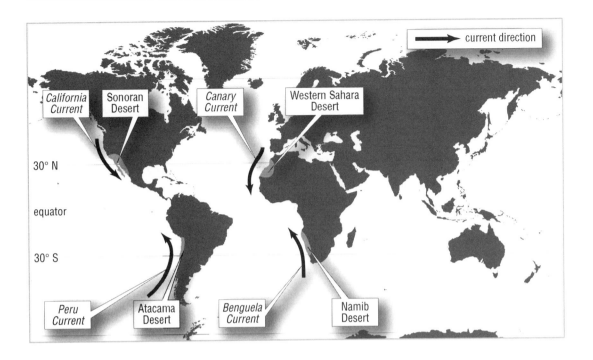

the southwestern United States and northern Mexico, the Atacama Desert in Chile, the Western Sahara Desert in Western Sahara and southern Morocco, and the Namib Desert in Namibia. As the map shows, all of them lie along the western coasts of continents.

West Coast deserts. These deserts are affected by the cold ocean currents that flow parallel to the western coast.

Eastern boundary currents and the subtropical anticyclones

The map also shows that not far offshore there are ocean currents that flow parallel to the coast and toward the equator. The California Current flows along the western coast of North America, the Peru Current along the coasts of Chile and Peru, the Canary Current past the Canary Islands and the West African coast, and the Benguela Current along the coast of southwestern Africa. All of these currents carry cool water from the Arctic or Antarctic. They are eastern boundary currents (see the section "Ocean currents and sea-surface temperature" on page 51).

Subtropical deserts are produced by dry, warm air that is subsiding as part of the vertical air circulation in the Hadley cells (see the box on page 39 in the section "Air movements and the transport of heat"). This subsidence produces areas of permanently high surface pressure, known as the *subtropical anticyclones*. These are centered over the eastern sides of the Atlantic and Pacific Oceans.

Air circulates in a clockwise direction around anticyclones in the Northern Hemisphere and counterclockwise in the Southern Hemisphere.

The second map shows the approximate location of the subtropical anticyclones and illustrates the effect of the air movement around them. This is to bring cold air toward the equator. The resulting prevailing winds—northwesterlies in the Northern Hemisphere and southeasterlies in the Southern Hemisphere—drive the surface currents toward the equator. The winds continue around the anticyclones to become the northeasterly and southeasterly trade winds, and the currents also turn, to join the Equatorial Currents that flow parallel to the equator in both hemispheres.

Cold, dense air, carried on these winds, enhances the sinking motion of air on the eastern side of the anticyclones. This tends to reinforce the temperature inversions that are typical of all subtropical deserts. The temperature inversions inhibit convection, so no matter how moist the air in the lower layer of the atmosphere and how warm the desert surface beneath it, the air is unable to rise sufficiently for the development of clouds that are big enough to produce rain. The air is said to be very *stable*, which means that if anything forces it to rise, as soon as the force ceases the air will sink back to its former height. Convective clouds—cumulus and cumulonimbus—cannot develop in stable air and these are the clouds that bring rain showers (cumulus) or heavy storms (cumulonimbus).

Upwellings

The ocean currents carry cold water, but the water is made even colder by numerous upwellings of water from deep below the surface. These upwellings result from the *Ekman spiral*, a phenomenon that was first explained in 1902 and more fully in 1905 by the Swedish oceanographer Vagn Walfrid Ekman (1874–1954). In the 1890s the Norwegian Arctic explorer Fridtjof Nansen (1861–1930) had noticed that sea currents do not flow in the same direction as the wind driving them, but at an angle to the wind. Ekman found out why this is so.

Ocean currents are driven by the wind and, like the wind, they are subject to the Coriolis effect (CorF; see the box on page 53 in the section "Ocean currents and sea-surface temperature"). The balance between the CorF and the friction between the wind and ocean surface produces two component forces of equal strength, one acting in the direction of the wind and the other acting at right angles to the wind direction. The resultant force causes the current to flow at an angle of 45° to the wind direction— to the right of the wind in the Northern Hemisphere and to its left in the Southern Hemisphere. The diagram on the facing page illustrates this.

Below the surface, the influence of the wind decreases and so the CorF becomes the greater of the two forces. This has the effect of deflecting the current more and more with increasing depth, with the overall result that water near the bottom of the surface boundary layer, about 82 feet (25 m) below the surface, drifts at right angles to the wind. The current spirals downward from the surface. This is the Ekman spiral. Deeper water then rises to the surface (i.e. wells up) to replace it. It is a slow movement, often

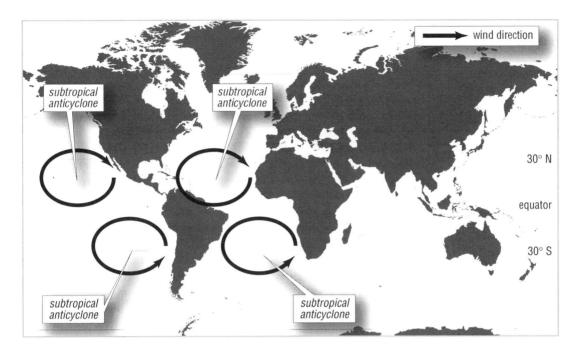

at less than 3.3 feet (1 m) per day. The surface boundary layer that is subject to the Ekman spiral is known as the *Ekman layer.*

Winds drive the eastern boundary currents parallel to a north-south coastline. The Ekman spiral pushes surface water away from the coast, and deep water rises from below. This is known as *coastal upwelling.* The boundary currents carry cold water, but upwelling increases their cold influence. The difference is very marked. In August, the temperature of the Atlantic off the coast of North Carolina is often 70°F (21°C) and it can be warmer. The Pacific, off the coast of California in the same latitude, is about 59°F (15°C). The climate is also markedly cooler on the western than the eastern side of South America. In July (winter) the difference is

Winds along western coasts. Prevailing winds around the subtropical anticyclones bring cold air to western coasts.

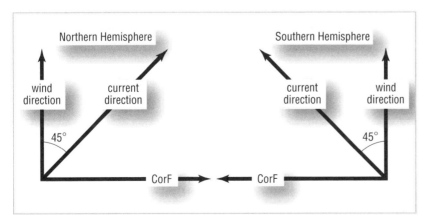

The Coriolis effect and ocean currents. The balance of forces causes the current to flow at about 45 degrees to the direction of the wind.

about 12°F (6.7°C). It is less in summer because every few years an El Niño event allows warmer water to flow southward, raising the summer average temperature.

Warm air and cold sea

The coastal deserts lie in the subtropics, straddling two belts of prevailing winds—the westerlies of middle latitudes and the easterly trade winds of the Tropics. Between the westerlies and easterlies the winds tend to blow toward the equator as part of the circulation around the subtropical anti-cyclones. Consequently, for much of the time the winds over the parts of the deserts nearest the equator blow from the land toward the sea, carrying dry air from the continental interior. This contributes to the aridity of the climate.

Prevailing winds are most dependable over the sea. Over land there are mountains to redirect them, and near coasts, especially tropical coasts, there are land and sea breezes that can dominate the wind direction (see the box on page 23). The interactions among these influences produce effects that differ from one desert to another.

Land and sea breezes dominate the climate of the Namib Desert. Although the prevailing winds are the southeasterly trades, the sea breeze starts by about 10 A.M. on most days. It is stronger in the south than in the north, but at its strongest it can blow at 30 MPH (48 km/h) and it raises a great deal of dust. Soon after sunset the wind dies down, and after a period of calm the land breeze begins and continues until morning. Easterly winds are also fairly common, especially on winter mornings before the sea breeze has had time to suppress them. They bring warm, dry air from the interior of the continent.

As warm, moist air over the ocean drifts across the cold Benguela Current, it is chilled and its water vapor condenses to form low cloud and fog. In the early hours of the morning the land breezes have often weakened sufficiently to allow this air to cross the coast. The heat of the Sun evaporates it soon after dawn, and the air is too stable for convection to make it rise and draw more moist air in from over the sea, but for a time there is low cloud, fog, and even drizzle. Walvis Bay has fog on an average of 55 days a year. Some plants and animals are able to survive with the water they obtain from the fog.

The Western Sahara (also called the Atlantic Sahara) has a climate very similar to that of the Namib Desert, dominated by land and sea breezes and the cold Canary Current. Low cloud and fog are fairly common and the sea breezes keep temperatures much lower than those of the central Sahara. In July, the average daytime temperature at In Salah is 113°F (45°C). At Nouakchott, very near the coast in Mauritania, it is 89°F (32°C). Humidity is much higher at Nouakchott, often exceeding 80 percent in summer, compared with a relative humidity at In Salah that never reaches 70 percent and is often below 40 percent. Yet, like the Namib, the

Land and sea breezes

A sea breeze blows from water to land during the day. A land breeze blows from land to sea by night.

During the day, the land warms faster than the water. Warm air rises over the land and cool air is drawn in from over the water to replace it. As it rises, the air over land cools. It then moves over the water surface, where it subsides and flows back toward the land.

At night the opposite happens. The land loses heat faster than the water. Consequently, air subsides over the land and flows out over the water as a land breeze. There it pushes beneath the air next to the water surface, which has not yet cooled. This air rises and flows back toward the land. The diagram shows what happens.

sea breeze day

land breeze night

Land and sea breezes. By day, air rises over land, and cool air flows from the sea or lake toward the shore. By night, air flows from land toward the sea or lake.

Western Sahara is exceedingly dry. Nouakchott receives an average of only 6.2 inches (157 mm) of rain a year and 4.1 inches (104 mm) of that falls in August, during the monsoon season.

The climate of the Atacama Desert is also affected by a cold boundary current—the Peru Current. Water vapor condenses in the warm, moist air that comes into contact with the cold ocean surface, producing low cloud and fog just as it does off Namibia and the Western Sahara. The cloud and fog seldom reach the desert, however, because a range of mountains up to 9,000 feet (2,745 m) high lie between the Atacama and the coast. Air crossing the mountains loses its moisture as it does so, leaving the Atacama in a rain shadow. To the east of the desert, the Domeyko Mountains, which are part of the Andes, and beyond them the high Andean plateau known as the *altiplano*, prevent any moisture from traveling from east to west.

The Sonoran Desert is affected by the California Current, but the desert is farther inland than the other West Coast deserts. This moderates the effect of the current. High ground in Baja California traps much of the moisture entering from the Pacific, but the desert benefits from monsoon rains in summer and occasional frontal systems that move in from the Pacific to bring rain in winter. Farther inland, however, the climate is dry. Yuma, Arizona, receives an average of only 3 inches (76 mm) of rain a year.

Polar deserts

When Captain Robert Falcon Scott (1868–1912) crossed Antarctica in 1903 in his first attempt to reach the South Pole, to his surprise he and his party came across a sheltered valley. No snow or ice was to be seen, and the sand on the valley floor felt warm as he let it trickle through his fingers. What the expedition had found was one of several *dry valleys.* Together they occupy about 2,200 square miles (5,700 km²). This is a tiny fraction of the 5,400,000 square miles (13,986,000 km²) that is the area of the entire continent, but the valleys are interesting. Very little lives there. Scott saw no sign of life, although there are bacteria and a few mosses and lichens. In fact, apart from their much lower temperature they are very similar to the dry deserts found elsewhere, despite being surrounded by vast amounts of snow and ice. The dry valleys are so cold and inhospitable they resemble Mars more closely than any other places on Earth. They are dry partly because the small amount of snow that falls on them is swept away by winds that often exceed 100 MPH (160 km/h), and partly because their dark-colored rocks and sand absorb enough warmth from the Sun to melt any snow that does settle.

Most of Antarctica lies beneath ice. The thickness of the ice varies greatly from place to place, but on average the ice sheet is almost 7,000 feet (2,100 m) thick. Around 90 percent of all the ice in the world lies on the surface of the continent of Antarctica. There is even liquid water, in the form of at least 70 freshwater lakes beneath the ice sheet. These are kept liquid by heat from the radioactive decay of elements in the underlying rock (the main source of heat in the Earth's crust) and are insulated by the thick layer of ice above them. The discovery of what may be the largest lake was announced in June 1996. Lake Vostok, lying beneath more than 13,000 feet (4,000 m) of ice near the Russian Vostok station (at about 78° S), is about 125 miles (201 km) long, covering an area of 5,400 square miles (14,000 km²), and in places it is more than 1,500 feet (458 m) deep. The map shows the outline of the coast of Antarctica, the ice shelves that extend over the large bays, the way the territory is shared among nations for research purposes, and the location of the Vostok station. The continent is not short of water. Indeed, it contains about 95 percent of all the freshwater in the world.

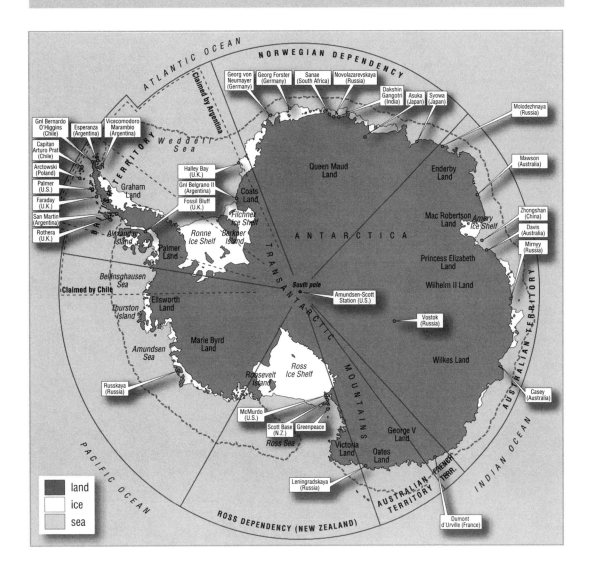

Antarctica

Roaring forties, furious fifties, shrieking sixties

If you are ever fortunate enough to visit Antarctica by sea, there is a good chance you will sail through some very bad weather. You will pass through latitudes sailors rounding the southern tips of South America and Africa called the "roaring forties," "furious fifties," and "shrieking sixties." As their names suggest, the gales intensify the farther south you go.

You will also cross the polar front, where tropical air to the north meets polar air to the south, in summer at about 45°S and in winter rather farther to the north. This front produces violent storms that lash the coast. Heavy snow and blizzards are common, but in summer there are long spells of clear weather. When you arrive, assuming the weather then is fine, you will be greeted by spectacular scenery sculpted entirely from ice.

Wet or dry?

What with the fierce snowstorms, the huge icebergs your ship will have passed, and the landscape of endless snow, you may well conclude that Antarctica has a wet climate. Indeed, that does describe the part of it you will have seen, where the annual precipitation is equivalent to about 15 inches (380 mm) of rain, but Antarctica is a big continent and, as the map shows, the coastal weather does not travel far inland. In its deep interior Antarctica is desert, and possibly the driest desert in the world.

Apart from the dry valleys, the land is everywhere covered by ice, but this does not mean the climate is moist. It is too cold for the ice to melt even in summer and the Antarctic climate has been like this for many millions of years. When snow does fall, it adds to what has fallen before. The ice sheet is the result of a very long, very slow, accumulation.

Measuring snowfall is difficult under Antarctic conditions. The snow itself is usually fine and powdery. It blows easily and the winds are always strong—they have been known to blow at 200 MPH (320 km/h), which is as strong as a category-5 hurricane. The trouble is, the winds tend to blow the snow across the snow gauges rather than letting it fall into them, so

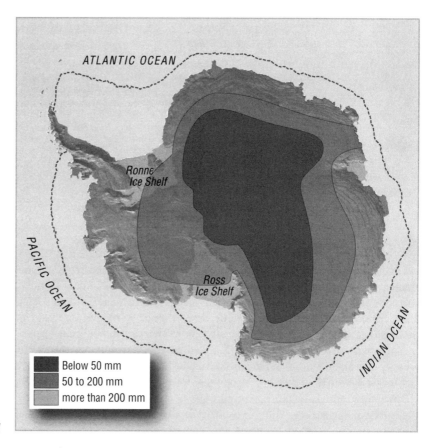

Antarctic snowfall

that when the snowfall ends there is no way of distinguishing between what has just fallen and the snow onto which it fell. Even if that were possible, the wind drives the snow into drifts, so its thickness varies widely.

To allow for the many different kinds of snow, measurements of snowfall are usually converted into the equivalent amount of rainfall. The interior of Antarctica probably receives an average of little more than two inches (50 mm) of rainfall-equivalent a year. The South Pole receives 2.4–3.1 inches (60–80 mm) a year. Regardless of temperature, if the annual rainfall is less than 10 inches (250 mm) the land is likely to be a desert. So Antarctica is a desert.

Why are the gales so fierce?

Most pictures of Antarctica depict vast fields of snow and ice. These exist, of course, but the pictures are misleading. Most of them are taken on the surface of the ice shelves that extend outward from the coast over the huge bays in the Ross and Weddell Seas. Others are taken on the Peninsula, in the British Territory on the map. These areas are far from typical of the continent as a whole. Farther inland the ground rises and the continent is divided into two unequal parts by the Transantarctic Mountains—just one of several mountain ranges. Near the center of the continent, the average elevation of the rock surface beneath the ice is about 8,000 feet (2,440 m) above sea level. The thickness of the ice sheet must be added to that to calculate the elevation of the surface exposed to the sky. If you stand on the ice anywhere near the South Pole you will be about 15,000 feet (4,575 m) above sea level.

Temperature decreases with increasing height above sea level by 5.5°F every 1,000 feet (10°C per km) in the dry Antarctic air. If the temperature at sea level is 13.5°F (–10.3°C), at 15,000 feet (4,575 m) it will be –69°F (–56°C), which is the average maximum temperature at the South Pole in winter. The elevation explains why the interior of Antarctica is so much colder than the Arctic, where the surface is at sea level.

Air in contact with the surface becomes very cold indeed and as it cools it also contracts and becomes denser. The dense air then moves downhill, away from the high ground, cutting beneath the slightly warmer air nearer the coast, and as it moves it accelerates. A wind that flows downhill is called a *katabatic wind*. Over Antarctica, the katabatic winds frequently reach gale and even hurricane force by the time they reach sea level.

Greenland, or Kalaallit Nunaat

Greenland, or Kalaallit Nunaat, to give the country its correct, Inuit, name, also lies beneath an ice sheet. The map shows the location of the principal towns, with their modern Inuit names. The average thickness of the ice sheet is about 5,000 feet (1,525 m). Qaanaaq (Thule), at latitude 76.5° N, receives about 2.5 inches (63.5 mm) of precipitation a year, well below the 10-inch (250-mm) threshold. The equation $r \div (t + 14)$ gives a value of 2.2 (see the section on subtropical deserts). This is more than 1, the upper limit of a desert, but nevertheless it indicates a dry climate and, like all the towns, Qaanaaq is on the coast. The climate of Qaanaaq is believed to be typical of that over most of the interior, but probably moister because of its coastal location. More rain and snow fall farther south but, like the interior of Antarctica, northern Greenland and much of the interior is a dry desert situated on top of an ice sheet.

Over both poles, cold, dense air is subsiding, much as air does over the deserts in low latitudes. This movement is part of the global circulation of the atmosphere, illustrated in the diagram, in which warm air moves from the equator toward the poles and cool air moves from the poles to the equator in a series of three vertical cells.

The circulation pattern that makes polar regions dry deserts begins with the tropical Hadley cells (see the box on page 39 in the section "Air

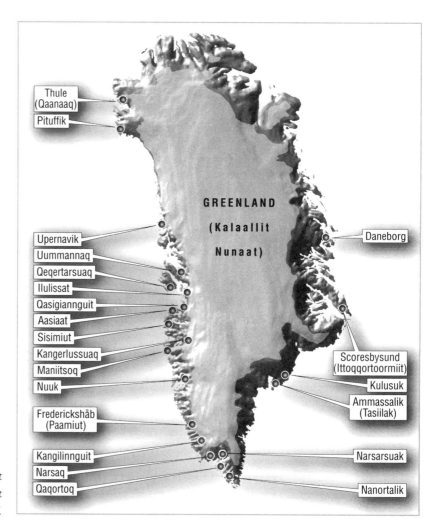

Greenland (Kalaallit Nunaat), the largest island in the world.

Three-cell model. Cold, dense air subsides over the Arctic and Antarctic, producing areas of permanently high pressure. Warm air rises over the equator. The equatorial and polar cells drive the third cell in middle latitudes.

movements and the transport of heat"). It is subsiding air from the Hadley cells that produces deserts at around latitude 30° in both hemispheres, but not all the air sinks into the subtropics. Some continues to move away from the equator, all the way to the poles. Near the surface, some of the air subsiding into the subtropics returns to the equator, but some turns the other way, heading toward the poles. When air reaches the poles it can travel no farther, because it meets air that is also traveling poleward from all around the world. Air accumulates and becomes dense enough to sink. This is what generates the subsiding air over the central Arctic and Antarctic regions. At the surface, the air has no choice but to flow away from the poles until, at around latitude 60° in both hemispheres, it meets air moving away from the tropical Hadley cells. The converging air rises and joins the high-level flow, some of the air moving toward the pole and some toward the equator.

In reality, the air movements are more complicated, but this general description is called the *three-cell model* of atmospheric circulation and it gives a fair impression of the way air moves. The first cell, closest to the equator, is the tropical Hadley cell. The second is the polar cell, of subsiding air over the pole and rising air at about 60°. These two cells drive the third, mid-latitude cell.

Cold poles

Just as the geographic equator does not coincide with the climatic equator (see the section "Air movements and the transport of heat"), so the climatic poles are not in precisely the same place as the geographic poles. This makes little difference at the South Pole, where the two are close together, but the two North Poles are a long way apart. The climatic North Pole, often called the *cold pole*, is close to Verkhoyansk in Siberia, at 65° N 133.5° E. Verkhoyansk and Oimyakon, a small town about 300 miles (480 km) to the southeast, are the coldest places in the Northern Hemisphere, with an average January temperature of –58°F (–50°C). Sometimes the temperature can fall as low as –90°F (–68°C).

The South Pole is colder. At the Vostok Station, located at the southern cold pole, in 1997 scientists measured the temperature as –131.8°F (–91°C). That is the lowest temperature ever known on the surface of Earth. Vostok is a Russian base that opened in 1957; it is no longer manned throughout the year. Scientists at the Amundsen-Scott Station, the United States base at the South Pole itself, have recorded a temperature of –117°F (–83°C) in June—midwinter in the Southern Hemisphere, of course. Unlike central Antarctica, Verkhoyansk is not cold all year round. In July the average temperature is 56°F (13°C), but it has been known to exceed 90°F (32°C).

Like the area around the South Pole, Verkhoyansk has a dry climate. Its annual rainfall averages 5 inches (127 mm), falling mainly in summer. The average temperature is 1.4°F (–17°C) and $r \div (t + 14) = -4.5$. This is less than 1, so Verkhoyansk lies within a very dry desert.

Relative humidity (RH, see the box on page 14 in the section "Subtropical deserts") at Verkhoyansk ranges from 45 to 78 percent during the day, but at night it sometimes exceeds 80 percent. This makes it sound as though the climate should be wetter than it is, but remember that the relative humidity refers not to the actual amount of water vapor in the air, but to the amount of water vapor as a proportion of the amount needed to saturate the air at that temperature. As the temperature falls the relative humidity rises, because cold air can hold less water vapor than warm air. In May, when the average daytime temperature is 43°F (6°C), the average RH is 47 percent; if the temperature were 68°F (20°C) the same amount of atmospheric moisture would give an RH of 19 percent.

Survival in the polar desert

It may seem that the problems of survival are quite different in the polar deserts from those facing the plants and animals in a subtropical desert, but in fact they are very similar. It is true that in Antarctica and Kalaallit Nunaat there is no shortage of water, but water is abundant there only for humans. We can light fires and melt the ice. Plants cannot do that and it is only as a liquid that their roots can absorb water, without which they die (see the section "Why plants need water" on page 102). Frozen water is not available to them, so as far as plants are concerned, frozen ground is no different from completely arid ground.

Predictably, very few plants grow in the polar deserts. Despite the hostility of the climate, in dry valleys and on mountainsides, where bare rock and sand are exposed, mosses and lichens are able to grow for a few days in summer, when the dark-colored surface absorbs enough heat to melt a little water for them. In sheltered places, the absorption of sunlight in midsummer, when daylight is almost continuous, can briefly raise the temperature of rocks to more than 80°F (27°C). For the rest of the year these simple plants remain dormant.

Mammals might be able to melt ice with the warmth of their bodies, but all animals need food and all food is obtained in the first instance from plants. Meat-eaters may consume no plants themselves, but they eat plant-eaters, which do. With so few plants, polar deserts are even more devoid of animal life than hot deserts. It is also almost impossible for the continent to be colonized, because Antarctica is very isolated. From the northernmost tip of the Antarctic Peninsula it is 600 miles (965 km) across the Drake Passage to the southernmost tip of South America. This is no barrier to fish, marine mammals such as seals, or birds—including the penguins, of course, which travel by sea rather than by air—but few land-dwelling animals have managed to cross it. The only animals native to Antarctica are about 100 species of invertebrates and half of them are parasites of seals or birds.

Low-latitude deserts are hot during the day and much cooler, or even cold, at night. It is never hot in polar desert, but temperature is no less of a problem. Plants can adapt to limited periods of very low temperatures, but photosynthesis ceases below about 20°F (–7°C). If respiration continues, the plants will "starve," just as plants do at very high temperatures (see the section "Why plants need water").

Polar deserts are as dry as the more familiar subtropical deserts and conditions in them are, if anything, even harsher. Compared with them, the hot deserts of America, Africa, Asia, and Australia are teeming with life.

Air movements and the transport of heat

Oceans cover more than two-thirds of the surface of Earth. Ours is a watery planet. Water evaporates from the oceans, condenses to form dew, frost, fog, or cloud, and falls as precipitation—hail, drizzle, rain, or snow. Some of that precipitation falls over land, from where it returns to the sea, thus completing the *hydrological cycle*, illustrated in the diagram on page 32.

Precipitation does not fall on all land equally, however. Some regions receive very much more than others. Kisangani, in the Democratic

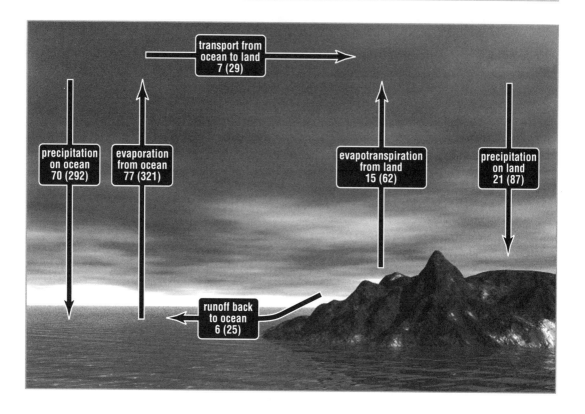

Hydrological cycle. Republic of Congo, receives on average 67 inches (1,700 mm) of rain a year, for example, and Timbuktu, in Mali, receives an average of only nine inches (229 mm). Both cities are in Africa and both are far from the sea. Kisangani lies less than one degree north of the equator, Timbuktu just south of 17° N. The difference in latitude is about the same as that between St. Louis, Missouri, and Edmonton, Alberta, both inland cities like Kisangani and Timbuktu. With an average annual rainfall of 39.4 inches (1,001 mm), St. Louis has a climate more than twice as wet as that of Edmonton, with 17.3 inches (439 mm), but Kisangani is more than seven times wetter than Timbuktu.

What makes the difference is not the latitudinal distance between the cities, but where that distance is located. The Democratic Republic of Congo lies close to the equator and Mali is in the subtropics. Both North American cities lie in temperate latitudes.

Sunshine, tropics, and seasons

All the energy Earth receives comes from the Sun. Most of that radiation passes through the atmosphere and warms the surface of the land and sea. Air is warmed by contact with the warm surface. In other words, the land and sea are heated from above, but the air is heated from below. It is this solar energy that drives our climates, but sunshine does not fall every-where with the same intensity.

As Earth orbits the Sun, you can picture the path it follows as mark-ing out the edge of a flat disk (called the *plane of the ecliptic*). If you imag-ine a line through the center of Earth at right angles to the plane of the ecliptic and compare this with the axis of Earth's rotation, you will see that the axis of rotation is tilted by approximately 23.5°. This means that at noon the Sun is directly overhead somewhere close to the equator (but precisely over the equator only on two days in the year, called the *equinoxes*) and that sunlight falls more intensely in equatorial regions than it does in higher latitudes.

This tilt produces the Tropics. These are two belts, one on either side of the equator, bounded by the highest latitude at which the noonday Sun is directly overhead on at least one day in the year. The tropic of Cancer is at latitude 23.5° N and the tropic of Capricorn at 23.5° S, and as the dia-gram below shows, this is also the angle of axial tilt. The two days in the year—at present June 21–22 and December 22–23—when the Sun is directly overhead at noon at one of the tropics are known as the *solstices*. These are Midsummer Day in one hemisphere and Midwinter Day in the other. The equinoxes, which are the two days when the noonday Sun is directly overhead at the equator, fall on March 20–21 and September 22–23. At the equinoxes there are 12 hours of daylight and 12 hours of night in both hemispheres.

As Earth moves in its orbit around the Sun, the axial tilt also produces the seasons. They occur because first one hemisphere and then the other is tilted toward the Sun, so each in turn receives more sunlight. As the drawing on page 34 shows, this difference is most extreme at the solstices and there is no difference at the equinoxes.

Why the Sun is overhead in the Tropics. As the Earth travels around the Sun in the course of a year. the line where the plane of the ecliptic meets the surface moves from the tropic of Can-cer. across the equator. to the tropic of Capri-corn. then back again. This movement of the plane of the ecliptic means the Sun is directly overhead at noon some-where between the two tropics on every day of the year.

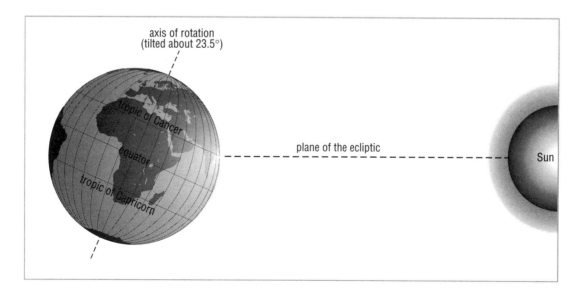

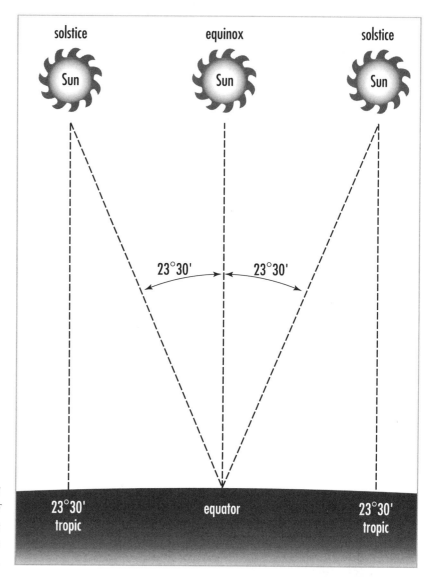

Tropics, solstices, and equinoxes. It is the tilt of the Earth's axis that determines the latitude of the Tropics.

Evaporation and convection

Equatorial regions are therefore heated more strongly than other regions throughout the year. Glance at a map of the world and you will see that for most of its length the equator crosses the oceans. Water is very abundant along the equator and, because the surface is warmed strongly by the Sun, the rate of evaporation is high.

Air expands when it is warmed, because its molecules absorb energy and move farther apart. This reduces the density of the air. It is being warmed from below, so the air closest to the surface becomes less dense than the air immediately above it. This allows denser air to sink beneath it, forcing it to rise. The process is called *convection* and because it is due to the sinking of denser, heavier air, in fact it is caused by gravity. Convection would not happen out in space. The air continues to rise until it reaches a level where it is at the same density as the air around it. As it rises, the air cools *adiabatically* (see the box on page 13 "Adiabatic cooling and warming" in the section "Subtropical deserts").

Water evaporates into the warmed air and rises with it as water vapor. How much water vapor air can hold depends on the air temperature. Warm air can hold more water vapor than cool air, and as the air temperature falls, the relative humidity (RH, see the box "Humidity" on page 14 in the section "Subtropical deserts") rises. The temperature at which air becomes saturated (its RH reaches 100 percent) is known as its *dew-point* temperature. When this temperature is reached, water vapor will start to condense, and this is one way to measure dew-point temperature.

Over the equator, a great deal of warm, moist air rises and cools. Soon it reaches its dew-point temperature. Water starts to condense, clouds form, and when the cloud droplets grow too large and heavy for the rising air currents to support them, they fall as rain. That is why rainfall is high in equatorial regions. Air rises in some places, and between those places sinking air brings dry weather, as shown in the illustration on page 36. Even over the equator it does not rain all the time.

Most of the rising air travels upward until it reaches the tropopause. This is a boundary, over the equator at a height of about 10 miles (16 km), above which the temperature and density of air do not decrease with height, so it traps rising air beneath it. Once the air can rise no farther it spills away from the equator, to the north and south. At this height the air

Seasons and the Earth's orbit. Because of the tilt of the Earth's axis, when it is summer in one hemisphere, it is winter in the other. As the Earth travels around the Sun, these alternate.

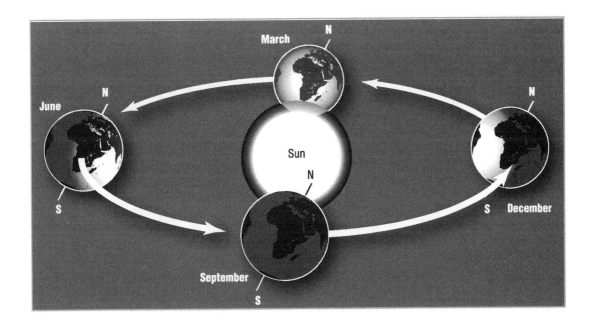

temperature is usually between –94°F (–70°C) and –120°F (–84°C), so it can hold almost no water vapor at all. It is extremely dry.

Sinking to produce subtropical deserts

Fed constantly by an endless supply of rising air and chilled to a very low temperature, the high-level air moves away from the equator—but, despite its low temperature, it does not sink (to find out why, see the box "Potential temperature" on page 37). At about latitude 30°, the tropical air meets air moving toward the equator and the two merge. That is where they sink all the way to the surface. Sinking air is compressed, because the lower it descends the greater is the weight of all the air in the atmosphere above it. As it sinks and is compressed it warms adiabatically. By the time it reaches the surface the air is hot, but still extremely dry. Where it reaches the surface, it creates dry, desert conditions.

Look again at a map of the world and you will see a belt of deserts in both hemispheres with their centers just outside the tropics of Cancer (Northern Hemisphere) and Capricorn (Southern Hemisphere). These are the subtropical deserts produced by warm, dry, sinking air. The Sahara, Arabian Desert, Thar Desert of India, Australian Desert, and the desert of Central America are generated by this movement of air. Subsiding air over the poles also produces deserts—the polar deserts.

Air circulation over the Tropics and subtropics. Air rises over the equator, moves away at high altitude, then sinks over the subtropics.

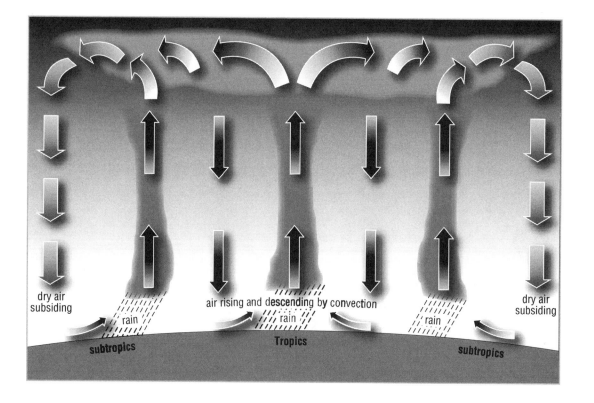

Potential temperature

Cold air is denser than warm air, because its molecules are closer together. Consequently a given volume of cold air has a greater mass than a similar volume of warm air and so it weighs more. Warm air rises because it is less dense than the cold air above it. The cold, dense air sinks beneath the warm, less dense air, and pushes it upward.

Air temperature decreases with height. If you climb to the top of a mountain, you expect the air to be colder there. High mountaintops are covered in snow, even in summer, and climbers take warm clothes with them. Why is it, then, that the cold, dense air at the top of a mountain, or at the top of the troposphere, does not simply sink to the surface? How does it manage to stay up?

To answer that you must imagine what would happen to the air if it did descend. Suppose, for example, that the air is fairly dry, with no clouds in the sky, and the temperature near to ground level is 80°F (27°C). Near the tropopause, 33,000 feet (10 km) above the surface, suppose the air temperature is –65°F (–54°C). The air near the tropopause is dense, because of its temperature, but this really means it is denser than the air immediately above it. Because air is very compressible, its density also decreases with height.

If the high-level air were to subside all the way to ground level, as it descended it would be compressed by the increasing weight of air above it, and it would heat adiabatically (see the box "Adiabatic cooling and warming" in the section "Subtropical deserts"). Because it is dry, the air would warm at the dry adiabatic lapse rate (DALR; see the box "Lapse rates and stability" in the section "Precipitation, evaporation, sublimation, deposition, and ablation"). The DALR is 5.4°F per 1,000 feet (9.8°C per 1,000 m). As the air descends 33,000 feet (10 km), its temperature will rise by 5.4 × 33 = 178.2°F (98°C). Add this increase to its initial temperature, and its temperature when it reaches the ground will be 178.2 – 65 = 113.2°F (44°C). This is much warmer than the actual ground-level temperature of 80°F (27°C). The air could not reach the ground, because it would be less dense, and therefore lighter, than the air below.

The temperature that air at any height above the surface would have if it were subjected to sea-level pressure of 1,000 mb (100 kPa, 29 in. of mercury) and warmed adiabatically as it was compressed is known as its *potential temperature* (usually symbolized by ϕ, which is the Greek letter phi). Potential temperature depends only on the actual pressure and temperature of the air. Meteorologists calculate the potential temperature of air to determine its stability.

The desert belt is wider than it would be if Earth were upright in relation to the plane of the ecliptic. Geographically, the equator is the line drawn on maps around the center of Earth, equidistant from the two poles, but the *thermal equator* has to be defined differently, as the line joining all points where the temperature is greatest. Earth's axial tilt causes the thermal equator to move with the seasons, from 23° N to between 10° S and 15° S. Its mean location over the year as a whole is about 5° N. The vertical movement of air by convection is centered on the thermal equator rather than the geographic one, so this also moves north and south with the seasons. Since the region in which air is rising moves, so does the region in which subsiding air produces hot, dry conditions. This spreads the desert belts into higher latitudes than they would otherwise occupy.

Not all the deserts in the world result from this circulation of tropical and subtropical air. Deserts also occur in the deep interior of Asia, where the air reaching them has traveled so far over land as to have lost its moisture, and in the lee of mountains on the western sides of continents in midlatitudes. Since midlatitude weather systems move from west to east, these areas are dry because the air loses its moisture as it rises over the mountains. They are in the rain shadow of the mountains. The deserts to the east of the Rockies in the United States are of this type.

General circulation of the atmosphere

This is part of the mechanism by which warmth moves from the equator into higher latitudes, and it was discovered more than 250 years ago. At that time, no one was thinking of explaining why deserts are where they are, of course. That would have been much too ambitious a project and, in any case, another consequence of this circulation was of far greater importance. If air is rising, air must also be flowing in at a low level to take its place. Air moving horizontally is a wind, and on either side of the equator the winds are very predictable. They blow from the northeast in the Northern Hemisphere and the southeast in the Southern, and are so predictable that sailors called them the *trade winds*, a name derived from the old German word for a track and referring to the fact that they are (almost) always there, and they always move in the same direction. It was the reliability of the trade winds that needed explaining and the large-scale circulation of tropical air was the mechanism that supplied the explanation.

Several scientists attempted the task, but the name most closely associated with this circulation is that of George Hadley (see the box on page 39), and the tropical convection he described is called a *Hadley cell*. It also explained something else of interest to sailors, which they called the *doldrums*. These are areas close to the equator where winds are almost always very light and variable in direction, and often no wind blows at all. Ships could be becalmed in them. They occur because converging trade-wind air also rises, quite gently, as it crosses the warm sea. Close to the thermal equator the air can be almost still because the air is moving vertically rather than horizontally. The result is the doldrums, on the eastern sides of the Atlantic and Pacific Oceans from October to June, but spreading far to the west from July to September. The doldrums also cover much of the equatorial Indian Ocean and western Pacific between October and December and in March and April.

Precipitation, evaporation, sublimation, deposition, and ablation

Imagine it is early in the winter and you are outdoors looking at a small lake. Ice has begun to form around the edges of the lake and now covers part of the surface. You can see ice and liquid water and the air around you

George Hadley and Hadley cells

When European ships began venturing far from their home ports, into the Tropics and across the equator, sailors learned that the trade winds are very dependable in both strength and direction. They made use of them, and by the end of the 16th century their existence was well known.

Many years passed, however, before anyone knew why the trade winds blow so reliably. Like many scientific explanations, this one developed in stages.

Edmund Halley (1656–1742), the English astronomer, was the first person to offer an explanation. In 1686 he suggested that air is heated more strongly at the equator than anywhere else. The warm equatorial air rises, cold air flows in near the surface from each hemisphere to replace it, and this in-flowing air forms the trade winds. If this were so, however, the trades on either side of the equator would flow from due north and south. In fact, they flow from the northeast and southeast.

There the matter rested until 1735. In that year George Hadley (1685–1768), an English meteorologist, proposed a modification of the Halley theory. Hadley agreed that warm equatorial air rises and is replaced at the surface, but he said that Earth's rotation from west to east swings the moving air, making the winds blow from the northeast and southeast.

Hardley was right about what happened, but not about the reason for it. This was discovered in 1856 by the American meteorologist William Ferrel (1817–91), who said the swing is due to the tendency of moving air to rotate about its own axis, like coffee stirred in a cup.

In accounting for the trade winds, Hadley had proposed a general explanation for the way heat is

(continues)

Three-cell model. The tropical (Hadley) and polar cells are directly driven by convection. The middle-latitude (Ferrel) cell is indirect, because it is driven by the polar and tropical cells.

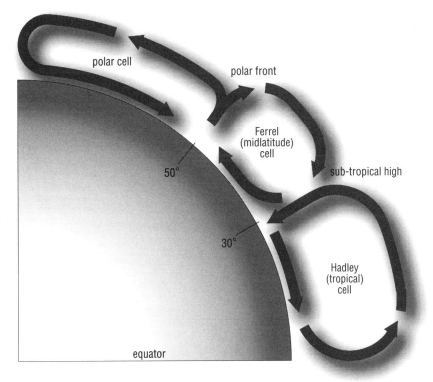

(*continued*)

transported away from the equator. He suggested that the warm equatorial air moves at a great height all the way to the poles, where it descends. This vertical movement in a fluid, driven by heating from below, is called a *convection cell*, and the cell Hadley described is known as a *Hadley cell*.

The rotation of Earth prevents a single, huge, Hadley cell from forming in each hemisphere. What really happens is more complicated. In various equatorial regions, warm air rises to a height of about 10 miles (16 km), moves away from the equator, cools, and descends between latitudes 25° and 30° N and S. These are the Hadley cells. When it reaches the surface in the Tropics, some of the air flows back toward the equator and some flows away from the equator.

Over the poles, cold air descends and flows away from the poles at a low level. At about latitude 50° it meets air flowing away from the equatorial Hadley cells. Where the two types of air meet is called the *polar front*. Air rises again at the polar front. Some flows toward the pole, completing a high-latitude cell, and some flows toward the equator until it meets the descending air of the Hadley cell, which it joins.

There are three sets of cells in each hemisphere. This is called the *three-cell model* of atmospheric circulation by which warm air moves away from the equator and cool air moves towards the equator.

General circulation of the atmosphere

The tropics of Cancer in the north and Capricorn in the south, mark the boundaries of the belt around Earth where the Sun is directly overhead at noon on at least one day in the year. The Arctic and Antarctic Circles mark the boundaries of regions in which the Sun does not rise above the horizon on at least one day of the year and does not sink below the horizon on at least one day in the year.

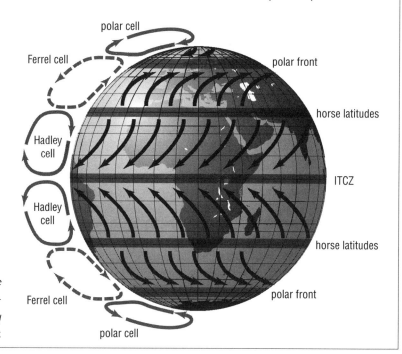

General circulation of the atmosphere. Air movements carry heat away from the equator.

contains water vapor. Water is present in its solid, liquid, and gaseous forms all in the same place at the same time.

The vapor is invisible, of course, but it is there all the same. Air always contains some water vapor. In really dry weather you might think the air was as dry as the ground, but even then there is moisture in the air and there is even some in the soil that seems completely dry.

Water is the only common substance that can exist in all three states at ordinary temperatures. We take it for granted, and everyone knows that water freezes at 32°F (0°C) and boils at 212°F (100°C), though this is true only of pure water at sea-level atmospheric pressure: impurities dissolved in it and changes in pressure alter its freezing and boiling points.

Polar molecules

Commonplace it may be, but this property of water is remarkable. Substances with molecules of approximately similar size usually freeze and boil at about the same temperatures. Water molecules, comprising two atoms

---

Imagine a beam of sunlight just a few degrees wide. This beam illuminates a much smaller area if the Sun is directly overhead than it does if the Sun is at a low angle in the sky. The amount of energy in each beam is the same, because they are of the same width, so energy is spread over a smaller area directly beneath the Sun than it is when the Sun is lower. This is why the Tropics are heated more strongly than any other part of Earth and the amount of heat we receive from the Sun decreases the farther we are from the equator.

The Sun shines more intensely at the equator than it does anywhere else, but movements of the air transport some of the warmth away from the equator. Near the equator, the warm surface heats the air in contact with it. The warm air rises and, near the tropopause, at a height of around 10 miles (16 km) it moves away from the equator, some heading north and some south. As it rises, the air cools, so the high-level air moving away from the equator is very cold—about –85°F (–65°C).

This equatorial air subsides around latitude 30°N and S, and as it sinks it warms again. By the time it reaches the surface it is hot and dry, so it warms this region some distance from the equator. At the surface, the air divides. This is a region of calm winds, sometimes called the horse latitudes

(because when supplies of fresh water ran low on ships carrying horses as cargo, some of the horses died and were thrown overboard). Most of the air flows back toward the equator and some flows away from the equator. The air from north and south meets at the Intertropical Convergence Zone (ITCZ), and this circulation forms a number of Hadley cells.

Over the poles, the air is very cold. It subsides and when it reaches the surface it flows away from the poles. At about latitude 50–60° N and S, air moving away from the poles meets air moving away from the equator. The colliding air rises to the tropopause, in these latitudes about 7 miles (11 km) above the surface. Some flows back to the poles, forming polar cells, and some flows toward the equator, completing Ferrel cells (discovered by the American meteorologist William Ferrel, 1817–91).

Follow this movement and you will see that warm air rises at the equator, sinks to the surface in the subtropics, then flows at low level to around latitude 55°, then rises to continue its journey toward the poles. At the same time, cold air subsiding at the poles flows back to the equator.

If it were not for this redistribution of heat, weather at the equator would be very much hotter than it is, and weather at the poles would be a great deal colder.

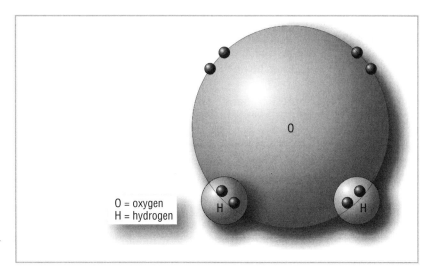

O = oxygen
H = hydrogen

The water molecule. The black circles indicate the positions of the outer-shell electrons. which explains why the water molecule is polar.

of hydrogen and one of oxygen (H_2O), are much the same size as those of ammonia (NH_3), hydrochloric acid (HCl), and methane (CH_4), but water freezes and boils at much higher temperatures than any of these. Ammonia freezes and boils at –108°F (–78°C) and –28°F (–33°C); hydrochloric acid at –175°F (–115°C) and –121°F (–85°C); and methane at –299°F (–184°C) and –263°F (–164°C).

It is not the size of its molecules that gives water its peculiar properties, but their composition and structure. Each water molecule consists of an atom of oxygen bonded to two hydrogen atoms, both of which are on the same side of the oxygen atom, separated by an angle of 104.5°. The water molecule is shaped like a rather open V and its atoms are held together by attraction between opposite electrical charges. The diagram above shows how the atoms are arranged. The nucleus of each atom carries a positive charge (because the nucleus contains protons, with positive charge), which is balanced by the negative charge on its electrons (the negative charge on an electron is equal to the positive charge on proton). The atoms in a water molecule share some of their outermost electrons. This is called a *covalent* bond. Four of the oxygen electrons (negative charge) are on the oxygen side of the molecule and the other four are shared with hydrogen atoms on the opposite side of the molecule. The result is a small negative charge at the oxygen end of the molecule, a small positive charge at the hydrogen end, but a molecule that is electromagnetically neutral overall. A molecule of this type is said to be *polar.*

Hydrogen bonds

When hydrogen forms a molecule with oxygen (O), fluorine (F), or nitrogen (N), each of which carries a strongly negative charge, a further bond can form between the hydrogen in the molecule and the negatively charged O, F, or N atom in a neighboring molecule. This is called a hydrogen bond and it links water molecules together as groups of molecules in the liquid and more firmly in ice.

Molecules are in constant motion and the more energy they have the faster they move and the greater the distance between them. In a gas, the molecules move independently of one another in straight lines, ricocheting when they collide with one another or with any other object. Cool them and they lose energy, move closer together, and become a liquid. At still lower temperatures they lock together so tightly they can only vibrate, and form a solid. In order to change from solid to liquid or liquid to gas, the molecules must absorb enough energy to accelerate them to the required speed. In most cases, how much energy this takes depends on the size of the molecules, but if molecules in the liquid and solid are linked by hydrogen bonds, additional energy is needed to break those bonds. This raises the melting and boiling points of substances with hydrogen bonds. Ammonia and water molecules are linked by hydrogen bonds and without them would melt and boil at lower temperatures.

The energy needed to break the attraction between molecules has no effect on the temperature of the substance. It is called *latent heat* and, because of its hydrogen bonds, the latent heat of water is higher than that of most substances (see the box on page 44).

Evaporation

Pure water boils at 212°F (100°C), but it will evaporate at any temperature. Within the liquid, all the molecules are moving, the hydrogen bonds that link them into small groups constantly breaking and reforming, and the warmer the water the faster they move. If you heat water, individual molecules absorb the added heat. This addition of energy accelerates them and some move fast enough to break from the surface into the layer of air immediately above the surface. Water molecules in this layer are also entering the liquid, so it contains molecules moving in both directions. They exert a pressure on the liquid surface, called the *vapor pressure*, and there is a vapor pressure at which the layer is saturated and can contain no more water molecules. This is known as the *saturation vapor pressure* and it varies with the temperature, so that as the temperature increases the amount of water vapor needed to saturate the air also increases. Saturation vapor pressure reaches a maximum of 1,013 millibars (100 kPa; 14.5 lb. in.^{2}; 29.5 inches of mercury) at 212°F (100°C). At saturation vapor pressure the layer can hold no more water vapor, so if any water molecules enter, an equal number instantly condense into liquid.

If molecules that escape from the liquid surface enter a layer that is below its saturation vapor pressure, they are able to pass through it and into the air beyond. That is evaporation.

Sublimation and deposition

In really cold but sunny weather, when the temperature is well below freezing, thin patches of snow and ice sometimes dwindle in size and even-

Latent heat and dew point

Water can exist in three different states, or phases: as gas (water vapor); liquid (water); or solid (ice). In the gaseous phase, molecules are free to move in all directions. In the liquid phase, molecules join together in short "strings." In the solid phase, molecules form a closed structure

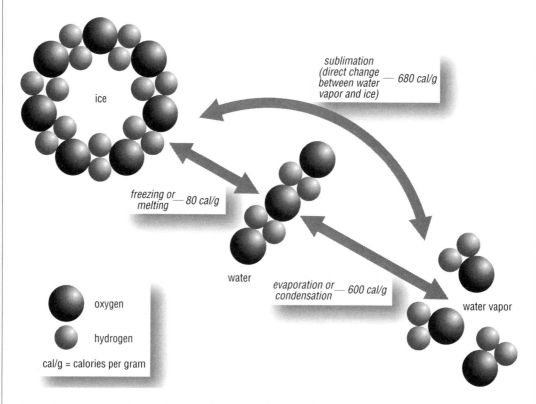

sublimation (direct change between water vapor and ice) — 680 cal/g

ice

freezing or melting — 80 cal/g

water

evaporation or condensation — 600 cal/g

water vapor

oxygen

hydrogen

cal/g = calories per gram

Latent heat. As water changes between the gaseous, liquid, and solid phases, the breakage and formation of hydrogen bonds linking molecules release or absorb energy as latent heat.

tually disappear. The ice has evaporated directly into the air. This is called *sublimation*. Water molecules in the ice or snow crystals have absorbed enough energy from the sunshine for them to break their hydrogen bonds and escape. This requires more energy than the escape from liquid, because there are more hydrogen bonds linking the molecules in ice. The air must also be very dry, because at low temperatures it can hold only a little water vapor.

There is a single value for the saturation vapor pressure at any temperature above freezing, but there are two values at temperatures below freezing. This is because the saturation vapor pressure over an ice surface with a space at the center. As water cools, its molecules move closer together and the liquid becomes denser. Pure water at sea-level pressure reaches its densest at 39°F (4°C). If the temperature falls lower than this the molecules start forming ice crystals. Because these have a space at the center, ice is less dense than water and, weight for weight, has a greater volume. That is why water expands when it freezes and why ice floats on the surface of water.

Molecules bond to one another by the attraction of opposite charges and energy must be supplied to break those bonds. This energy is absorbed by the molecules without changing their temperature, and the same amount of energy is released when the bonds form again. This is called *latent heat*. For pure water, 600 calories of energy are absorbed to change one gram (1 g = 0.035 oz.; 600 cal g^{-1} = 2,501 joules per gram; joules are the units scientists use) from liquid to gas (evaporation) at 32°F (0°C). This is the *latent heat of vaporization* and the same amount of latent heat is released when water vapor condenses. When water freezes or ice melts, the *latent heat of fusion* is 80 cal g^{-1} (334 J g^{-1}). Sublimation, the direct change from ice to vapor without passing through the liquid phase, absorbs 680 cal g^{-1} (2,835 J g^{-1}), equal to the sum of the latent heats of vaporization and fusion. Deposition, the direct change from vapor to ice, releases the same amount of latent heat. The amount of latent heat varies very slightly with temperature, so this should be specified when the value is given. The standard values given here are correct at 32°F (0°C). The diagram on page 49 illustrates what happens.

Energy to supply the latent heat is taken from the surrounding air or water. When ice melts or water evaporates, the air and water in contact with them are cooled, because energy has been taken from them. That is why it often feels cold during a thaw and why our bodies can cool themselves by sweating and allowing the sweat to evaporate.

When latent heat is released by freezing and condensation, the surroundings are warmed. This is very important in the formation of the storm clouds from which hurricanes and tornadoes develop. Warm air rises, its water vapor condenses, and this warms the air still more, making it rise higher.

Warm air is able to hold more water vapor than cool air can, and the amount of water vapor air can hold depends on its temperature. If moist air is cooled, its water vapor will condense into liquid droplets. The temperature at which this occurs is called the *dew-point* temperature. It is the temperature at which dew forms on surfaces and evaporates from them.

At the dew-point temperature, the air is saturated with water vapor. The amount of moisture in the air is usually expressed as its *relative humidity* (RH). This is the amount of water present in the air expressed as a percentage of the amount needed to saturate the air at that temperature.

is always lower than that over a water surface at the same temperature. Water that remains liquid below freezing is said to be *supercooled*. Most clouds contain at least some supercooled water droplets. Under laboratory conditions water droplets can be cooled to as low as –40°F (–40°C) before they freeze spontaneously.

Water vapor can also freeze directly into ice without passing through a liquid phase. This is called *deposition*. It happens on clear, cold nights when frost, rather than dew, forms on plants and in the morning drivers have to scrape the ice from their windshields before they can move their cars.

Ablation

Glaciers and snowfields also lose snow and ice, even in the coldest conditions, by a combination of melting and sublimation. The overall effect is called *ablation* and the rate at which it occurs depends on the air temperature, humidity, the intensity of the sunshine, and various other factors.

One of these is the wind. Water evaporates or sublimes much more readily in a wind than when the air is still, and the stronger the wind the faster it carries away water vapor. We have been making use of this throughout history, of course, every time we have hung out washing to dry in the wind. It happens because of air turbulence. As the wind blows across the land surface, small irregularities produce eddies. These carry much of the water vapor aloft and replace it at the surface with dry air from a higher level, into which more water can evaporate or sublime.

Condensation and clouds

Once airborne, water vapor may be carried in air that cools to a temperature at which it becomes saturated, and the vapor starts to condense into droplets (see the box below). This is called its *dew-point temperature*.

Evaporation, condensation, and the formation of clouds

When air rises it cools adiabatically. If it is dry, at first it will cool at the *dry adiabatic lapse rate* of 5.5°F every 1,000 feet (10°C per km). Moving air may be forced to rise if it crosses high ground, such as a mountain or mountain range, or meets a mass of cooler, denser air at a front. Locally, air may also rise by convection where the ground is warmed unevenly.

There will be a height, called the *condensation level*, at which its temperature falls to its dew point. As the air rises above this level the water vapor it contains will start to condense. Condensation releases latent heat, warming the air, and once the relative humidity of the air reaches 100 percent and the air continues to rise, it will cool at the *saturated adiabatic lapse rate*, of about 3°F per 1,000 feet (6°C per km).

Water vapor condenses onto minute particles, called *cloud condensation nuclei* (CCN). If the air contains CCN consisting of minute particles of a substance that readily dissolves in water, water vapor will condense at a relative humidity as low as 78 percent. Salt crystals and sulfate particles are common examples. If the air contains insoluble particles, such as dust, the vapor will condense at about 100 percent relative humidity. If there are no CCN at all, the relative humidity may exceed 100 percent and the air will be supersaturated, although the relative humidity in clouds rarely exceeds 101 percent.

Cloud condensation nuclei range in size from 0.001 μm to more than 10 μm diameter, but water will condense onto the smallest particles only if the air is strongly supersaturated, and the largest particles are so heavy they do not remain airborne very long. Condensation is most efficient on CCN averaging 0.2 μm diameter (1 μm = one-millionth of a meter = 0.00004 inches).

At first, water droplets vary in size according to the size of the nuclei onto which they condensed. After that, the droplets grow, but they also lose water by evaporation, because they are warmed by the latent heat of condensation. Some freeze, grow into snowflakes, then melt as they fall into a lower, warmer region of the cloud. Others grow as large droplets collide and merge with smaller ones.

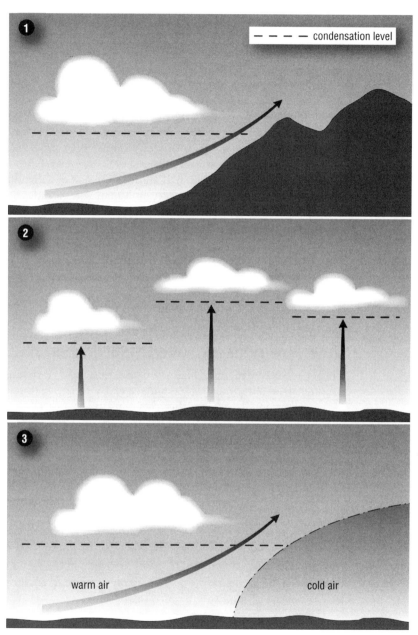

Why air rises. 1) Air is forced to rise over high ground (orographic lifting). 2) Air rises by convection, due to uneven heating of the ground. 3) Air is forced to rise along a weather front.

During a drought, water continues to evaporate, but often without condensing again. The air is so dry that it can hold all the water vapor entering it without becoming saturated. Even if clouds do form, no rain falls from them.

Watch the puffs of white cloud that drift across the sky on a fine day and they look quite stable—almost solid enough to touch. Study them through binoculars, however, and you will see they are constantly changing. Small bulges and wisps appear from them constantly, only to vanish a few moments later, and the whole cloud may last no more than a few hours before all its water evaporates. The cloud is surrounded by dry air. If cloud droplets—fragments or wisps of cloud—are blown into the surrounding air, they evaporate almost instantly.

It can take no more than half an hour for one of these little clouds to grow into a huge storm cloud seven miles tall and six miles across and yet an hour later that great cloud can have disappeared completely. Even in really cloudy weather, when a solid sheet of cloud covers the entire sky for days on end, individual parts of the cloud may last no longer than a day or two. Air moves through the cloud so fast that it soon carries bits of cloud away from the main mass and into drier air, where its droplets evaporate. Inside any cloud the individual water droplets and ice crystals last much less than an hour before they evaporate or sublime.

How do clouds manage to survive at all?

Clouds are very dynamic. Their water is constantly evaporating and condensing again, but some droplets and ice crystals manage to remain in a liquid or solid state. To achieve this, they must reach a certain size. They can do this only if the air immediately around them is slightly supersaturated (its relative humidity is greater than 100 percent; see the box "Humidity" in the section "Subtropical deserts"). This prevents their molecules escaping as vapor, and if air movements around them can bring more water vapor to them and carry away the latent heat of condensation, the droplets will grow.

They start very small, no more than about 0.2 μm (0.000008 inch) in diameter, but once they start to grow their size increases very rapidly. As soon as the droplets are more than about 100 μm (0.04 inch) across, they start to fall. As they fall, they collide and merge with other droplets. When they are more than 200 μm (0.08 inch) in diameter, they are heavy enough to fall from clouds in which there are only very weak upcurrents of air. If they reach the ground they are drizzle.

Droplets grow this way only in warm clouds, however, and most clouds are cold, even in the middle of summer and even over a hot desert. If the temperature at ground level is 90°F (32°C), it will be 30°F at 11,000 feet (–2°C at 3,350 m) if air temperature decreases with height at the dry adiabatic lapse rate (see the box on page 49). In parts of the cloud where the temperature is below freezing, supercooled water vapor will not condense into droplets, but will change directly into ice crystals. Once there are ice crystals present, water will evaporate from supercooled liquid

Lapse rates and stability

Air temperature decreases (or lapses) with increasing height. The rate at which it does so is called the *lapse rate*. When dry air cools adiabatically, it does so at about 5.5°F for every 1,000 feet (10° C per km). This is known as the *dry adiabatic lapse rate* (DALR).

When the temperature of the rising air has fallen sufficiently, its water vapor will start to condense into droplets. This temperature is known as the *dew-point temperature*, and the height at which it is reached is called the *lifting condensation level*. Condensation releases latent heat, which warms the air. Consequently, the air cools at a slower rate, known as the *saturated adiabatic lapse* rate (SALR). The SALR varies, but averages 3°F per 1,000 ft (6°C per km).

The actual rate at which the temperature decreases with height is calculated by comparing the surface temperature, the temperature at the tropopause (about –67°F; –55°C in middle latitudes), and the height of the tropopause (about seven miles; 11 km in middle latitudes). The result is called the *environmental lapse rate* (ELR).

If the ELR is less than both the DALR and SALR, rising air will cool faster than the surrounding air, so it will always be cooler and will tend to subside to a lower height. Such air is said to be absolutely stable.

If the ELR is greater than the SALR, air that is rising and cooling at the DALR and later at the SALR will always be warmer than the surrounding air. Consequently it will continue to rise. The air is then absolutely unstable.

If the ELR is greater than the DALR but less than the SALR, rising air will cool faster than the surrounding air while it remains dry, but more slowly once it rises above the lifting condensation level. At first it is stable, but above the lifting condensation level it becomes unstable. This air is said to be conditionally unstable. It is stable unless a condition (rising above its lifting condensation level) is met, whereupon it becomes unstable.

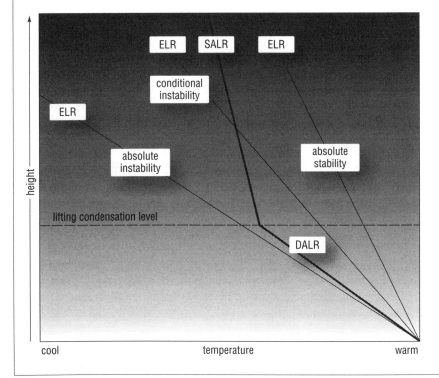

Lapse rates and stability. If the environmental lapse rate (ELR) is less than both the dry adiabatic lapse rate (DALR) and the wet adiabatic lapse rate (SALR), the air is absolutely stable. If the ELR is greater than the SALR, the air is absolutely unstable. If the ELR is less than the SALR but greater than the DALR, the air is conditionally unstable.

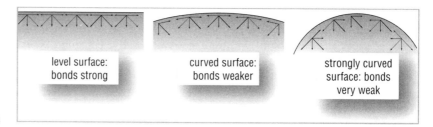

Curvature effect.

droplets and be deposited as ice onto the crystals. This happens because the saturation vapor pressure over ice is lower than that over liquid, but also because water evaporates much more easily from a droplet than from a large, level surface, and more rapidly from a small droplet than from a big one. As the diagram shows, this is because molecules are held more securely at a level surface than they are at a curved surface. Below the surface, each molecule is held by hydrogen bonds to molecules on all sides. At the surface, there are no molecules above, so molecules in this layer are held only from the side and below. If the surface is curved, molecules to the sides are in fact slightly below, so the bonds to the sides are weaker. The greater the curvature of the surface, the more weakly the surface molecules are held, and so the more likely they are to escape into the air, causing small droplets to evaporate faster than large droplets.

Once deposition begins, it proceeds much faster than the condensation of vapor into liquid droplets, as supercooled droplets evaporate and ice crystals grow at their expense. The cloud may then contain ice crystals near the top and water droplets in the lower levels, which are warmer. Ice crystals falling through the cold layers will grow as more supercooled droplets freeze onto them, but when they reach levels where the temperature is a degree or two above freezing they start to melt. In most clouds, even over the equator, droplets grow by a mixture of freezing and the growth of ice crystals, and the collision and merging of water droplets.

Eventually, when they are heavy enough, droplets fall from the base of the cloud. In fact, though, much smaller droplets are leaving the cloud all the time. The bulges and wisps that appear only to vanish again all around the fine-weather cloud you examine with binoculars are made from water droplets or, near the top of a tall cloud, ice crystals. After they emerge from the main mass of the cloud, they do not disappear because they have returned into it. Rather, they evaporate. Water vapor condenses because the relative humidity reaches saturation, but this does not happen everywhere. Where it does, cloud forms, and where it does not the air remains clear. Droplets that leave the cloud enter unsaturated air and simply evaporate, or ice crystals sublime. That is why clouds have shapes and why they also have clearly defined bases.

How big is a raindrop?

The air between the base of a cloud and the ground is not saturated. If it were, water vapor would condense in it and the cloud would extend to ground level, as fog. This means that water falling from the cloud enters unsaturated air. Consequently, it immediately starts to evaporate. Only drops of more than a certain minimum size can reach the ground before they vaporize.

The bigger the droplets, the greater is their mass in relation to their surface area. If the droplet is spherical, with a diameter of, say, 2 units, its volume $(4/3\pi r^3)$ will be 4.18 and its surface area $(4\pi r^2)$ 12.6; if its diameter is 4 units its volume will be 33.5 and its surface area 50.3. The ratio of volume to surface area for the first is 1:3.0 and for the second 1:1.5. Having a smaller surface area in relation to its weight (or mass), the bigger droplet will encounter relatively less air resistance than the smaller one, so it will fall faster. A drizzle droplet 200 μm in diameter falls at about 2.5 feet per second (0.76 m s^{-1}) and a rain droplet 500 μm in diameter falls at about 13 feet per second (4.0 m s^{-1}). Not only does the bigger droplet contain more water, allowing it to survive longer before it vaporizes, but it also falls faster, so it spends less time in the air.

Even so, the rain may never reach the ground. During a drought, and over a desert, the relative humidity of the air is low. The condensation level, marking the cloud base, will be fairly high and water falling from the cloud will have to travel a considerable distance through extremely dry air. Clouds do appear over even the driest deserts, and some of them may be big enough to produce rain, but the rain evaporates in the dry air just below the cloud. The evaporating rain is often visible below a cloud as what looks like a thin, gray veil, called *virga*. Only towering storm clouds can release water fast enough to saturate the air beneath the cloud as drops evaporate, allowing those that follow to fall to the ground.

Ocean currents and sea-surface temperature

Sunshine warms the ground, and the ground warms the air that is in contact with it. At the equator, the warm air rises and moves away to north and south. Thus begins the circulation of the atmosphere by which heat is carried from the equator to the poles (see the box "General circulation of the atmosphere" on page 40 in the section "Air movements and the transport of heat"). Without it, tropical climates would be very much hotter than they are and polar climates very much colder.

It is only part of the story, however, for the Sun shines on both land and sea and, unlike the rocks and soil of the land, the waters of the sea can move. Their movements also carry warmth from low to high latitudes, but the patterns the waters make are rather different from those of air movements.

The outcome is similar, however. Water is warmed near the equator, moves north and south, and its place is taken by cooler water flowing in from higher latitudes. In other words, heat is transported, with the result that it is distributed more evenly.

Ocean gyres

In each of the major oceans (the North and South Atlantic, the North and South Pacific, and the Indian), there are water currents that follow approximately circular paths, flowing clockwise in the Northern Hemisphere and counterclockwise in the Southern. These major currents are called *gyres*.

Ocean currents that flow near the surface are driven by the wind. On either side of the equator the prevailing winds are the northeasterly and southeasterly trades. The currents do not flow in the same direction as the wind, however, but at an angle of 45° to the right of it in the Northern Hemisphere and to the left of it in the Southern Hemisphere. The reason for this is explained in the section "West Coast deserts." The result is that the tropical currents flow from east to west in both hemispheres. As they approach the continents, the currents are deflected. As they move away from the equator, the currents are increasingly influenced by the Coriolis effect (see the box on page 53), the magnitude of which increases from zero at the equator to a maximum at the poles.

Below the surface, the effect of the wind decreases, and therefore the Coriolis effect becomes relatively stronger and the angle of deflection increases with depth. The direction of the current changes with increasing depth in what is called an *Ekman spiral*, down to an *Ekman depth* at which the current is flowing in the opposite direction from the surface current (see the section "West Coast deserts" on page 18).

The major currents

To either side of the equator, the North and South Equatorial Currents flow from east to west. As it approaches North America, the North Equatorial Current in the North Atlantic turns northward (to the right). It then becomes in turn the Antilles and Florida Currents and then the Gulf Stream, which flows along the North American coast, out into the Atlantic, and turns south in the latitude of Portugal and Spain to rejoin the North Equatorial Current.

As it starts to turn south, however, part of the Gulf Stream breaks away as the North Atlantic Drift. This current washes the coasts of northwestern Europe and becomes the Norwegian Current as it passes the coast of Norway and enters the Arctic Ocean. A current also flows northward along the western coast of Greenland and then south, as the Labrador Current, along the Canadian eastern coast. It meets the Gulf Stream near Newfoundland, where the reaction between warm and cold water generates frequent fogs.

The South Equatorial Current in the South Atlantic turns to the south as it approaches the South American continent. It becomes the Brazil Current, flowing down the eastern coast of South America all the way to the

The Coriolis effect

Any object moving toward or away from the equator and not firmly attached to the surface does not travel in a straight line. As the diagram illustrates, it is deflected to the right in the Northern Hemisphere and to the left in the Southern Hemisphere. Moving air and water tend to follow a clockwise path in the Northern Hemisphere and a counterclockwise path in the Southern Hemisphere.

The French physicist Gaspard Gustave de Coriolis (1792–1843) discovered the reason for this in 1835, and it is called the Coriolis effect. It happens because Earth is a rotating sphere, and as an object moves above the surface, Earth below is also moving. The effect used to be called the Coriolis "force" and it is still abbreviated as CorF, but it is not a force. It results simply from the fact that we observe motion in relation to fixed points on the surface.

Earth makes one complete turn on its axis every 24 hours. This means every point on the surface is constantly moving and returns to its original position (relative to the Sun) every 24 hours, but because Earth is a sphere, different points on the surface travel different distances to do so. If you find it difficult to imagine that New York and Bogotá—or

(continues)

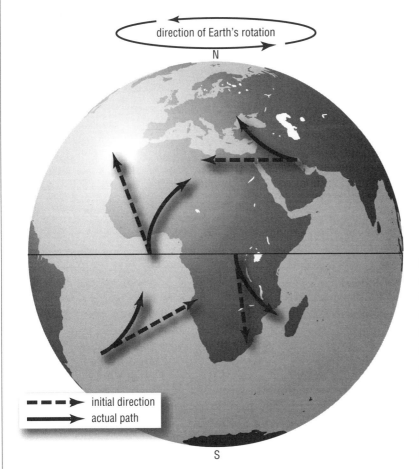

direction of Earth's rotation

N

initial direction
actual path

S

Coriolis deflection. Moving air masses, winds, and ocean currents are deflected to the right in the Northern Hemisphere and to the left in the Southern Hemisphere. The Coriolis effect is at a maximum at the poles and does not exist at the equator.

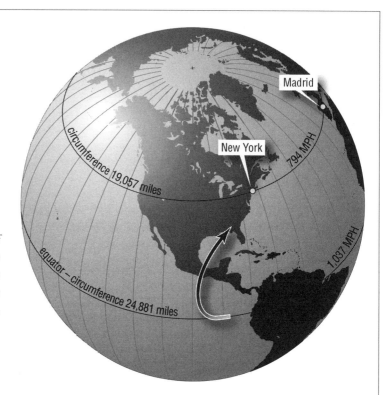

The Coriolis effect. The track of an aircraft flying from the equator to a destination in a higher latitude appears to be deflected to the east.

(continued)

any other two places in different latitudes—are moving through space at different speeds, consider what would happen if this were not so: the world would tear itself apart.

Consider two points on the surface, one at the equator and the other at 40° N, which is the approximate latitude of New York and Madrid. The equator, latitude 0°, is about 24,881 miles (40,033 km) long. That is how far a point on the equator must travel in 24 hours, which means it moves at about 1,037 MPH (1,668 km/h). At 40° N, the circumference parallel to the equator is about 19,057 miles (30,663 km). The point there has less distance to travel and so it moves at about 794 MPH (1,277 km/h).

Suppose you planned to fly an aircraft to New York from the point on the equator due south of New York (and could ignore the winds). If you headed due north you would not reach New York. At the equator you are already traveling eastward at 1,037 MPH (1,668 km/h). As you fly north, the surface beneath you is also traveling east, but at a slower speed the farther you travel. If the journey from 0° to 40° N took you 6 hours, in that time you would also move about 6,000 miles (9,654 km) to the east, relative to the position of the surface beneath you, but the surface itself would also move, at New York by about 4,700 miles (7,562 km). Consequently, you would end not at New York, but (6,000−4,700 =) 1,300 miles (2,092 km) to the east of New York, way out over the Atlantic. The diagram illustrates this.

The size of the Coriolis effect is directly proportional to the speed at which the body moves and the sine of its latitude. The effect on a body moving at 100 MPH (160 km/h) is 10 times greater than that on one moving at 10 MPH (16 km/h). Sin 0° = 0 (the equator) and sin 90° = 1 (the poles), so the Coriolis effect is greatest at the poles and zero at the equator.

Antarctic Circle. There it joins the West Wind Drift (also called the Antarctic Circumpolar Current), which flows from west to east right around Antarctica, but with a branch flowing north along the west coast of Africa as the Benguela Current. The West Wind Drift is the only ocean current that flows all the way around the world—it is able to do so because there are no land masses to interrupt its progress. This also means there is nothing to interrupt the winds. The height of an ocean wave is proportional to the strength of the wind and the distance over which the wind blows. Both are greater in the Southern Ocean than anywhere else and consequently that is where the fiercest winds and biggest sea waves are encountered (see the section "Polar deserts" on page 24).

In the Pacific, the Kuroshio and Oyashio Currents flow northward along the Japanese and mainland Asian coasts and the California Current flows south along the western coast of North America. To the south, the East Australia Current flows down the eastern coast of Australia and into the West Wind Drift, and the Peru (or Humboldt) Current flows northward along the western coast of South America.

There are currents flowing close to but in the opposite direction from certain of the major currents. The Equatorial Countercurrent flows from west to east close to the equator, between latitudes 5° and 10°, so it flows between the Equatorial Currents. There is also a current that flows from west to east between latitudes 1.5° N and 1.5° S, beneath the surface of the tropical Pacific Ocean. It was discovered in the 1950s by the oceanographer Townsend Cromwell and is called the Cromwell Current. Easterly winds blowing off the continent of Antarctica also drive a current, known as the Antarctic Polar Current, flowing from east to west, close to the coast.

North Atlantic Deep Water

Winds are the principal force driving ocean currents, but they are not the only one. In the North Atlantic, near the edge of the Arctic sea ice, dense water sinks beneath less dense water to its south, forming the North Atlantic Deep Water (NADW) that flows close to the floor of the Atlantic all the way to Antarctica.

Two factors, salinity and temperature, combine to increase the density of the water adjacent to the sea ice and cause it to sink to become the NADW. Common salt is sodium chloride (NaCl). Its sodium atom carries a positive electrical charge (written as Na^+) and its chlorine atom a negative charge (Cl^-). As the diagram on page 56 shows, when salt dissolves in water its sodium and chlorine separate. The sodium is attracted to the oxygen end of the water molecules (O^-) and its chlorine to the hydrogen end (H^+).

When the water freezes, its molecules move closer together and the sodium and chlorine are ejected, so ice consists of fresh water. The ejected salt (still as separate sodium and chlorine) goes into the water that is still unfrozen and, because that water now contains more salt, the density of the saltier solution increases. At the same time, the water near the edge of the ice is very cold, but not quite at freezing temperature. Sea water reaches its greatest density at about 32°F (0°C), which is the approximate temperature of the chilled water.

The water sinking to become the NADW is replaced at the surface by warmer water flowing north. This mechanism accounts for the North

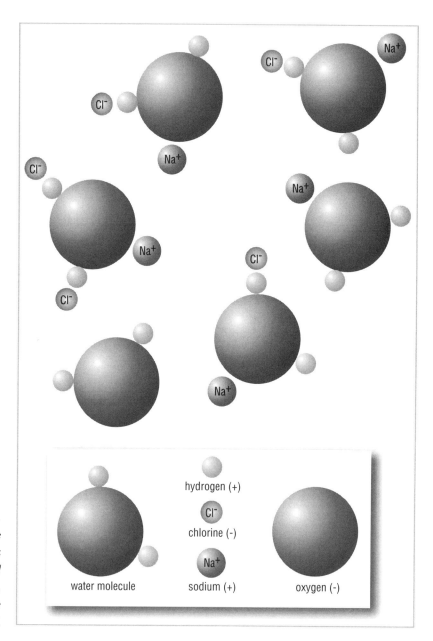

Common salt in solution. The sodium and chlorine separate. Sodium is drawn to the oxygen end of the water molecule, and chlorine, to the hydrogen end.

hydrogen (+)

chlorine (-)

sodium (+)

water molecule   sodium (+)   oxygen (-)

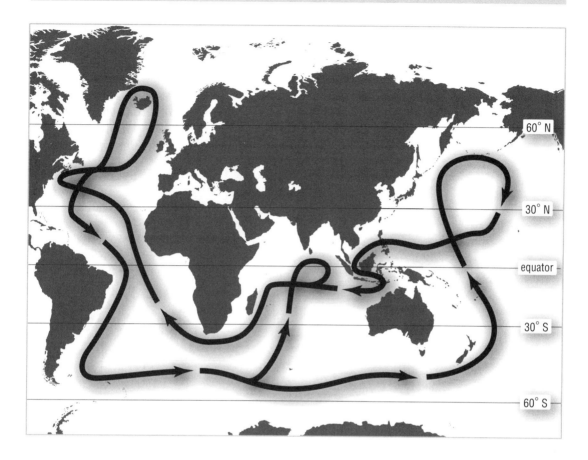

Atlantic Drift and contributes to the entire circulation of the Atlantic. Scientists believe changes in the formation of NADW, leading to changes in the ocean circulation, have been responsible for major changes in climate in the past. Should the formation of NADW change again in years to come, this would have a large effect on climate (see the section "Will climate change bring more droughts?").

The Great Conveyor. This system of currents carries warm water away from the equator and cold water toward it.

When it reaches the Southern Ocean, the NADW is joined by Antarctic Bottom Water, which is formed in exactly the same way. Together, these two deepwater currents follow a path that takes them through the Pacific and Indian Oceans before they finally return to the Atlantic. The map above shows the route they follow.

Boundary currents

In general, the ocean circulation brings warm water to the eastern coasts of continents and cool water to the western coasts. Currents that flow parallel to the coasts of continents are known as *boundary currents*. Because of the way the ocean gyres circulate, the boundary currents that pass close to the eastern coasts of the continents are carrying warm water away from the equator and those passing close to the western coasts carry cold water toward the equator.

Western boundary currents (on the western sides of oceans) are warm and eastern boundary currents (on the eastern sides of oceans) are cold, but that is not the only difference between them. Western boundary currents are deep, narrow, and swift. The Gulf Stream, for example, transports about 1,940,000 cubic feet (55 million m^3) of water, the Kuroshio about 2,295 million cubic feet (65 million m^3), and the Brazil about 353 million cubic feet (10 million m^3) every second. Eastern boundary currents are usually shallow, broad, and slow. The Canary Current, which is the current on the eastern side of the North Atlantic corresponding to the Gulf Stream on the western side, carries 565 million cubic feet (16 million m^3) per second.

The direct climatic effect of boundary currents is small, but significant, because coasts washed by warm currents enjoy milder winters than those washed by cold currents. More important, the current system carries warm water into high latitudes and thus contributes to the overall transport of heat.

The North Atlantic Drift and Norwegian Current are the exception to the general rule, because they bring warm water to northwestern Europe and this strongly influences the climate. At Vancouver, for example, the average daytime temperature in January is 41°F (5°C) and in Cherbourg, France, also on a west coast and in the same latitude, it is 47°F (8°C). The difference is small, but whereas the lowest January temperature recorded in Vancouver is 2°F (–17°C), in Cherbourg it is a much milder 21°F (–6°C). Poolewe, in a sheltered location on the western coast of Scotland at 57.77° N, is especially favored. A garden there contains plants more typical of a Mediterranean climate. Poolewe is in the same latitude as Kodiak Island, Alaska.

Scientists still have much to learn about the influence of ocean currents on climates, but there is no doubt that it is considerable.

Climate cycles and oscillations

We tend to think of the climate as eternally unchanging. There are good summers and bad summers, mild winters and hard winters, of course, but over a few decades these cancel one another. Travel back in time 100 or 1,000 years and everything would be different—except for the weather. Now we are told this may be changing.

Scientists are warning us that gases we release into the air may be altering the climate. Their warnings have caused widespread alarm, but that alarm is based at least partly on our belief that climate change is unusual and necessarily for the worse. This is wrong. The climate has changed many times in the past. One hundred years ago, at the beginning of the 20th century, the climate was still emerging from the prolonged cold period known as the *Little Ice Age*. One thousand years ago, early in the 10th century, people were living in a relatively warm period, when Viking settlers were establishing colonies in Iceland and Greenland—but the warm period they enjoyed was soon to end.

These are changes on the scale of centuries. Other changes, such as the onset and ending of ice ages, take place on the scale of tens of thousands or hundreds of thousands of years.

People living at these times would have been quite unaware of the changes that were happening. They move too slowly compared with a human lifetime, and in any case temperatures fluctuate during cold or warm periods. Even ice ages relent from time to time, and despite its name, the Little Ice Age included many warm summers. It is only by studying records that have been accumulated over a very long time that we are able to identify periods when the average temperature deviated from the average calculated over a much longer term. The people who lived during the medieval warm period, when Britain exported wine to France, or during the Little Ice Age, when the Thames froze so firmly that winter fairs were held on it, complete with fires roasting meat, would not have known that the weather familiar to them was in fact unusual and would change. So far as they were concerned, there were good years and bad years, but on balance the weather remained pretty much the same from one decade to the next.

There would have been those who said the weather had been different in the past. Those reports were misleading, however, because they were based on a trick our memories play. We remember events that stand out against a uniform background. Consequently, we remember the very hot summers of long ago, and the bitterly cold winters, but forget the many more years of ordinary weather that separated them. By forgetting conditions that were, quite literally, unmemorable, it is easy to suppose the hot summers and cold winters were much more common than in fact they were.

Recurring drought and Pacific salmon

Nevertheless, there are types of weather that recur at apparently regular intervals. Droughts occur on the Great Plains of North America approximately every 20 to 22 years, for example, and they have done so at least since the early 19th century.

The drought that afflicted the Sahel region during the 1970s attracted widespread attention and aroused fears that the Sahara was spreading rapidly along its southern border. These fears were based on the belief that the drought was a unique event, but there have been similar droughts in the past—and famines resulting from them. Sahel droughts occur when the intertropical convergence zone (ITCZ; see the box on page 60) remains well to the south of its usual summer position. The ITCZ moves with the seasons, bringing tropical rain with it. It reaches its most northerly position in the middle of August. That is the peak of the rainy season in the Sahel, but if the ITCZ remains farther

Intertropical convergence and the equatorial trough

The trade winds blow toward the equator in both hemispheres. Consequently, there is a region close to the equator where the winds meet. When two bodies of air flow toward each other, they are said to *converge*. The meeting of the trade winds is therefore the intertropical convergence and the region where it happens is the intertropical convergence zone (ITCZ). Because the ITCZ forms a boundary between air from the two hemispheres, it is sometimes called the intertropical front (ITF), although it is not a front strictly comparable to those in middle latitudes between polar and tropical air.

The ITCZ is more strongly developed over the oceans than over the continents, and even over the oceans it is evident only as an average. The convergence of the trade winds varies in strength, and disturbances form in it and then travel westward.

The position of the ITCZ changes through the year. The map shows its approximate location in February and August, as this is revealed by bands of clouds that are clearly visible on satellite images. As the map shows, the ITCZ is more often to the north of the equator than to the south and it seldom coincides with the equator itself.

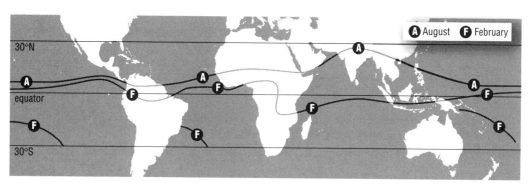

Location of the Intertropical Convergence Zone (ITCZ). The map shows the approximate location of the ITCZ and equatorial trough in February and August.

south, the rains fail to arrive. If it moves farther north than usual, the rainfall increases in the Sahel. During the summer of 2000, the ITCZ was much farther south than usual over the eastern side of Africa—and the weather was dry in Ethiopia and Somalia.

This is one of the cycles that may be linked to El Niño–Southern Oscillation (ENSO) events, which occur at intervals of five to seven years (see the section "El Niño and La Niña" on page 64). ENSO events are also believed to be the principal cause of another cycle that affects climates over the Pacific. From 1896 to 1914 the weather over the coastal regions of northwestern North America was generally wet and cool. There were relatively warm and dry years during this period, but the cool, wet years heavily outnumbered them. This period was followed by warm, dry weather lasting from 1915 until 1946, during which there were several

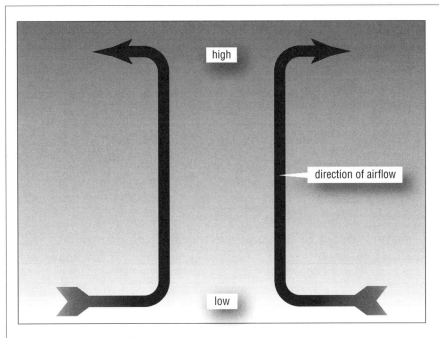

Convergence. Air converges and rises, producing low surface pressure and high pressure in the upper atmosphere.

Instead, its position coincides with the *thermal equator.* This is the region where the surface temperature is highest. Any change in the sea-surface temperature is likely to cause the ITCZ to move. The highest sea-surface temperature also produces the most highly developed convection, with the formation of convective clouds and heavy rain.

Both convergence and convection cause air to rise. This reduces air pressure near the surface and produces a region of high pressure in the upper air, where air diverges. The diagram shows what happens. The low surface pressure is known as the equatorial trough. The trough does not coincide precisely with the ITCZ, but is a short distance from it on the side farthest from the equator.

droughts lasting longer than one year. The weather was cool and wet again from 1947 until 1975, then warm and dry from 1976 until 1994. While the Pacific Northwest was experiencing one phase in this cycle, Alaska was experiencing the other, so that warm, dry weather in one was accompanied by cool, wet weather in the other. These four periods lasted for 18, 31, 28, and 18 years.

What drew them to the attention of scientists was a curious correlation with salmon populations. For reasons no one understands, salmon numbers increase during cool, wet periods and decline during warm, dry periods.

The Pacific Decadal Oscillation (PDO) is another cycle. It is an alternation of warm and cold phases affecting the lower atmosphere that occurs over a period of several decades in the ocean-atmosphere system in the Pacific basin.

Yet another cycle affects the warmest part of the Pacific Ocean. This is a region in the far west, around Indonesia, called the *warm pool*, where the sea-surface temperature can rise as high as 95°F (35°C). The temperature in the warm pool rises and falls over an approximately 20-year cycle. Most of the time, these changes have only a small climatic effect, altering the humidity of the air over the western Pacific and the Indian Ocean. During an El Niño year, however, the state of the warm pool becomes important. During an El Niño, water in the tropical western Pacific is cooler than normal. If this coincides with a cool phase in the warm pool, the El Niño is amplified considerably, bringing extreme weather to Australia and the midwestern United States.

Madden-Julian Oscillation

In 1971 Roland Madden and Paul Julian discovered a further cyclical change in conditions over the tropical oceans. This is now known as the *Madden-Julian Oscillation* (MJO). It occurs over a period of 30 to 60 days, and it is the principal fluctuation responsible for variations in tropical weather through the year—remember that the equatorial climate does not have strongly marked seasons.

The MJO moves eastward along the equator at about 11 MPH (5 m s^{-1}) and its effects are most pronounced in the Indian Ocean and the western Pacific. It involves changes in wind, cloudiness, rainfall, and sea-surface temperature. As the MJO approaches, the trade-wind inversion (see the box "Temperature inversions" on page 12 in the section "Subtropical deserts") strengthens over an area where the sea-surface temperature is lower than it is elsewhere. This suppresses convection, reducing the amount of cloud and rainfall. At the same time the trade winds strengthen. Increasing sunshine, due to the clear skies, warms the sea surface and, together with the stronger winds, increases evaporation. The wind strength weakens as the MJO continues to pass overhead, and this reduces the rate of evaporation. Moist air moves into the area, over what is now a warm sea, producing vigorous convection and clusters of huge clouds, with heavy rain.

North Atlantic Oscillation

Apart from the El Niño–La Niña seesaw, the most dramatic weather cycle of all is called the North Atlantic Oscillation (NAO). It was once thought to affect only the climates of northwestern Europe, but we now know that the NAO influences the weather over almost all of the temperate regions of the Northern Hemisphere. This has led some scientists to call it the Northern Hemisphere Annular Mode (*annular* means "like a ring")—although North Atlantic Oscillation is still the most widely used name.

The NAO involves a change in the distribution of surface atmospheric pressure. There is an area of low pressure permanently centered on Iceland and an area of permanently high pressure in the subtropics, centered approximately on the Azores. The map below shows the location of these two pressure systems and hints at their implication.

The oscillation in the NAO affects the pressures in these centers and it is measured on an index. The NAO index gives a zero value to the average situation, then records deviations from it. The index is positive when pressure is higher than average in the Azores high and lower in the Iceland low, increasing the difference between the two. It is negative when the difference is below average.

Air circulates (in the Northern Hemisphere) counterclockwise around centers of low pressure and clockwise around centers of high pressure. Consequently, as the map indicates, the Iceland low and Azores high combine to generate westerly winds over middle latitudes. The westerly winds drag weather systems with them. The greater the pressure difference between the high and low, the stronger are the winds and the more rapidly

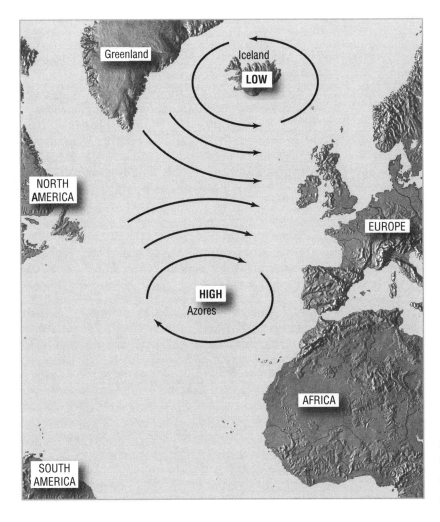

North Atlantic Oscillation. Weather systems are driven by pressure differences.

weather systems move. When the NAO index is positive, more storms cross the ocean in winter and the storms themselves are stronger. They also follow a track that is farther north than it is when the index is neutral or negative. With a positive index, western Europe has mild winters, winters are mild and wet in the eastern United States, and northern Canada and Greenland have cold, dry winters. When the NAO index is negative, there are fewer winter storms and the storms are weaker. The Mediterranean region has wet winters, winters are cold and dry in northern Europe, but winters are mild in Greenland. There are more cold air outbreaks in the eastern United States, so there is more snow.

During the latter part of the 19th century the cycle oscillated from positive to negative about every 10 years, but the negative troughs were more pronounced than the positive peaks, so the overall effect was more negative than positive. This changed during the 20th century. The index was positive most of the time from 1900 to about 1925, mainly negative from the 1930s to the 1970s, and mainly positive since then.

The effect is important. A strongly positive index increases average winter temperatures in Europe and the eastern United States by about 9°F (5°C). This is sufficient to account for the mild winters of the 1980s and 1990s. The positive NAO index may also account for a reported thinning of the sea ice in the Arctic Ocean. When the index is positive, average wind speeds increase over the North Atlantic. They blow from the west at about longitude 20° W, and approximately from the southwest at about 10° W. Their effect is to accelerate the North Atlantic Drift. Water moves more rapidly beneath the sea ice and because it travels faster it has less time to cool as it enters higher latitudes, so the water is warmer. The relatively warm, fast-flowing current melts the Arctic sea ice from below, reducing its thickness.

Climates are constantly changing for entirely natural reasons. Cycles and oscillations move, sometimes haltingly, over periods of decades, alternating warm and wet with cold and dry conditions. These repeating changes can bring drought. As the cycle advances, the drought ends, but the message of all recurring patterns is that sooner or later the drought will return.

El Niño and La Niña

Irregularly, at intervals of two to seven years, climates over some parts of the world are affected by a change in the circulation of air, and an associated change in a particular ocean current. The effects of these events are occasionally so dramatic as to provide a clear demonstration of the extent to which our weather systems are linked to the transport of heat by the oceans. Ordinarily, this is not easy to see. Like some obscure component of a car engine, it is only when it goes wrong that we become aware of its existence. In this case nothing has gone wrong, of course—the change is entirely natural.

Although the effects of the change have been noticed and recorded for centuries, it is only over the last few decades that scientists have discovered the reason for them. The change in an ocean current linked to the effects was known, but until the middle 1970s this change was thought to be much too small to be important, except very locally, perhaps. Then, in 1976, it was linked to drought, famine, and the collapse of one of most important fisheries in the world, all of which had taken place in 1972 and 1973. After that, the scientific investigation of the phenomenon accelerated and much more has been learned about it. One of the discoveries is that its influence is less widespread than it was thought to be.

The first reported instance of this particular change in the weather is believed to have been in 1541, but there is evidence showing it has occurred at intervals over the last 5,000 years. Clearly it is not a new phenomenon. More recently, it has occurred on a large scale in 1925, 1941, 1957, 1965, 1972, 1982, 1987, and 1997–98. It was also recorded in 1992 and 1995, but more detailed studies revealed that a single episode began in 1990 and continued until the middle of 1995.

Walker circulation and the Southern Oscillation

Despite having been overlooked for so many years, what is now regarded as the first clue to what happens was discovered in 1923 by Sir Gilbert Walker (1868–1958). Walker, a British meteorologist who had been director of the Indian meteorological service since 1904, had a particular interest in the causes of the Asian monsoons. These are extremely important in the subcontinent, because if the monsoon is weaker than usual or fails entirely, the crops also fail. Monsoon failures had caused severe famine in India in 1877 and 1899. The government asked Walker to find out whether monsoon failures could be predicted early enough to allow emergency food supplies to be prepared for distribution. What Walker found is that the easterly trade winds are balanced by a westerly (west to east) airflow close to the tropopause. This is known as the *Walker circulation*. He also found that the monsoons are greatly affected by the distribution of air pressure and winds over the Tropics and subtropics in both hemispheres. (It is still not possible to predict monsoon failures reliably.)

This is where he made his most important discovery. In some years, for reasons scientists still do not understand, atmospheric pressure is lower than usual over Indonesia and the eastern side of the Indian Ocean and higher than usual over Easter Island and the southeastern Pacific. In other years the pattern is reversed, with higher than usual pressure over Indonesia and lower than usual pressure over Easter Island. This changing pattern of pressure distribution continues all the time, reaching its maxima at intervals of two to seven years. He called this periodic change the *Southern Oscillation* (it is conventionally written with initial capital letters).

Low pressure over Indonesia brings heavy rain there, associated with rising air. On the opposite side of the Pacific, near the western coast of South America, air is subsiding. This pressure pattern strengthens the trade winds, and these drive the Equatorial Current, which flows from east to west parallel to the equator. The sea surface is warm and often close to the highest temperature that seawater can attain—about 85°F (29°C). It can rise no higher than this with the available amount of solar energy, because of the high rate of evaporation at this temperature. Evaporation cools the surface by drawing latent heat from it (see the box on page 44 in the section "Precipitation, evaporation, sublimation, deposition, and ablation"). When the temperature reaches about 85°F (29°C), evaporative cooling balances the accumulation of warmth from the Sun.

Ocean currents and upwellings

The Equatorial Current flows at the surface, carrying warm water away from South America and toward Indonesia. It is replaced by the Peru (or Humboldt) Current, which flows northward close to the South American coast. This is a cool current. When it enters the Tropics, its waters are at about 68°F (20°C) or lower, and sometimes as low as 61°F (16°C), making it the coldest seawater anywhere in the Tropics. The Peruvian coast bulges into the Pacific and deflects the Peru Current to the west. Eventually it joins the Equatorial Current.

As it flows northward the Peru Current is pushed away from the coast by the Ekman spiral (explained in the section "West Coast deserts") and this generates numerous upwellings of water from near the seabed. The bottom water brings up nutrients scoured from the seabed sediments that encourage vigorous growth of marine plants (phytoplankton). These, in turn, support a vast fish population, and the fish are food to huge flocks of seabirds.

Economically the cold upwellings are extremely important. Peru has one of the world's largest fishing industries, based mainly on the Pacific anchovy *(Engraulis ringens)*. Seabird droppings form *guano* (from the Quechua word *huanu*, meaning "dung"), a rich fertilizer that used to be mined and exported.

Not all the consequences are beneficial, however. Air crossing the tropical Pacific from east to west is chilled and loses most of its moisture before arriving at the coast, producing very dry conditions along the coasts of Chile and Peru. Lima, Peru, receives an average of only 1.6 inches (41 mm) of rain a year, most of it in winter (May to September). Applying the equation for effective precipitation (see the section "Subtropical deserts" on page 9), $r \div t = 0.2$, makes the climate that of a very dry desert.

Trade winds and the warm pool

The Sun warms the surface of the ocean. Warm water forms a surface layer overlying much cooler water. Ordinarily, the Equatorial Current carries warm surface water away from South America and it accumulates around Indonesia in the warm pool (see the section "Climate cycles and oscillations" on page 58). Consequently, the layer of warm water is deep around Indonesia and shallow near the South American west coast. It is the shallowness of the warm-water layer that allows the cold upwellings of nutrient-rich bottom water to rise almost to the surface.

During a Southern Oscillation, however, the pattern changes. Atmospheric pressure increases over Indonesia and decreases over Easter Island and the southeastern Pacific. This reduction of the difference in pressure weakens the mechanism driving the trade winds. These slacken and occasionally cease entirely or even reverse their direction. The weakening of the trade winds reduces the force driving the Equatorial Current, so the current also weakens. Its weakening reduces the rate at which warm water is being shifted westward. The layer of warm water around Indonesia grows shallower and warm water accumulates near South America. From June to December 1972, for example, the sea-surface off the Peruvian coast warmed to 6–7°F (3–4°C) above its usual temperature. In effect, the warm surface water forms a small current of its own.

El Niño

This current had been known locally for centuries. Usually it develops in the middle of summer, which in the Southern Hemisphere is Christmastime. That is why local people called it *El Niño*, the boy-child. Like the infant Jesus, it brings good fortune, at least to some. Air crossing the ocean is no longer chilled and dried as it approaches the coast. Instead, moisture evaporates into it from the warm surface and falls as rain on the arid coastal strip. A place in northern Peru that received less than one inch (25 mm) of rain between November 1981 and June 1982 received 156 inches (3,960 mm) between November 1982 and June 1983. That is what El Niño can do. Despite causing floods and mudslides, on the whole it is good for farmers, who enjoy an *año de abundancia*, a year of plenty.

Unfortunately, not everyone benefits. When the depth of warm water increases, the cold upwellings of the Peru Current are suppressed. The nutrient-rich waters no longer reach the surface layer, and marine plants starve. As their population decreases, the fish feeding on them also starve, or migrate to richer waters far out at sea, and fish catches decrease sharply. The fishermen enjoy a Christmas vacation, but it is a vacation that extends long into the following year. Peruvian fishermen caught almost 14 million tons of fish in 1970. In 1973, following a strong El Niño, they caught only 2.4 million tons. To all intents and purposes the fishery collapsed, bringing great hardship to the communities dependent on it. Catches recovered very slowly in the years that followed and conservation measures have since been introduced to make the industry more sustainable. It takes a long time for the numbers of fish to grow again and stocks remain vulnerable to El Niño episodes. They fell drastically in 1983, following the 1982 El Niño, although later ones have had less effect.

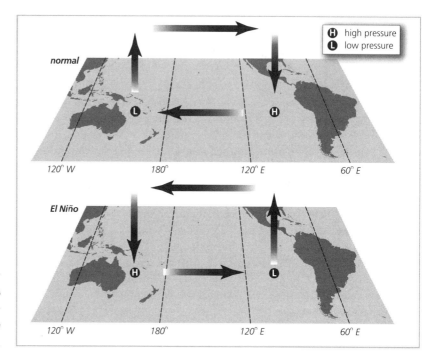

El Niño/Southern Oscillation (ENSO) cycle. A reversal of pressure distribution allows warm water to flow eastward.

Once the link between El Niño and the Southern Oscillation was recognized, it became customary to join their names, because a reference to one clearly implicates both. Today the phenomenon is known as an *El Niño–Southern Oscillation*, or ENSO. It is best known and most pronounced in the Pacific, but a much weaker ENSO is believed to occur in the tropical Atlantic, affecting the weather in West Africa.

Southern Oscillations can work in both directions, of course. Sometimes the ordinary distribution of pressure strengthens, the trade winds blow harder, and the pool of warm water around Indonesia grows deeper while waters off South America grow cooler. For want of a better name, scientists have called this *La Niña*.

Serious though it is for the fishermen of Peru, the effects of ENSO extend much further than the eastern tropical Pacific and last much longer than the years in which they occur. The disturbance they produce in the oceanic circulation sends out what are known as *Rossby waves* after Carl-Gustav Rossby (1898–1957), the Swedish-American meteorologist who discovered such waves in the atmosphere. The waves move slowly, at about $\frac{1}{10}$ of a mile per hour (0.16 kmh), and are very long, measuring some thousands of miles from one wave crest to the next. Ten years after the 1982–83 ENSO, the Rossby waves associated with it had crossed the Pacific and altered the path of the Kuroshio Current, raising the sea-surface temperature in the northwestern Pacific by about 2°F (1°C). This was an increase comparable to the original warming in the Tropics. It was believed to be affecting the climate of North America, and scientists expected its effects to continue for at least another 10 years.

El Niño and the weather

Minor ENSO events have little effect outside the Tropics. They produce drier conditions over Indonesia, Papua New Guinea, eastern Australia, northeastern South America, the Horn of Africa, East Africa and Madagascar, and in the northern part of the Indian subcontinent. Conditions are wetter over the central and eastern tropical Pacific, parts of California and the southeastern United States, eastern Argentina, central Africa, southern India, and Sri Lanka.

A strong association has also been found between ENSO events and corn (maize) yields in Zimbabwe. Corn is the most important food crop in Zimbabwe, and yields depend on the amount of rainfall between January and March. Drought, with low crop yields, is usually unexpected, but now that ENSO events can sometimes be predicted, it is possible to warn farmers in advance, and governments can anticipate possibly reduced harvests. Surplus food from a previous good harvest can be taken into government stores, for example, or food can be imported and stockpiled before world prices start to rise. ENSO prediction has already benefited Brazil. There, the drought caused by the 1987 ENSO reduced crop yields by 85 percent, but by 1992 the ENSO was predicted long enough in advance for farmers to prepare, by installing irrigation or changing to crop varieties that need less water, and the harvest was only slightly lower than normal.

Intense ENSO events may affect a wider area. Vigorously rising air produces two cells of high pressure in the upper troposphere, centered at about latitudes 20° N and S. They intensify the Hadley-cell circulation (see the box on page 39 in the section "Air movements and the transport of heat"). The cells also cause high-level easterly winds to develop, and they feed air into the jet stream.

This should carry the influence of El Niño and La Niña into middle latitudes, but no two ENSO events are identical and the climates of middle latitudes are highly changeable. It is difficult to confirm any link to weather outside the Tropics, although El Niño does weaken hurricanes by strengthening the jet stream. El Niño winters are usually mild over western Canada and parts of the northern United States and wet over the southern United States. El Niño is only one of many factors influencing the weather, however, and its effect is easily overwhelmed. Consequently, predicting an ENSO event is not at all the same thing as predicting the weather that may or may not be associated with it.

There is a *Southern Oscillation Index* (also called an *El Niño Index)*, calculated by subtracting the average monthly atmospheric pressure in Darwin, Australia, from that measured at Tahiti. Ordinarily, the result is positive (greater than 1), but during an ENSO event it is strongly negative (less than 1). Another index, called the Trans-Niño Index, is based on changes in sea-surface temperature in the equatorial Pacific. These indices are used to identify and help predict ENSO events, and also to compare one ENSO with another.

Predicting ENSO

Since about 1985, scientists have been developing techniques for predicting forthcoming ENSO events. Prediction is becoming possible as scientists learn more about the behavior of the tropical ocean and atmosphere and as satellite monitoring alerts them to small changes in sea-surface temperatures. During the second half of 2001, for example, strong 30–60-day fluctuations in conditions due to the Madden-Julian Oscillation (see the section "Climate cycles and oscillations" on page 58) warned them that a warm-phase El Niño might be developing. The observed conditions suggested the gradual warming would continue. It would produce no major changes before the middle of 2002, but an El Niño might possibly begin late in 2002. Predicting ENSO events will be an important achievement, offering real benefits to people living in the Tropics.

There is no evidence that either the frequency or intensity of ENSO events will increase should the climate become warmer in years to come. Indeed, it is much more likely that they will weaken and become less frequent. Evidence of conditions in the remote past show that El Niño occurs most often when the climate is cold and that during ice ages there is a permanent El Niño. El Niños become less frequent during warm periods. They have become more frequent since early in the 20th century, however, while the global climate was warming, so the link with temperature may be weak.

Jet streams and storm tracks

Where air is rising, the atmospheric pressure at the surface is reduced. Where air is subsiding, the surface pressure is increased. These vertical movements of air produce patterns of high and low pressure that move and change constantly. Over the world as a whole, however, the large-scale atmospheric circulation produces regions in which pressure is usually higher or lower than it is elsewhere.

At the equator, air rises into the Hadley cell (see the box on page 39) system, and surface pressure is low. That air subsides into the subtropics, producing high pressure. Subsiding air over the poles produces high pressure there and in midlatitudes, where the tropical and polar cells drive a third cell (called the *Ferrel cell*), air is generally rising and pressure is low. The diagram illustrates the overall pattern. This pressure distribution is only an average, of course, and pressure often varies locally.

Prevailing winds

The vertical movement of air and distribution of pressure also produce patterns of *prevailing winds*—the direction from which the wind blows more often than it does from any other direction. Again, these are averages, although the easterly trade winds are very reliable. Near ground level, the wind is often deflected by hills or tall buildings, but in most places it will blow more frequently from one direction than from others. It means measuring the wind at regular intervals over a long time, but you can find out the commonest, or prevailing, wind direction around your home.

Over the world as a whole, the winds cancel one another. Winds blow with as much force from the east as they do from the west and there is no need to measure the winds to prove the fact. Wind is moving air and, because it is moving, the air possesses *kinetic energy*—the energy of motion. When the wind blows over the ground or surface of the sea, friction slows it. What happens is that a proportion of its kinetic energy is transferred from the moving air to the surface with which it is in contact. In other words, by blowing against the ground, the wind pushes it and over a large area the force is considerable. Think how the wind blowing against a

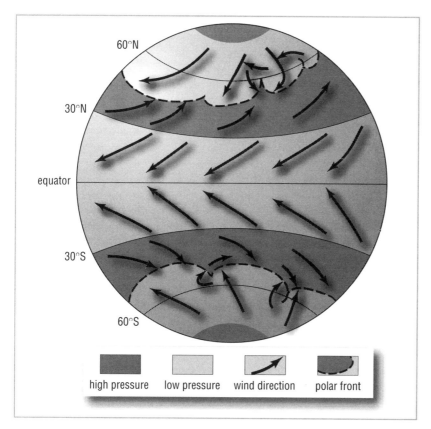

high pressure   low pressure   wind direction   polar front

Distribution of winds and pressure. Pressure and winds form distinct latitudinal belts. Low-pressure belts are associated with westerly winds; high-pressure belts, with easterlies.

mountain must be pressing against it. Continued for long enough, a wind from the west, in the same direction as Earth's rotation, could make Earth spin faster on its axis, and a wind from the east could slow it. Consequently, if the winds blew more strongly from one direction than the other, Earth would be either accelerated or slowed.

Occasionally this happens, but the effect is fairly brief. It happened in January 1990, for example, when winds blowing strongly across Asia and the Pacific slowed Earth by an amount that made one day (a full rotation) $\frac{1}{2000}$ of a second longer. That is a tiny difference, but if it continued for thousands of years it would build into a substantial slowing. Other factors also slightly accelerate or slow the rotational speed of Earth from time to time, but since there is no sustained change due to air movements, over the years the easterly and westerly winds must balance. They must also be constantly replenished by pressure systems. If more energy were not being fed into them all the time, friction would quickly slow the winds to a standstill.

Geostrophic wind

Friction slows the layer of moving air that is in direct contact with the surface. This layer is then moving more slowly than the layer above it. This causes friction between these layers, slowing the upper layer, which in turn slows the layer above it. The effect of friction against the surface extends to a height that varies according to the nature of the surface—it is higher over rough ground than over the sea, for example—but that seldom exceeds about 1,700 feet (518 m). Air between the surface and the maximum height at which friction can be detected comprises the *planetary boundary layer.*

Above the planetary boundary layer, well clear of the ground, the wind is not subject to friction with the surface and so it usually blows with more force. Its direction also changes with increasing height through the boundary layer, as the influence of friction diminishes. Above the boundary layer the wind blows parallel to the isobars—map lines joining points where the pressure is the same—and it is said to be *geostrophic.* The geostrophic wind results from a balance between the forces that cause the wind to blow.

Air moves away from centers of high atmospheric pressure and toward centers of low pressure. The force with which it does so depends on the difference in pressure between the two centers. You can think of the pressure difference as a sloping surface, or *pressure gradient.* This appears on weather maps as the distance between isobars. The steeper the gradient, the faster the air flows, like a ball rolling downhill, and the force pushing it is called the *pressure-gradient force.*

Once the air starts to move, however, it comes under the influence of the Coriolis effect (see the box on page 53). This deflects air moving away from the equator to the right in the Northern Hemisphere and left in the Southern, and pushes at right angles to the pressure-gradient force. These two forces oppose each other and achieve a balance with the air flowing parallel to the gradient, rather than across it, at a speed proportional to the gradient. This is the geostrophic wind. The wind in the planetary boundary layer is not geostrophic, because when friction slows the wind, the Coriolis effect (which is proportional to wind speed) is reduced. The pressure-gradient force is then the stronger of the two by a small amount, and so the wind blows across the isobars. It crosses at an average angle of about 45° over land and 30° over the sea, where there is less friction.

Constant-pressure surfaces and constant-height surfaces

When you climb a hill, the gradient is often steeper in some places than in others. A line at right angles to the contours will also change direction. Atmospheric pressure often changes with height in the same way. That is why you sometimes see high-level clouds moving faster than clouds below them (the pressure gradient has steepened) or in a different direction.

Isobars are often likened to the height contours on ordinary maps, but this can be misleading. If you could remove all the land above a certain height contour, the result would be a level plane. Obviously, everywhere on the plane would be at the same height. If you could do the same with isobars, the resulting surface would be at the same pressure everywhere, but it would not all be at the same height. The diagram illustrates this. On the left a hill has been cut through at the 500-foot contour, exposing a flat surface, all at the same height. On the right, the exposed surfaces are at different atmospheric pressures. They are *pressure surfaces*. These would be

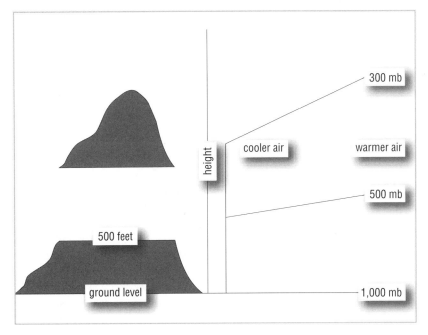

Height contours and isobars. The section on the left shows a constant-height surface. The three on the right are constant-pressure surfaces.

shown on a map as contour-like isobars, but, as you see, they slope in relation to ground level.

The layers of air between the 1000 mb level and 500 mb level and between the 500 mb level and 300 mb level are thicker on the right of the diagram than they are on the left. This shows that the layers of air at a particular pressure are not all of the same thickness. What is more, the layer between 500 mb and 300 mb thickens to the right more than does the layer below it, so its pressure surface slopes more steeply. These differences in thickness are due to the different rates at which pressure decreases with height in adjacent columns of warm and cool air.

Air expands when it warms, so the thickness of a layer of air between two pressure surfaces is proportional to its temperature. In the diagram, the air to the right is warmer than the air to the left. Cool air occupies a smaller volume than warm air. It is more compressed. As a result, pressure decreases with height more rapidly in cool air than in warm air.

Now imagine a horizontal line drawn across one of these layers from left to right and you will see that pressure changes along it. Starting, say, at the 400-mb level on the left, a line parallel to the ground surface would be almost at 500 mb on the right. This pressure difference produces a wind and, because it is the relationship between temperature and the thickness of the layers that causes the wind, it is called the *thermal wind*. A thermal wind blows wherever two adjacent bodies of air are at different temperatures at the same height, and its force is proportional to the temperature difference between them. In the Northern Hemisphere a thermal wind blows with the cooler air on its left, in the Southern Hemisphere with the cooler air on its right.

Fronts and jet streams

There are belts around Earth where the general circulation of the atmosphere produces very sharp temperature differences of this kind. Where the air moving away from the equator in the Hadley cells starts to subside, it is adjacent to subsiding air flowing toward the equator from middle latitudes. That is one region where a sharp temperature difference causes a strong thermal wind. The other is where cold air flowing away from the poles meets warm air flowing away from the Tropics. The low-latitude boundary between air at quite different temperatures is called the *intertropical front* and that in high latitudes is the *polar front*. These are the two regions where the thermal wind is strongest, and it is especially strong near the tropopause (the upper boundary of the lower atmosphere), at a height of about 30,000 feet (9,000 m), because that is where the temperature difference, or pressure gradient, is greatest.

At the polar front, the height of the tropopause is greater on the side where the air is warmer than it is on the cooler side, because the warm air forms a thicker layer. Warm air slightly overlaps cold air and the thermal wind is strongest of all where the warm air wraps around. Like a long tube of moving air snaking around the world, this wind blows from west to east in both hemispheres at speeds up to 150 MPH (240 km/h) and in winter, when the temperature difference is greatest, it can reach 300 MPH (480 km/h). This is the polar front jet stream. The subtropical jet stream at the intertropical front blows more constantly, but not so fast.

Wandering jet streams

Its position is quite variable, but in summer the polar-front jet stream usually lies across North America, very nearly following the Canadian border. In winter it is farther to the south, approximately along a line from the tip of Baja California, then running northeast to Cape Hatteras. It crosses Europe and Asia in summer along a line through the Mediterranean and Caspian Seas, north of the Himalayas to Japan, and in winter it passes across North Africa, northern Arabia, just to the south of the Himalayas, and to Indonesia.

If you were a jet pilot, often flying at high altitudes, the location and strength of the jet stream would be important to you. Indeed, it was aircrews who discovered it. During World War II, when military aircraft began flying higher than aircraft had flown before, American crews found journey times across the Pacific were sometimes radically reduced on the west-to-east leg and increased on the return. German aircrews reported a similar phenomenon over the Mediterranean region. The meteorologists who sought an explanation for this concluded that there must be a narrow belt of very strong wind at high level, rather like the fast-moving exhaust from the jet-pipe of a jet engine. They called it the jet stream.

It is more difficult to see why those of us who stay on the ground should worry about a wind, even a strong one, several miles above our heads. In fact, though, the jet stream has a powerful effect on the weather. Weather fronts and depressions tend to form beneath it and move along it. These often bring rain and they can bring storms, sometimes severe ones. The tracks that storms most frequently follow in the United States are more or less parallel to the jet stream lying above them.

Jet streams are not constant, however. They twist and snake, but according to well-defined rules, and every so often they die away altogether. When they do that, weather systems become stuck in one place. We may experience a spell of wet weather or a spell of fine weather. We may also experience a drought.

Blocking highs

In middle latitudes the prevailing winds blow from west to east in both hemispheres, carrying weather systems with them. This is called *zonal flow*. It is what brings us our "ordinary" weather, but from time to time the pattern breaks down. Instead of moving mainly from west to east, parallel to the equator, the air moves north and south, in what is called a *meridional flow* because it follows the lines of longitude, or *meridians*. Meridional flow brings unusual or unseasonal weather, because it carries air into a higher or lower latitude. If you live at 40° N, for example, you might suddenly be exposed to cold air that had been at 60° N only a day or two ago, or to warm air that had moved northward from 20° N. Depending which it is, people will either shiver and complain about the cold weather, or take off their coats and enjoy the heat wave. They will say the weather is unusual for the time of year.

It can also happen that the movement of air ceases entirely over a large region. The weather becomes "stuck" and remains the same for weeks or occasionally even for months on end. This condition is called *blocking*. If the resulting weather happens to be fine and dry, then prolonging it is likely to cause drought.

European heat waves and droughts

Northwestern Europe, from western France north to Sweden, experienced a drought of this kind from May 1975 until the end of the summer of 1976. For day after day in June and July 1976, temperatures over England reached more than 90°F (32°C), and television weather reports showed satellite photographs of the whole of Britain with not a single cloud to be seen anywhere. The entire country was laid out like a map. It is extremely rare for all of Britain to enjoy cloudless skies at the same time, and since 1976 no blocking high has continued for so long. Unfortunately, the fine weather led to water shortages. Rainfall had been below average in 1975, and so the levels in reservoirs were already low when the 1976 blocking began.

The weather became stuck in the same way in Finland in July 1972, when people living close to the Arctic Circle enjoyed temperatures of 90°F (32°C). It is also partly what caused the 1972 drought in the Sahel region of Africa. That was associated with an ENSO event (see the section "El Niño and La Niña"), but it involved the same kind of "seizure" of the weather. The droughts on the American plains east of the Rockies that produced the Dust Bowl conditions of the 1930s (see the section "The Dust Bowl") and that occurred as well in the 1890s, 1910s, 1950s, and 1990s were also due to blocking.

The polar front and Rossby waves

The polar front, with the polar front jet stream at its top, marks the boundary between polar and tropical air. Cold air subsides over the poles and flows away from the poles at a low level. Warm, tropical air subsides in the subtropics. Most of it flows back toward the equator, but some flows at low level away from the equator. The polar front is where polar air moving toward the equator encounters tropical air moving away from the equator (see the box "General circulation of the atmosphere" in the section "Air movements and the transport of heat"). The front moves with the seasons, lying farther from the equator in summer and closer to the equator in winter.

Air—and therefore the weather—on the poleward side of the front is colder than air on the side closest to the equator and air flows parallel to the polar front on either side of it. This flow is zonal—parallel to the lines of latitude. When the zonal flow is drawn on a map, however, the line it follows is not quite straight. Middle-latitude air does not move in a precisely easterly direction right around the world. It is deflected by mountain ranges that produce waves in the pattern, so the air follows a slightly wavy path.

These waves were discovered in 1940 by the Swedish-American meteorologist Carl-Gustav Rossby and they are known as *Rossby waves.* They are very long, with about 4,000 miles (6,400 km) between one wave crest and the next, and they affect the whole of the polar front. Provided the airflow does not move in relation to the surface features producing the waves, the wave pattern is quite stable. Near the surface, large eddies, up to 1,200 miles (1,900 km) across, produce areas of relatively high and low atmospheric pressure along the polar front, and weather fronts (see the box on page 78) form along it. All the resulting weather systems travel eastward (in both hemispheres), dragged along by differences in the high-level air pressure produced by the jet stream. These systems bring us the weather we expect for the time of year.

The index cycle

When the polar front moves farther away from the equator in spring, however, the waves become unstable. The Coriolis effect (see the box on page 53) increases in strength as the airflow moves into a higher latitude, so air is deflected. Because it is already following a curved path due to the Rossby waves, the air possesses vorticity (see the box). Increasing the magnitude of the Coriolis effect is equivalent to increasing the planetary vorticity, and in order to maintain a constant absolute vorticity, the relative vorticity of the airflow decreases. This turns the moving air back toward the equator, which reduces its planetary vorticity and increases its relative vorticity, turning it away from the equator again.

Over a period of about three to eight weeks, the undulations of the Rossby waves grow bigger and bigger, until much of the flow is meridional rather than zonal. The diagram "The index cycle" on page 82 illustrates this. In A, the waves are small, and the general flow is zonal. Flow becomes increasingly meridional in B, as the waves grow bigger, and in C, flow is mainly meridional. Then, in D, the waves break into cells, where the air flows in a series of circles with the larger waves weaving around them. At this stage the zonal flow has broken down completely and the cells cease to move. They are stuck and can remain so for some time. Meteorologists calculate the extent to which the flow of air is zonal and the value they give it is known as the *zonal index*. The cycle of changes in the zonal index, shown in the diagram, is therefore called the *index cycle*.

Mountain ranges that are aligned approximately from north to south, such as the Rocky Mountains and the Andes, also divert weather systems

Weather fronts

During World War I, a team of meteorologists led by the Norwegian Vilhelm Bjerknes (1862–1951) discovered that air forms distinct masses. Because each mass differs in its average temperature, and therefore density, from adjacent masses, air masses do not mix readily. He called the boundary between two air masses a *front*.

Air masses move across the surface of land and sea, and so the fronts between them also move. Fronts are named according to the temperature of the air *behind* the front compared with that ahead of it. If the air behind the advancing front is warmer than the air ahead of it, it is a warm front. If the air behind the front is cooler, it is a cold front.

Fronts extend from the surface all the way to the tropopause, which is the boundary between the lower (troposphere) and upper (stratosphere) layers of the atmosphere. They slope upward, like the sides of a bowl, but the slope is very shallow. Warm fronts have a gradient of 1° or less, cold fronts of about 2°. This means that when you first see, high in the sky, the cirrus clouds marking the approach of a warm front, the point where the front touches the surface is about 350–715 miles (565–1,150 km) distant. When you see the first, high-level sign of an approaching cold front, the front is at the surface about 185 miles (300 km) away.

Cold fronts usually move across the surface faster than warm fronts, so cold air tends to undercut warm air, raising it upward along the cold front. If the warm air is already rising, it will be raised even faster along the front separating it from cold air. The front is then called an *ana-front* and there is usually thick cloud and heavy rain or snow associated with it. If the warm air is sinking, an advancing cold front will raise it less. This is a *kata-front*, usually with only low-level cloud and light rain, drizzle, or fine snow. The diagram on pages 79–80 shows these frontal systems in cross-section, but with the frontal slopes greatly exaggerated.

After a front has formed, waves start to develop along it. These are shown on weather maps and as they become steeper, areas of low pressure form at their crests. These are *frontal depressions*, or *extratropical cyclones*, and they often bring wet weather. Just below the wave crest, there is cold air to either side of a body of warm air. The cold front moves faster than the warm front, lifting the warm air along both fronts until all the warm air is clear of the surface. The fronts are then said to be *occluded* and the pattern they form is called an *occlusion*.

Once the fronts are occluded and the warm air is no longer in contact with the surface, air to both sides of the occlusion is colder than the warm air. Occlusions can still be called cold or warm, however, because what matters is not the actual temperature of the air, but whether air to one side of a front or occlusion is warmer or cooler than the air behind it. In a cold occlusion the air ahead of the front is warmer than the air behind it and in a warm occlusion the air ahead is cooler, but both of these are cooler than the warm air that has been lifted clear of the surface. The diagram shows this in cross-section. As the warm air is lifted, clouds usually form and often bring precipitation. Eventually the warm and cold air reach the same temperature, mix, and the frontal system dissipates. Often, however, another similar system is following behind, so frontal depressions commonly occur in families.

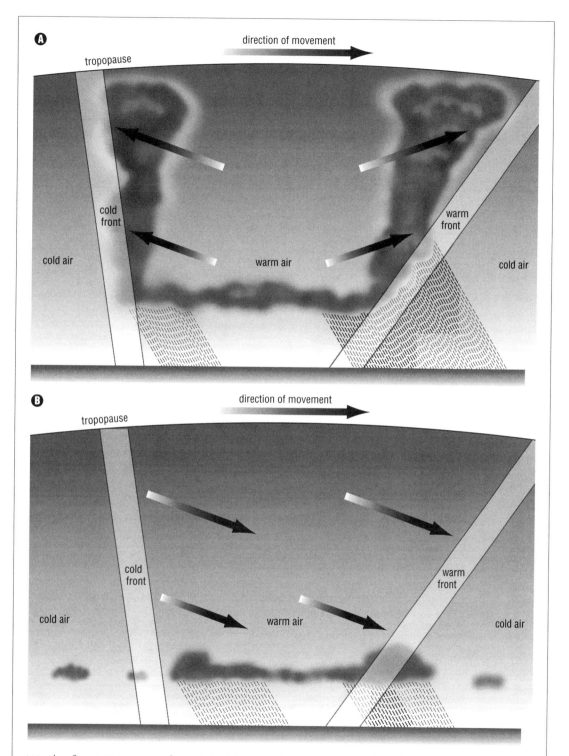

Weather fronts. A) At an ana-front, air is rising along both fronts. B) At a kata-front, air is subsiding along both fronts.

(continues)

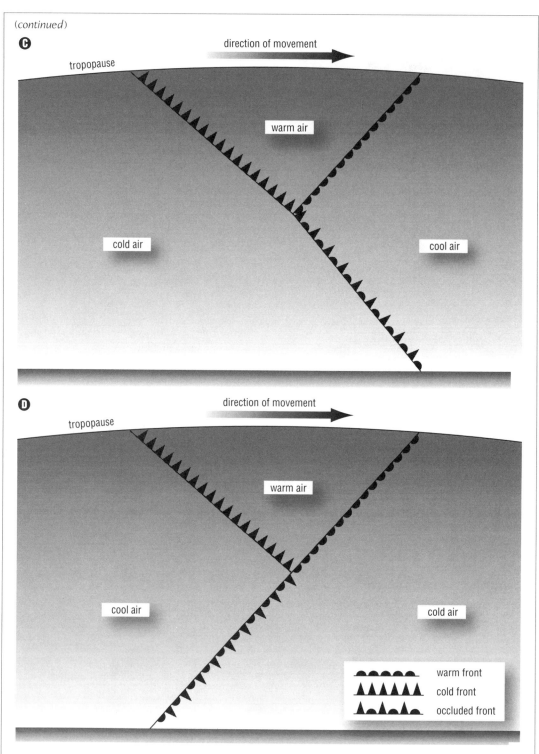

Occluded fronts. C) A cold occlusion, in which the air behind the occlusion is cooler than the air ahead of it. D) A warm occlusion, in which the air behind the occlusion is warmer than the air ahead of it. In both cases, the air to either side of the occlusion is cooler than the warm air that has been lifted clear of the surface.

Vorticity and angular momentum

Any fluid moving in relation to Earth's surface tends to rotate about a vertical axis. This is called *vorticity*. Vorticity in a counterclockwise direction (seen from above) is said to be positive and clockwise vorticity is said to be negative.

On a large scale, the rotation of Earth also imparts vorticity to a moving fluid everywhere except at the equator. This vorticity is equal in magnitude to the Coriolis effect and is positive in the Northern Hemisphere and negative in the Southern. It is called *planetary vorticity*, and the vorticity of the fluid itself is called *relative vorticity*. The two together are called *absolute vorticity*. For any body of air or liquid possessing vorticity, absolute vorticity tends to remain constant. In other words, if one of its components increases, the other decreases in proportion.

The speed with which a body rotates about an axis is called its *angular velocity* and is measured in the number of degrees through which it travels in a given length of time, or in radians. The radian is the unit of circular measure. One radian (rad) is equal to the angle subtended at the center of a circle by an arc on the circumference that is of the same length as the radius (r) of the circle. The circumference of a circle is $2\pi r$ and subtends an angle of $2\pi r/r = 2\pi$ radians (dividing throughout by r). Consequently, $360° = 2\pi$ rad; 1 rad = 57.296°. Earth, for example, rotates through 360° (2π rad) in 24 hours. This is its angular velocity.

The body also has *angular momentum*. This is calculated by multiplying together its angular velocity (V), its mass (M), and its radius of rotation (R) measured from the axis of its rotation to its most distant point. For a body of a particular mass, angular velocity, and radius of rotation, the angular momentum is a constant. That is, $M \times V \times R = $ a constant. Ignoring friction, which slows all motion, this constant remains the same; technically, angular momentum is said to be conserved. This means that if one variable alters, the others must alter to compensate so that the constant remains the same. If the radius decreases, for example, and the mass remains unaltered, the angular velocity will increase.

that are moving from east to west. Scientists do not understand just why this should be so, but there is no doubt that blocking occurs more often in parts of the world with such mountain ranges than it does elsewhere.

Weather systems continue to travel eastward, but the cells remain stationary and advancing systems go around them. This is called blocking, and once the cells are firmly established they can remain in position for a long time. The polar front jet stream has then split into two, very wavy branches with the stationary cells between them. As the diagram shows, high-pressure areas are trapped to the north and low-pressure areas to the south, with the main airflow, including the jet stream, traveling around them and carrying the surface weather systems with them. Areas of stationary high pressure that divert weather systems around them are called *blocking anticyclones* or *blocking highs*. The map on page 82 shows the extent to which the jet stream is diverted when there is a blocking anticyclone over the North Atlantic. Sometimes it shifts by as much as 20–30° of latitude from its usual track.

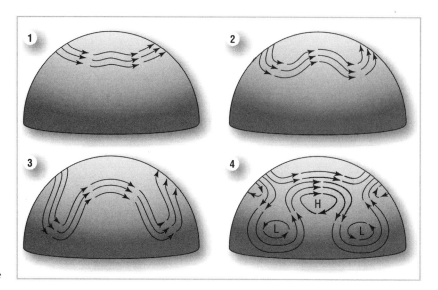

The index cycle

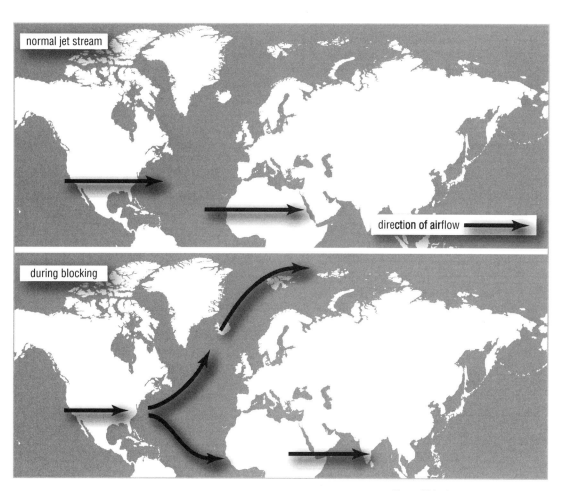

normal jet stream

direction of airflow

during blocking

Effect of blocking on the jet stream

As the undulations become more pronounced, polar air is carried a long way south and tropical air a long way north, because the jet stream also marks the position of the polar front, with cold air on one side and warm air on the other. Some regions then experience temperatures much lower than are usual and others temperatures that are higher, and rainfall also changes. High pressure, with subsiding air, brings fine, dry weather, which is very warm in summer and very cold in winter. Drought is less likely in winter, because the rate of evaporation is relatively low, but blocking in winter does bring dry weather. If this is followed by further prolonged blocking during the following summer, as it was in Europe in 1975 and 1976, drought is probably inevitable. Closer to the equator, *blocking cyclones* or *blocking lows* bring prolonged periods of wet weather.

Location is important

The location of a blocking anticyclone is very important. In 1975 and 1976, a blocking anticyclone centered over northwestern Europe brought the most severe drought since the first reliable records were made, in 1727. Britain lay directly beneath the anticyclone and the drought reduced the water content of soil over the entire country to its lowest value since 1698 (as measured at the Royal Botanic Gardens, Kew, London, which was established in the late 17th century). This blocking anticyclone diverted depressions approaching from the Atlantic by 5° to 10° to the north, so they missed Britain. Further east, however, that summer was cool. Winds over Russia were mainly from the north and temperatures were as much as 7°F (4°C) below normal.

In 1954, on the other hand, a blocking anticyclone over Scandinavia and eastern Europe gave those regions a warm, dry summer and Britain a cool, wet one. The Sahel drought (see "The Sahel" on page 141) was caused partly by the blocking of Atlantic depressions by a northward movement of the subtropical anticyclone over the Sahara.

Blocking weather seems to occur for several years in succession, then disappear for several more years. It is rather like the periodic changes of the Southern Oscillation (see the section "El Niño and La Niña" on page 64) that lead to ENSO events, but in both cases the oscillation is irregular. It is simple enough to identify blocking patterns when they occur and even to forecast them a short time ahead, but not to predict them reliably years in advance. Nevertheless, droughts in the Great Plains do seem to recur at intervals of 20 to 23 years. So do variations in the temperature records for central England, which are complete back to 1659, and also in temperatures in other parts of the world. Over Europe, blocking seems to be commoner in the '30s and '80s of each century than at other times, and severe winters are more likely in the '40s and '60s. One day, scientists may succeed in unraveling the complexities of these cycles. If and when they do, they will be able to warn of blocking that brings drought, in time for farmers and water utilities to make adequate preparation.

WATER AND LIFE

Desert life

Walk out into the desert and you will see rock, gravel, dust, sand, and very little else. There may be no sign of anything living. The place appears lifeless. Our word *desert* is from the Latin *desertus*, meaning "forsaken." Without water nothing can live, and over most of the desert there is no water. It is a forsaken place indeed.

Nor can most plants and animals survive for long in very high temperatures. Photosynthesis is the process by which plants manufacture the carbohydrates that supply the energy they need to live and grow. Like all living organisms, they also respire. Respiration is the process by which carbohydrates are broken down to release energy. Plants, therefore, must strike a balance between their rates of photosynthesis and respiration. At temperatures above about 100°F (38°C), plants respire faster than they photosynthesize. This means that carbohydrates are being broken down in their tissues faster than they can be replaced, and so the plant starves. Very bright light makes the problem worse, and desert plants are often exposed to high light intensity. At most light levels, the more intense the light a plant receives the faster it photosynthesizes, but at very high intensities photosynthesis slows; the phenomenon is called *solarization.*

High temperatures can also damage enzymes, the proteins that regulate most of the chemistry of living organisms. If the enzymes are made inactive, or even destroyed, body chemistry is severely disrupted.

Osmosis and explosive heat death

Water evaporates rapidly into hot, dry air, and the loss of body fluids leads to dehydration. This is the most immediate and obvious danger to both plants and animals, and it conceals a vicious trap. Many organisms use the evaporation of water to keep cool. Humans do it when we sweat. This works, but the water must be replaced; otherwise its loss leads to dehydration. The choice is between overheating and dehydrating.

Living cells are bounded by *selectively permeable membranes.* These are membranes that allow water molecules to pass through them under certain conditions. If a selectively permeable membrane separates two solutions, one of which is much more concentrated than the other, the membrane will allow molecules of the solvent to pass but hold back molecules of the solute (the dissolved substance).

The solvent in our bodies, and those of plants and other animals, is water. When the body loses more water than it takes in, the concentration of dissolved substances increases in the fluid bathing its cells, and water flows out of the cells, from the weaker to the stronger solution. This process is called *osmosis*, illustrated in the drawing. Water continues to cross the membrane until the solutions on either side are at the same concentration. The effect is to drain water from the cells until, in extreme cases, the cells no longer function normally and start to die.

Under these conditions a plant simply wilts and eventually dies. Mammals, including humans, respond differently. Water is drawn from the blood to keep the concentrations equal inside and outside body cells. This allows the cells to survive a while longer, but it causes the blood to thicken. Eventually the blood thickens so much that it ceases to flow fast enough to carry body heat to the skin, where it can be lost. Then the body temperature rises rapidly. Human victims become disoriented, confused, deaf, and insensitive to pain. Death follows swiftly from heat stroke. It is sometimes called *explosive heat death*. It is why dehydration is so dangerous.

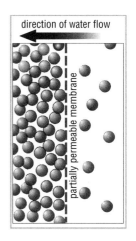

Osmosis

Making do with very little water

Facing such a formidable array of difficulties, it is not surprising that most organisms avoid deserts. For any plant or animal that can tolerate the harsh conditions, however, there are several important advantages. Deserts are not crowded, so there are plenty of places for an animal to find shelter or to nest, and the lack of competition means nutrients are abundant for those plants able to reach them. Seizing the opportunities is not easy, but some have managed to adapt, at least partially, and by no means is the desert so barren as it appears.

Avoidance or tolerance are the two strategies available to plants facing harsh conditions. Many choose avoidance. Some are visible but appear to be dead. Others spend most of the time as seeds, buried in the soil. The seeds of some desert plants can remain buried for many years and still germinate as soon as they are moistened by rain. The ground will not remain moist for long and the plants must grow, flower, and produce a new crop of seeds before the water disappears. After it has rained, the apparently lifeless desert is briefly a mass of green plants and brightly colored flowers. *Boerhaavia repens*, a small herb of African deserts, may hold the record. It is said to take eight to 10 days to germinate, mature, produce big, bright flowers pollinated by insects, and a crop of seeds. Then it dies and disappears. Plants that appear and disappear rapidly in this way are called *ephemerals* and they waste no time growing elaborate roots. *Eschscholzia minutiflora*, a close relative of the Californian poppy, is a North American equivalent, but with tiny, yellow flowers rather than big ones.

Plants that appear to be dead may also be waiting for the rains. The ocotillo, or coachwhip *(Fouquieria splendens)* of North American deserts is typical. Most of the time it is a bunch of thin, unbranched stems, up to 15 feet (4.5 m) tall, swaying in the wind. It has no leaves, but its stems are green and contain chlorophyll, so the plant is photosynthesizing. When it rains, the ocotillo covers its stems in a mass of tiny leaves. These increase the area available for photosynthesis, allowing it to grow faster. When the rains cease and the air becomes dry, the leaves rapidly wither and fall. Each spring buds develop at the tips of its stems and open as red flowers. Its close relative, the boojum tree *(Idria columnaris)* is very similar, but it grows as a single, thick, conical stem like an upside-down carrot up to 60 feet (18 m) tall, with a few branches and yellow flowers. The branches start erect, but they grow so long, they often fall sideways under their own weight into weird shapes.

Storing water

The boojum tree stores water in its carrotlike stem. Plants that do this are called *succulents* and the most famous examples are the cacti. Cacti are American plants, although they are now grown all over the world and have established themselves in the wild in many places. Their equivalents in the deserts of Africa, Asia, and Australia belong to the spurge family (Euphorbiaceae), and some of them closely resemble cacti.

Succulents have few leaves and many species have none at all. Instead, they have green stems in which photosynthesis takes place. The thick, fleshy stems store water. All plants have small pores, called *stomata*, through which they exchange gases with the atmosphere. This is essential. Plants need carbon dioxide for photosynthesis. Respiration provides some, but most of the time it is not enough. Plants can also use some of the oxygen, which is the by-product of photosynthesis, for respiration, but not all of it, and the excess must be removed.

Stomata are essential, but it is not only carbon dioxide and oxygen that pass through them. So does water vapor, and while its stomata are open a plant is losing water. This is not a problem for a plant that is rooted in moist soil from which its lost water can be replaced, but it might have serious consequences for a plant growing in arid desert soil. To make matters worse, if the temperature of the plant surface rises above that of the air next to it, the rate of evaporation from the open stomata increases sharply.

Desert plants deal with the problem in several ways. Some cacti have "ribs," and their stomata are confined to the "valleys" between them, where they are shaded from direct sunlight and remain cooler. Other plants open their stomata early in the morning, and close them later, as the air grows warmer. Still others have very small leaves with an outer waxy coating that reduces evaporation.

This is the method adopted by possibly the most familiar plant of North American deserts, the creosote bush *(Larrea divaricata)*. In addition to its small, waxy leaves, it is covered in hairs. These reflect light, which helps keep the plant cool. Its stomata are sunk into recesses in its leaves, and in very dry conditions the plant sheds its leaves altogether to conserve water. It also stores water in its tissues. The acacias of Africa are very similar, and they are able to function efficiently at high temperatures. They photosynthesize best at 99°F (37°C), compared with 64°F (18°C) for most plants of temperate climates.

Cacti, euphorbias, and acacias are often thorny or covered in spines. This is protection. A plant that stores water in its tissues cannot afford to lose it, and animals know there is water to be had if only they can break into the plant.

Collecting dew

Thorns, spines, and hairs also serve another purpose. Dew condenses on them at night, and this provides the plant with some water it can absorb. Welwitschia *(Welwitschia mirabilis)*, one of the most remarkable of all plants, relies on collecting water from the air. It grows in the Namib Desert of southwestern Africa. It has only two leaves, which curl and are split into straps by the wind. They grow continuously, but wear away at their ends. Even so, their total surface area amounts to about 25 square yards (21 m²). The leaves collect dew and also moisture from sea mists that roll up to 50 miles (80 km) inland from the South Atlantic.

The welwitschia does everything slowly. When one of its seeds germinates, the seed leaves (cotyledons) last for five years before true leaves appear, during which time the plant grows a taproot up to 60 feet (18 m) deep. The plant itself lives for up to 2,000 years.

There are also animals that obtain moisture from the mists over the Namib. At dawn, darkling beetles (family Tenebrionidae) stand on top of sand dunes with their abdomens raised. The beetles have cooled during the night, and water condenses on their bodies and trickles down to their mouths.

Making do with less

All animals obtain some water from the food they eat, even if the food is very dry. This is not water that is contained in the food but a by-product of respiration. When carbohydrates are oxidized to release energy (which is what respiration means), water is one of the products. The general equation is: carbohydrate + oxygen → carbon dioxide + water + energy. This water is removed from the body along with the carbon dioxide. It is why your breath condenses on a cold mirror or windowpane.

Animals that live in the desert cannot afford to waste water, and they have evolved ingenious ways to economize. Some, like the kangaroo rat, spend much of their time below ground, which is also where they store their food. As they breathe, their store of dry plant material absorbs moisture from their breath, so they recover it whenever they eat. Kangaroo rats never need to drink, and all desert animals must be able to survive a long time without drinking. Many of the small mammals have noses that cool their breath before it leaves their bodies, so water condenses from it and is absorbed, and most desert animals excrete a very concentrated urine from which most of the water has been removed. The skins of reptiles and scorpions are almost completely impermeable, so no water can be lost by that route. The camel is the animal we immediately associate with deserts, of course. It is superbly adapted to the harsh environment (see the box on page 88).

The "ship of the desert"

The single-humped camel or dromedary (*Camelus dromedarius*) is the most famous of all desert animals. Trucks now carry most of the goods that were once transported by camel trains, but in years gone by camels provided the only long-distance transport, and its ability to carry cargoes justly earned the camel its nickname "ship of the desert".

A camel can walk across the Saharan dunes without its feet sinking into the loose sand. It can tolerate the heat of the desert afternoon. And it can survive for very long periods without food or drink. In winter, some camels do not drink at all, and a camel has been known to go for 17 days without drinking in summer. How does it do it?

To start with, it has very broad feet. These spread its weight over a large area of the surface and allow it to walk across loose sand (or snow) without sinking. A camel is a hoofed mammal, but its hoofs, unlike those of cattle and sheep, are turned forward, at the tips of its toes, and the animal does not walk on them. A thick pad of skin covers its toes and the camel walks on this.

Its hind legs are also unique. They are attached to the pelvis only at the top of the thigh bone (femur), rather than by muscles extending all the way to the knee, as they are in other hoofed animals. This arrangement allows a camel to lie down with its legs tucked completely beneath its body—and in the shade. Thick pads of hard skin on its chest and knees provide additional insulation from the hot surface when the camel lies down.

When they are not working, camels spend most of their time resting. They lie close together, so they shade each other, and they lie facing the Sun. This minimizes the area of body surface they expose to its direct rays. As the Sun moves across the sky, the camels turn around so they can continue to face it.

A camel has a thick coat. This absorbs the heat of the Sun and traps a layer of air next to the camel's skin. If the camel sweats to keep cool, its sweat evaporates into this layer of air, cooling the air beneath the coat. Its coat provides good insulation against the heat, and losing body heat is made easier by the fact that the camel does not have a

Walk barefoot over sand on a very hot day and the sand will burn your feet. This is because the sand itself is hot and, therefore, so is the air immediately above it. It is contact with the sand that burns your feet, but your ankles are also warm, because they are surrounded by warm air. The air around your head is much cooler. It is at ground level that the temperature is highest. Just a few feet higher or lower, the air is much cooler. A camel stands about eight feet (2.4 m) tall to the top of its hump and the midday temperature there may be 60°F (33°C) lower than the temperature at ground level. Even a short distance helps. Some lizards climb into bushes, where the air is cooler, and others, such as *Palmatogecko rangei*, a gecko that lives in the Kalahari, stand with one foot raised, from time to time replacing the foot and raising another.

Life below ground

Five feet (1.5 m) below ground, however, which is where many small animals rest during the hottest part of the day, the temperature may be as layer of fat beneath the skin. Other animals use this fat to store food. The camel stores food in its hump, which is made mainly from fat. Located on its back, and exposed to the Sun, the hump absorbs heat without transferring it to rest of the body. The camel's hump provides insulation.

Camels sweat very little, however, in order to conserve water. A camel does not begin to sweat until its body temperature rises above 105°F (40.5°C). It takes several hours for the animal to warm up to this temperature, because at night its body temperature is allowed to fall, sometimes to as low as 93°F (34°C). In winter, and in summer if water is plentiful, body temperature varies by only about 4°F (2.2°C).

A camel has a highly efficient digestive system that allows it to thrive on a diet containing very little protein. It does this by recycling food internally, with the result that its urine is very concentrated. As well as economizing on food, this also reduces the amount of liquid the animal loses in urine. In summer, a camel may excrete no more than one quart (1.14 liters) of water a day. The camel obtains some of the water its body needs by oxidizing the hydrogen contained in the fat in its hump. A full hump may contain fat equal to around 6.5 gallons (25 liters) of water.

Desert journeys by camel train are traditionally undertaken in winter and spring, rather than in the heat of the summer. At this time of year a camel can walk more than 300 miles (480 km) in two to three weeks and drink nothing during this time. As its body becomes drier, the camel maintains a fairly constant volume of blood. Instead it loses water from its saliva, moisture in its lungs, and other bodily fluids. This prevents its blood from thickening—and it is thickening blood that leads rapidly to the death of humans and other animals that are denied water in the hot desert. The loss of bodily fluids makes the camel grow thinner and thinner. After a time it is so emaciated it looks seriously ill, but it can survive losing fluid equal to 25 percent of its body weight. Once it finds water, it can drink up to 27 gallons (103 liters) in 10 minutes. As it does so, its body fills out to its normal size.

Its apparently supercilious expression is also an adaptation to the desert. A camel has long eyelashes to keep dust out of its eyes. When a standing camel looks at a human, it has to look down because its head is higher than the human's head, and its eyelashes partly cover its eyes, making the animal appear disdainful.

much as 80°F (44°C) lower than it is at the surface. Underground is a good place to be when the white, blinding, desert Sun is at its fiercest.

Animals that do a great deal of burrowing through loose sand have become very good at it. Some lizards and snakes swim just below the surface, and so does Grant's desert mole (*Eremitalpa granti*) of the Namib Desert. It has no eyes or external ears, but despite this apparent handicap it is a successful underground hunter of insects and lizards that are also sheltering from the heat. Many burrowers have big feet to help with the shoveling, but skinks, a group of lizards with small legs and, in some species, no legs at all, manage differently. They hold their little legs to the sides of their bodies as they swim through the sand, like fish. In fact *Scincus philbyi*, a skink (with legs) that is about eight inches (20 cm) long and lives in the desert of Saudi Arabia, is called the "sandfish."

Some burrowers dive headfirst into the sand. Many lizards, with triangular heads, vanish this way. Others use a sideways movement, pushing sand away to make a trench into which they sink until they are deep enough for the loose sand to fall back and cover them.

Lying in wait

Once it is below ground, an animal is invisible. This makes burrowing a good way to hide from enemies, but it is also a good way to hide while waiting for prey or even while searching for it. The sidewinder rattlesnake *(Crotalus cerastes)* and the horned viper *(Cerastes cerastes)* are among several species of desert snakes that hunt in this way. They have short, thick bodies, can spread their ribs to flatten themselves, are covered in scales that give a good grip on loose sand, and their raised eyes are protected by horns. These snakes shuffle along below the surface with just their eyes above ground. Sand boas of western Asia are similar in overall design but are constrictors, rather than venomous snakes.

Sidewinders are best known for their curious method of locomotion. This works well on soft ground, but place them on a firm surface and they move like any other snake. If you place most snakes on soft sand, they will make an attempt at sidewinding.

Convergent evolution

Unrelated plants and animals living in areas thousands of miles apart often come to resemble one another. This is called *convergent evolution*, and it arises when the same solution to a particular problem appears more than once.

Extreme environments provide many examples, and none provide more than deserts. The cacti of America are very similar to some of the euphorbias of Africa and Asia. For example, the American creosote bush looks much like an African acacia, and among animals the similarities are even more striking. The greatest practitioners of sidewinding are the American sidewinder rattlesnake, the horned viper and carpet viper *(Echis carinatus)* of North Africa and the Middle East, and *Bitis peringueyi*, a South African viper.

The 70 or so species of American kangaroo rats (genus *Dipodomys*) live in a similar way and look much like the jerboas (genus *Jaculus*) of the Sahara and the Arabian Desert. In the North American desert you may see a kit fox *(Vulpes velox)*, a delicate animal with very large ears. Blood vessels passing through the thin cartilage of the ears carry heat away from the body, so big ears help an animal keep cool. In the Sahara the fennec *(Fennecus zerda)* is another fox that also has big ears.

The list is long, and the reason simple. Desert life is hard, and there are only a few ways a plant or animal can keep cool and save water. It is not surprising that identical solutions have evolved in widely separated places.

Life near the poles

Deserts are places where temperatures reach extremes. We think of deserts as hot places, but the arid lands surrounding the North and South Poles are very cold. At Qaanaaq (Thule), in the north of Kalaallit Nunaat (Greenland), the average summer temperature is 40°F (4.4°C), but the winter average is 1.5°F (–17°C). Qaanaaq (pronounced "kay-nak") is on the coast, at sea level; over the center of the ice sheet, about 10,000 feet (3,050 m) above sea level, the average temperature is –27°F (–33°C) in winter and 12.8°F (–10.7°C) in summer.

Winters on the Greenland ice sheet are not the coldest in the world, or even the coldest in the Northern Hemisphere. To experience those you must visit the town of Verkhoyansk, in Siberia, where the average annual temperature is 1.1°F (–17.2°C), but the average temperature in January, the coldest month, is –58.5°F (–50.3°C) and where the lowest temperature ever recorded is –89°F (–67°C). Snag, in the Yukon, in Canada, has the coldest winters in North America. In February 1947 the temperature there fell to –81°F (–63°C).

Antarctica is much colder. On July 21, 1983, the temperature at the Russian Vostok Station was –126.6°F (–89.2°C). In summer, temperatures at Vostok rise to an average –25.7°F (–32.1°C).

Plants of the permafrost

No plants are able to grow on the surface of the ice, but there is vegetation in places where the ground is exposed. The plants that manage to grow in and around the edges of the polar deserts form a type of vegetation called *tundra*, a Russian word that is derived from the Finnish word *tunturia*, meaning a treeless plain. The tundra landscape is mainly level, with some low hills. Large areas of bare rock separate scattered groups of plants, most of them no more than eight inches (20 cm) tall. Tundra vegetation is similar in many respects to the vegetation found in any other desert. The map on page 92 shows the extent of the tundra vegetation in North America. Together with the Greenland ice sheet, this is the part of North America that is made up of polar desert.

Inside the Arctic and Antarctic Circles, and in some areas farther south in Siberia, the ground is frozen for most of the year. It is called *permafrost*. This means that below the surface there is a layer in which all the water adhering to and held in the spaces between soil particles remains frozen throughout the year. It never thaws. The permafrost layer is solid as rock— and as impermeable. Water is unable to drain through it. This has important consequences for plants.

Plant roots cannot penetrate the permafrost layer and so there are no deep-rooting plants. Trees send their roots deep into the soil and so no trees are able to grow in areas with permafrost, although a few plants that grow as trees in warmer, moister climates are able to survive above the permafrost by remaining close to the ground. They include dwarf birch (*Betula nana*), arctic willow (*Salix arctica*), and dwarf juniper (*Juniperus communis* var. *nana*), none of which grows more than three feet (1 m) tall. There are also low-growing shrubs that form cushions, such as arctic white

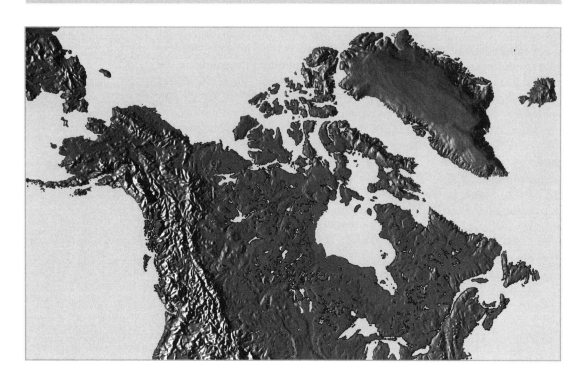

Tundra in North America. The shaded area shows the extent of tundra vegetation in North America. Together with the central ice sheet covering Greenland (Kalaallit Nunaat), this part of North America makes up a polar desert.

heather *(Cassiope tetragona)*, bearberry *(Arctostaphylos uva-ursi)*, and mountain avens *(Dryas octopetala)*.

These plants spread their roots in the layer of soil above the permafrost layer. This soil forms the *active layer*. It is up to 10 feet (3 m) deep, but much thinner in some places, and it thaws for a time in spring and summer. This releases water, but there is a problem. The underlying permafrost layer inhibits drainage and so the water in the active layer has nowhere to go. It accumulates in hollows and low-lying places, where the soil becomes waterlogged. Plants that cannot tolerate waterlogged soil grow on the better-drained higher ground. Over large areas, however, mosses and lichens are the only plants that can survive.

Brief life cycles

Plants growing in the active layer must make the most of the summer warmth and moisture while it lasts—and it does not last for long. Despite the very different temperatures they must endure, this is a need that plants of polar deserts and hot deserts share, and they satisfy it in similar ways. Waterlogged soil may be bad for most plants, but it suits insects that produce aquatic larvae. Arctic summers are notorious for the vast clouds of biting insects. Not all the insects feed on blood, however. There are some that pollinate flowering plants.

These plants have one advantage over the plants of hot deserts. Whereas rainfall is unpredictable in the southern deserts, in polar deserts the conditions for plant growth occur at the same time every year—in spring and summer. Consequently, plants can prepare for them by responding to changes in the length of daylight. In autumn, as the days shorten from 18 hours to 15 hours, for example, the alpine sorrel (*Oxyria dignya*) forms flower buds. These remain dormant throughout the winter, but they are ready to flower as soon as the days start lengthening again the following spring. For a brief time, before the other flowers open, alpine sorrel attracts hungry pollinators to the only flowers they can see.

The plants must work fast, and the tundra blooms in summer just like a southern desert after rain. Within four days of the disappearance of the snow, purple saxifrage (*Saxifraga oppositifolia*) and *Ranunculus nivalis*, a buttercup, are flowering. Many of the flowers are very brightly colored and some turn during the day so they always face the Sun. This makes the flower more conspicuous and it also makes it warmer—and insects are attracted to warmth.

Bright colors help attract insects to plants that grow close to the ground. This is an adaptation to the low temperature. Even in summer, a tall plant would lose heat rapidly in the incessant wind, and it would also dehydrate, because the wind would increase the rate of evaporation from its leaves.

Plants of Antarctica

This section describes the plant life of the Arctic, but not of the mainland of Antarctica. Antarctica has no tundra. Its climate is too cold and too dry.

Mosses and lichens are the only plants that grow in the "dry valleys" of Antarctica—areas covering a total of about 2,200 square miles (5,600 km^2) that are not covered by ice or snow. Only two species of plants grow naturally on the mainland of Antarctica: Antarctic pearlwort (*Colobanthus crassifolius*) and *Deschampsia antarctica*, which is a hair grass that has no common name. Both plants grow near sea level along the Antarctic Peninsula, no closer to the South Pole than 68° S, and although they produce flowers they reproduce vegetatively and do not set seed. In addition to these, visitors have introduced a few plants to the peninsula.

Arctic animals

Despite the summer abundance of blackflies, mosquitoes, and biting midges, flies are the most numerous insects of the tundra. Their eggs hatch in spring and they spend most of the summer as larvae, feeding on the dead plant material lying on the ground, before spending a few days as adults, during which time they mate and lay eggs. The biting insects that breed in water provide food for aquatic birds, such as eiders (*Somateria mollissima*), snow geese (*Anser caerulescens*), and whistling (or tundra) swans (*Cygnus columbianus*). The Lapland longspur (*Calcarius lapponicus*) and snow bunting *(Plectrophenax nivalis)* are among the birds that feed on the flies and other invertebrate animals that live on land.

Few birds are resident throughout the year, however. There is no food for most of them in winter, so they arrive in summer to take advantage of the temporary abundance of insects. Many of them have formed pairs before leaving their winter homes so they need waste no time before starting to raise their young. In species where only one parent raises the young, the other partner leaves again before the offspring are fully grown and in some cases even before the eggs have hatched. Some summer visitors remain for only a month or less.

Snowy owls *(Nyctea scandiaca)* and ptarmigans (three *Lagopus* species) are among the very few species that spend the winter in the tundra. Both have dense white plumage to keep them warm and camouflaged. Ptarmigans feed on berries and willow buds, so these birds are found only where their food plants are exposed. Snowy owls feed on voles and lemmings. The population of small rodents fluctuates, and in years when they are scarce the snowy owls move further south.

Adapted to cold

Small mammals can avoid the worst of the cold. Some of them hibernate and sleep through the winter—although hibernation is very different from ordinary sleep (see the box on page 95). Others spend the winter beneath the snow. This is how voles and lemmings survive, and it is a very successful strategy.

For one thing, they are out of sight. A small animal scurrying across the snow is highly visible to snowy owls, foxes, and most other predators looking for an easily won meal—although weasels and stoats can follow them underground. They are also sheltered from the wind. Wind chill in this climate can kill small animals very quickly. What is more, the covering of snow provides a layer of insulation.

Safe beneath the snow, the rodents excavate tunnels and nests. They move around freely in search of seeds and other plant material that is still lying on the ground. They breed during the winter and by the time the snow melts and they emerge in spring, their young are big enough to find their own food. Bigger animals, such as bears, also spend much of the winter in dens excavated in the snow.

Small animals do not have thick coats. Their bodies are too small to carry them. Large animals, such as the arctic fox *(Alopex lagopus)* and polar bear *(Thalarctos maritimus)*, have thick fur. They also have small external ears. Ears are thin, so their blood vessels are close to the surface and the blood in them loses heat to the outside air. That is why we cover our ears in cold weather. Small ears lose less heat. They are an adaptation to a cold climate.

Foxes, bears, and arctic birds must not have warm feet, however. If their feet were warm, walking would be very difficult, because they would melt the snow or ice by treading on it. Then, very quickly, it might freeze

Hibernation

Some small mammals hibernate during the winter, when food is very scarce. Hibernation is not common, however. Only animals with small bodies are able to hibernate. The biggest is the marmot (*Marmota* species), weighing an average 11 pounds (5 kg). Other animals, such as bears, retreat to a sheltered den and spend the winter inside it. They are asleep for much of the time, but this is not true hibernation.

Animals prepare for hibernation by choosing a sheltered place, hidden and out of the wind, in which they make a nest. Then they either feed voraciously, or gather food and store it in their winter nesting quarters, or both. Those that store food in their bodies secrete hormones that convert the food to a thick layer of fat.

As food starts to become scarce, the animal enters its nest, lies down in its usual sleeping position, and falls asleep. Blood vessels in the skin then begin to constrict. Its heartbeat slows to just a few beats every minute and then its body temperature starts to fall, in most species to about 40°F (4.5°C). This greatly reduces the amount of energy its body needs and its breathing slows until it takes just a few breaths a minute. The composition of the blood changes to prevent the slow-moving blood from clotting, but the animal's nervous system continues to function. Should its body temperature drop below a certain level the animal begins to shiver. This warms its body, but it also consumes energy, which is obtained by oxidizing some of its stored body fat. Shivering wakes the animal, which needs to eat some of its winter store of food before falling asleep once more.

In spring, the rising temperature arouses the sleeper. Its heartbeat accelerates rapidly and it starts shivering violently in the front of its body—the part that warms first. It starts breathing more rapidly, the blood vessels in its skin dilate, and very soon the animal is fully awake. Within about four hours the body temperature increases from 40°F (4.5°C) to the 95°F (35°C) that is usual for mammals.

again, leaving them literally frozen to the spot. Consequently, the parts of their feet that touch the ground are cold enough not to melt the surface. In other words, they are at or below freezing.

Blood flows from the heart to the toes. When it reaches the toes, the blood loses heat to the outside air. Cold blood then flows back toward the heart and, unless the body is able to burn enough energy to warm it again, the temperature of the internal organs—the *core temperature*—will drop, eventually to a dangerous degree. Food is scarce, however, so an animal cannot control its core temperature simply by burning food to generate heat. It needs a smarter trick—and, of course, it has one. Arctic mammals and birds have a *rete mirabile*, which is an anatomical name that means "wonderful net."

The net consists of many small blood vessels located close to where the feet join the main part of the body. These vessels run in both directions, toward and away from the heart, and they lie close together. As blood passes through them, the cold blood cools the warm blood and the warm blood warms the cold blood. Blood flowing toward the toes loses heat by warming the blood flowing away from the toes. This helps keep the toes cold. At the same time, blood flowing away from the toes is warmed, helping to prevent the core temperature from dropping. This system is called *countercurrent exchange*. Have you every wondered how penguins manage to waddle around without freezing to the ground? They have a very efficient "wonderful net."

Life at sea

Much of the life of polar deserts takes place at sea. Penguins breed on land, but they feed at sea. Indeed, penguins, southern (or silver-gray) fulmars *(Fulmarus glacialoides)*, snow petrels *(Pagodroma nivea)*, and seals are the only large animals that breed on land in Antarctica. Apart from them, the continent has just over 100 species of invertebrate animals and half of those are parasites of seals or birds.

Penguins feed on fish, squid, cuttlefish, and krill. Krill look like shrimps, but are only distantly related to them. There are about 85 species. One of the commonest, *Euphausia superba*, is about two inches (5 cm) long. It lives in the Arctic and also around the shores of Antarctica and beneath the edges of the ice shelves, where it forms swarms covering several square miles, often to a depth of more than 15 feet (4.5 m), and it provides food for seals, whales, and some fish, as well as penguins. A blue whale *(Balaenoptera musculus)* consumes about four tons (3.6 tonnes) of krill every day. Salmon feed on other krill species in arctic waters. Krill are now harvested by fishing fleets.

Polar bears, wolverines *(Gulo gulo)*, and wolves *(Canis lupus)* are the principal predators of the Arctic. The wolverine, a member of the weasel family (Mustelidae), eats berries, scavenges the carcasses of animals killed by other predators, and in winter it hunts caribou *(Rangifer tarandus,* known as reindeer in Europe). Wolves also hunt caribou as well as musk oxen *(Ovibos moschatus)*. Musk oxen are big animals, about seven feet (2 m) long, with a long, thick, waterproof coat. They have large, very heavy horns with which to defend themselves. When they are threatened, musk oxen form a circle, all facing outward, with the young inside. A wolf stands little chance of killing one unless it becomes isolated from its herd. In addition to land animals, polar bears hunt in the water.

Antarctica has no predators living on land. The southern equivalents of the polar bear and wolf are the leopard seal *(Hydrurga leptonyx)* and orca or killer whale *(Orcinus orca)*. The leopard seal is a fearsome hunter about 10 feet (3 m) long, with a slender body—spotted like that of a leopard—and long neck. Fast and highly maneuverable, it feeds on fish, squid, krill, and other seals, but penguins make up about one-quarter of its diet. Orcas hunt seals.

Peoples of the desert

You might think that no one would choose to live in a desert. What would they eat? How would they find enough water? People live there now, of course, but that is because nowadays there are roads, railroads, and air-fields for the trucks, wagons, and aircraft that bring food and other essentials, and pipes to carry water. Modern desert-dwellers can enjoy the dry climate without having to grow their own crops in it. What is more, those same roads, railroads, and airfields allow people to move around. They are able to leave the desert whenever they choose.

Droughts are disasters that bring hardship. Despite this, people have always lived in deserts, and they have done so from choice. There were people living in Arizona 25,000 years ago—long before many parts of North America were inhabited. Oraibi, a village in northern Arizona that is now the unofficial capital of the Hopi Reservation, has been occupied continuously since 1150 C.E., making it possibly the oldest continuously inhabited settlement in the United States—and it is in a desert.

Western civilization originated with the building of cities in the desert lands lying between the rivers Tigris and Euphrates, in what was then called Mesopotamia and is now Iraq, and in Egypt, along the shores of the Nile in the eastern Sahara. Life was possible in these places because the rivers supplied water that could be directed through irrigation canals into the cultivated fields. Crop farming began at about the same time in several parts of the world, and one of the most important centers lay in the dry lands of Turkey and southwestern Asia.

Farming communities must live close to their fields. This means they must build permanent settlements and it is these that sometimes grow into cities. Desert life is possible without farming, however, and there are people who have lived in deserts for many centuries without building cities or even permanent villages. All but the most inhospitable deserts are inhabited.

Life is possible, for those who understand the environment and how to find and exploit its resources, in the hot deserts of the Tropics and subtropics—such as the Sahara, Arabian, and American deserts—and in the cool deserts of continental interiors, such as the Gobi. The polar deserts of the north are also inhabited. Only the vast desert of Antarctica remains empty of people (except for visiting scientists and tourists) and its emptiness is due to its isolation rather than the harshness of its climate. No migrants from South America, Africa, or Australasia ever found their way across the wild Southern Ocean and survived to found a culture based on the abundant life around the Antarctic shores. There is no southern equivalent to the Inuit and Eskimo peoples.

Farmers of the desert

The Hopi of North America are farmers, as were the Anasazi people from whom they are descended. All the descendants of the Anasazi, as well as the Anasazi themselves, are known as *pueblo* people because they build towns, for which the Spanish word is *pueblo*.

Originally, the pueblo people built circular underground pits to store food. Later, they reinforced their stores with walls made from stone blocks bonded together with mortar and covered them with roofs. People then started living in them. Until that time they had moved from place to place, leaving stores of dry food to which they could return later. As their farming improved, they found it possible to remain permanently in one location. That is when they started building their homes above ground, along the sides of cliffs and beneath overhanging cliffs. Their buildings were several stories high, with each level set back from the level below so they were arranged in terraces. There were no doors or windows to the ground-floor rooms. Entry to those was by a ladder through a hole in the ceiling. Rooms on the upper floors had doors to adjacent rooms, but could also be entered through the ceiling. This arrangement made the dwellings very secure. An invader could gain access only by raising a ladder to the first terrace, and the defenders could easily throw the ladder down. The cliff dwellings were abandoned toward the end of the 13th century, perhaps because of a severe drought at this time or because of quarrels among the many tribes that lived in each pueblo. They were replaced by dwellings up to five stories high that were similar in design, but built away from the cliff sides. Adobe blocks became the predominant building material. These are made from wet clay that is shaped and then dried in the sun.

Corn was their staple food. This was not sweet and soft like modern corn. Its kernels were hard and were ground into a kind of flour that was used to make bread and soup. They also grew several varieties of beans, as well as gourds and squashes, and they hunted game. Their diet was balanced and nutritious, but everything depended on the careful use of water. In some places they developed irrigation systems, and in others they made skillful use of underground water.

Farming is an activity based on routine. Particular tasks must be performed at the same time each year. Not surprisingly, the pueblo farmers developed elaborate rituals that had to be performed at specified times and that were related to farming.

There are also farmers in the northern Sahara. Most of the Berber people grow crops. The Berbers are descended from the people known in ancient times as *Numidians*. They lived near Carthage, the city located close to the modern city of Tunis, and after the Romans had conquered the Carthaginians and destroyed their city, the region came to be called *Barbary*, from a Greek word meaning "foreign." The Berbers, then, are the people of Barbary. They live mainly in the Atlas and Rif Mountains of Algeria and Morocco. Although most Berber communities live by farming, some grow crops in the lowlands during the winter and spend the summer on the high pastures, watching over their flocks of sheep and herds of goats. This practice is called *transhumance*. Other Berbers are pastoralists. These are people who cultivate no crops, but live by herding cattle, sheep, goats, and camels.

Nomads

Pastoralists live in tents made from animal skins. Farmers who spend the summers on the high North African pastures also use tents, but build earth walls around them for added protection.

Nomadic peoples live in tents, for obvious reasons: they can be packed into loads that are transported by animals—usually camels—to a new site where they are quickly erected, and they are made and maintained using materials that are readily available. Several nomadic peoples live in the Sahara and the deserts of Arabia and western Asia. The best-known are the Tuareg, Fulani, and Bedouin.

The Tuareg are sometimes called "the blue people," because of the blue robes and turbans worn by the men. They make their tents from skins that they dye red and sometimes from plastic sheeting. Their ancestors were farmers in North Africa, but were driven from their lands in the 12th century by an invasion of Bedouin Arabs. Out in the desert the Tuareg learned to live by raising cattle and trading. They became the haulers of the desert, conveying goods by camel caravan. They regarded the desert as their own property and exacted "taxes" from non-Tuareg caravans crossing it, augmenting this income by robbing travelers.

Today the nomadic Tuareg are distributed throughout most of the western half of the Sahara and on the grasslands along the southern edge of the desert. Trucks now transport goods along desert roads and there is little demand for camel caravans, and many of their cattle died in the droughts of the 1970s. These changes impoverished them. Many have moved into refugee camps. Others have become farmers or settled in the cities. Many of their young men have become soldiers in the army of whichever country they happened to be in at the time.

The Fulani also live as nomads, moving their herds of cattle from one area of pasture to the next and trading dairy produce for the goods they need. They live throughout the western Sahara. Their way of life is changing, however, and many Fulani have settled in cities or taken up farming.

About 10 percent of the population of North Africa, the Near East, and the Middle East are Bedouin. They are the most numerous, most widespread, and therefore most typical of all desert peoples. Their name is derived from the Arabic word *bedu*, which means "desert-dweller." They wear long, flowing robes, ride horses and camels, and live among the sand dunes.

Their rectangular, low, black tents made from cloth draped from a line of poles along the center have appeared in countless movies. Plain on the outside, the tents are highly elaborate inside, where decorative hangings divide them into two sections. One section is occupied by the women and children, and is used for storage and for entertaining female visitors. It also has the hearth where food is cooked. The other section, with a hearth for heating, is occupied by the men and is used for entertaining visitors.

The Bedouin are pastoralists. They herd camels, sheep, and goats. In Sudan and southern Arabia there are Bedouin who herd cattle. The social position of a clan—an extended family group—depends partly on their animals, with the camel herders being the most highly regarded.

People of the Gobi

There are farms in some parts of the Gobi desert, but the rainfall is so unreliable that they do not produce a harvest every year. Most of the farmers are descended from Chinese immigrants. The true desert people are Mongolian, and traditionally they led a nomadic life, although many of them now live in towns. Not only do Mongolians not farm, traditionally they despise vegetables and refuse to eat them. Their diet consists mainly of meat and milk, with some dishes made from flour obtained by trading meat and dairy produce with farmers. They drink tea, also obtained by trading, and *airag*, made from fermented mares' milk. Milk is also eaten in the form of dried curds and cheese.

The typical Mongolian dwelling, called a *ger*, *yurt*, or *yurta*, is circular and made from a framework of wooden poles covered with skins or cloth, but most often with felt. There is a hearth at the center, from which the smoke rises through a hole at the highest point in the roof. Furnishings consist of brightly colored rugs. Each *ger* houses a family, and households form herding groups to collaborate in the care of the animals. They raise camels and horses, as well as sheep, goats, and cattle. Sheep supply the dung that is used as fuel for cooking and heating. This is possible because sheep feed during the day and defecate in the evening. They are led to the pasture every morning and brought back to the camp in the evening—partly to protect them from wolves—so the dung is easy to collect. Some cattle herds include yaks *(Bos grunniens)*. The camels are the two-humped Bactrian species *(Camelus bactrianus)*. These are used as pack animals, but they also produce milk, and wool from their long coats is spun and woven to make clothes and blankets.

Managing such a variety of animals would be almost impossible for a single family, because each species has its own requirements and they are all different. Consequently, the species are managed separately, and the families agree on who shall be in charge of each herd or flock. Grazing is carefully controlled, and when the resources within convenient reach are exhausted, the camp packs up and moves to a new site. As winter approaches, those animals that are unlikely to survive are slaughtered, and their meat dried and stored for the hungry months to come. The families then move to a winter site where there is shelter and food for the remaining livestock.

Inuit, Eskimos, and Aleut

Inuit means "the people" and is the name by which the native inhabitants of northern Canada and Greenland prefer to be known. Those who live in Alaska like to be called "eskimo," a name that is probably of Amerindian origin. *Aleut* is the Russian name for the inhabitants of the Aleutian Islands in southern Alaska, but these people refer to themselves as *Unganan* or *Unganas*. The Inuit, Eskimos, and Aleuts are closely related to one another, but Aleuts and Eskimos speak languages that are about as similar as English is to Russian.

The Aleut way of life has almost vanished, but originally these people were seafarers. They lived in coastal villages and caught fish, sea birds, seals, sea otters, sea lions, whales, and, occasionally, walruses, as well as gathering shellfish. They also hunted land animals such as bears and caribou. Although animals supplied most of their needs, there are more plants in the Aleutian Islands and along the southern coast of Alaska than there are farther north, and the Aleuts made bags and baskets from woven grass.

Most Inuit people also live in settled communities, fishing and hunting seals, although some used to spend the winter hunting on the sea ice and living in snow-houses ("igloos"). In spring and summer everyone moves to different hunting grounds. Some hunt bowhead whales *(Balaena mysticetus)*, others head inland, formerly traveling by dogsled but nowadays by snowmobile, in search of bears and caribou. The animals they hunt used to supply them with all their raw materials. They used bone to make tools and the frames of their buildings and boats, skins to make clothing and coverings for their tents, and blubber as fuel for light and cooking. Nowadays they have metal tools, snowmobiles, powered boats, rifles, and there are stores selling supplies.

Life in the desert is always hard, but over many generations the true desert peoples have learned how to increase their security and minimize their discomfort. A caribou or bear represents a large amount of food and raw material, for example, and a bowhead whale represents even more. A single successful hunt can feed and supply a family for a long time in an environment where meat freezes quickly and keeps for years. Nomadic pastoralists, moving their herds and flocks from one area of pasture to another, know the desert intimately. They are not wandering randomly, but heading for a destination where they have grazing rights.

Yet times change and the old ways of life are disappearing rapidly. Formerly nomadic people are encouraged to settle in villages, where they can receive better medical care, and their children can attend school. The transformation is sometimes disruptive and leads to social difficulties, but it is inevitable. Hunting was sustainable while the technology was based on dogsleds, bows and arrows, and hand-thrown harpoons, but snowmobiles, powered boats, harpoon guns, and rifles will rapidly deplete the animal populations on which the hunters depend.

Farther south, deserts are now intersected by national frontiers, oasis villages are growing into cities, and trucks arrive from distant farms to supply the markets for animal products. It is becoming increasingly difficult to make a living by pastoralism. At the same time, everyone now has access to radio, television, newspapers, and magazines. These describe a way of life that is more comfortable and safer than the old life, and that offers young people opportunities for education, employment, travel, and adventure they could never find in the desert. As they leave the desert to embrace the modern world, the old world of their ancestors gradually fades.

Why plants need water

Leave a plant without water and after a time it will wilt; its leaves will hang limp and unless it is a woody plant, with a rigid stem to support it, eventually the entire plant will collapse. All plants must have water and the amount they need can be surprisingly large. A birch tree, for example, with about 250,000 leaves, moves approximately 630 pints (359 liters) of water from the soil to the atmosphere every day and, while they are growing, peas use nearly 40 pints of water for every ounce of weight they gain (0.8 l g^{-1}). Living cells are 80 percent water by weight, and 60 percent of the weight of a human body is water. Even the most important or frightening person you can think of is 60 percent water.

Plants obtain their water from the soil. It enters through their roots, moves through their stems and leaves, and evaporates from two types of small pores, called *stomata* (the singular is *stoma*) in the leaves and *lenticels* in the stems. The loss of water through these pores is called *transpiration*, but in practice it is impossible to measure transpiration separately from other kinds of evaporation, and so the two are measured together, as *evapotranspiration*.

Area for area, water evaporates from small pores much faster than it does from an open water surface, such as a lake. This is because water molecules at the edges of the pore or lake spread to the sides and evaporate from there, but the smaller the diameter of the surface, the longer are its edges in proportion to its area, so water is able to spread more. It is a matter of geometry, as the diagram below shows.

Vapor pressure and saturation

Evaporation is the movement of water molecules from a body of liquid water into the air, as water vapor. Vapor molecules in the layer of air immediately above the surface of the liquid exert a pressure on the surface.

Surface area and edge length. The areas of A and B are the same, but whereas A is open, like the surface of a lake, B is divided into 16 smaller areas. Consequently, the total length of the edges in B is 2.5 times more than that in A.

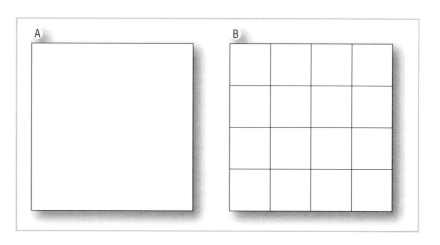

This *vapor pressure* increases as the number of molecules exerting it increases until it reaches the *saturation vapor pressure*. At this point the relative humidity (RH) reaches 100 percent and the water vapor is saturated, although the situation is usually described as the air being saturated (see the box "Humidity" on page 14 in the section "Subtropical deserts"). Until this point, more water molecules are entering the air than are returning to the surface of the liquid, but when the saturation vapor pressure is reached, the number leaving the liquid and the number returning to it are the same, and no more evaporation occurs.

The rate of transpiration from the surface of a plant depends on the difference between the water vapor pressure inside the plant tissues and that in the air outside. This depends partly on the temperature, because the pressure exerted by the same amount of water vapor is inversely proportional to the temperature. In other words, relative humidity (RH) decreases as temperature increases.

Inside a plant leaf, air spaces ordinarily contain water vapor at the saturation vapor pressure and a relative humidity of 100 percent. Suppose that the temperature both inside and outside the leaf is 50°F (10°C) and the relative humidity in the outside air is 60 percent. The vapor pressure inside the leaf (RH = 100 percent) will then be 12.3 millibars (mb) and that outside will be 7.4 mb, so there is a pressure difference of (12.3 − 7.4 =) 4.9 mb. With the same amount of moisture in the outside air, if the temperature increases to 80°F (27°C) the vapor pressure inside the leaf will be 35.7 mb (where the RH is still 100 percent), that outside still only 7.4 mb (where RH is then 21 percent), so the pressure difference increases to 28.3 mb. Even if the air becomes moister as it warms so that its RH remains at 60 percent, the difference in vapor pressure will still increase. At 80°F (27°C) the vapor pressure inside the leaf will be 35.7 mb, that outside 21.4 mb, and the difference will be 14.3 mb.

By day, leaves are exposed to the sunlight, which they need for photosynthesis. Their absorption of light also warms them, and the more intense the light, the more they are warmed by it. Dark leaves absorb more light than pale leaves, and if a dark leaf is exposed to direct, intense sunlight for several hours the temperature below its surface can be much higher than that of the outside air. The water vapor inside the leaf is still at saturation vapor pressure, but as the temperature increases so does the vapor pressure and, therefore, so does the difference between the internal and external vapor pressure. Strong sunlight alone can increase the rate at which a plant loses moisture.

It is this difference in vapor pressure that controls the rate at which water evaporates. The warmer and drier the outside air, the faster the plant will lose water through its open pores. If the RH of the air increases, the plant will lose water more slowly, but during a drought the RH of the air falls to a very low level. Even in temperate climates, and with ample water in the soil, plants often wilt in the middle of a summer day, when the rate of transpiration exceeds the rate at which their roots can absorb moisture. (Watering will not cure this type of wilting, because shortage of water is not what causes it.)

Water inside plants

Plants use water for mechanical and chemical purposes. Mechanically, it is what supports the structure of their leaves and other soft tissues. In large plants, such as trees, the hydrogen bonds linking liquid water molecules into groups are strong enough to allow columns of water to be drawn upward from the roots all the way to the crown. It is transpiration that drives the upward flow. As water evaporates from the leaves, more water is drawn up to replace it.

When plant cells have all the water they need, they are filled, and the cell contents press against their walls. This makes them rigid (the technical term is *turgid*). If they lose water, cell walls become flabby and the whole structure loses rigidity. The plant wilts and, unless it replaces the lost water, eventually it will die.

Chemically plants, like all living organisms, use water to transport the chemical compounds they need. Water is an excellent *solvent*. This means that a wide variety of substances will dissolve in water and their molecules will become dispersed evenly throughout the liquid. The water (the solvent) together with the dissolved substance (the *solute*) is then known as a *solution*. All the liquids found in plants and animals are solutions of various compounds in water.

Adaptation to dry conditions

Some plants have evolved to tolerate dry conditions. These are called *xerophytes* (the Greek *xeros* means dry and *phuton* means plant), and they grow in deserts. Many xerophytes have stomata only on the undersides of their leaves, where they are shaded and cooler, or in pits or grooves where they are sheltered from the drying wind. Some shed their leaves in very dry weather or reduce their leaves to a very small size. The leaves of cacti are their spines, for example, and they use their green stems for photosynthesis.

Cacti store water in their swollen leaves and stems. This is a common adaptation to environments where rain falls only very rarely, but when it does it sometimes falls very heavily. Many euphorbias store water in the same way. Plants that do this are called succulents (see the section "Desert Life" on page 84).

Plants have also evolved different ways to capture the carbon dioxide they use to manufacture sugars through the process of *photosynthesis*. These allow certain plants to grow more successfully than others in hot, sunny climates and in deserts (see the box on page 105, "C3, C4, and CAM plants").

Plants that grow in moister climates do not possess most of these adaptations, but they do have some. Many evergreens, for example, have dark green, thick, waxy leaves. The dark color increases their absorption of light, to help photosynthesis, their thickness increases the amount of water they can hold, and their waxy outer coating reduces the rate at which water evaporates from them. Coniferous trees have leaves that are shrunk to tiny scales or needles to reduce transpiration, and many broad-leaved

C3, C4, and CAM plants

All green plants use carbon dioxide from the air and water from the ground to assemble sugars. The process is called *photosynthesis*, but there are three versions of the way carbon is captured (the technical term is *fixed*) from carbon dioxide. Plants using these are known as *C3 plants*, *C4 plants*, and *CAM plants*.

Many common plants, including soybeans, rice, wheat, cabbage, and potatoes, are C3 plants. This means that the carbon dioxide (CO_2) entering their cells is made into glycerate 3-phosphate (GP), a compound in which each molecule contains three carbon atoms. C3 plants grow mainly in temperate climates. They must open their stomata to obtain the carbon dioxide they need, but this allows water to evaporate from inside the plant, so in hot, dry weather C3 plants must either cease photosynthesis or risk wilting. They also lose some of the carbon dioxide they absorb. This is because rubisco (ribulose biphosphate carboxylase), which is the enzyme that catalyzes the reaction that fixes carbon dioxide, can also combine with oxygen. In hot, sunny weather, most of the carbon dioxide in the immediate vicinity of photosynthesizing cells is being absorbed for photosynthesis and so the air is depleted of it, and rubisco starts combining with oxygen. This is called *photorespiration*, and it reduces the efficiency of photosynthesis without releasing energy the way ordinary respiration does.

C4 plants thrive better in hot, dry climates. Sugarcane and corn are C4 plants. Instead of using rubisco to make carbon dioxide react with ribulose biphosphate to form GP, they use a different enzyme, phosphoenolpyruvate carboxylase (PEP carboxylase).

This catalyzes a reaction between carbon dioxide and phosphoenolpyruvate (PEP) to make oxaloacetate, a compound in which each molecule contains four carbon atoms. PEP carboxylase will not combine with oxygen and so C4 plants do not suffer from photorespiration and photosynthesis can continue even when carbon dioxide levels are very low. Oxaloacetate is formed in specialized cells in the leaves, and it accumulates there until its carbon needs to be used. This means that C4 plants can continue photosynthesizing even when their stomata are closed, thus reducing the amount of water they lose.

Cacti and pineapples belong to the group known as CAM plants, as do the stonecrops, whose family name of Crassulaceae gives this version of carbon fixation its name: *crassulacean acid metabolism*. CAM plants open their stomata only at night and use the carbon dioxide entering their cells to make several organic acids. These are stored in spaces (*vacuoles*) in the cell. During the day they release their carbon for photosynthesis, but without needing to open their stomata at all. CAM plants are able to grow in dry places, because they are highly economical in their use of water, but they grow rather slowly, because they do not photosynthesize very efficiently.

CAM plants grow well in deserts, but C4 plants thrive better than CAM plants where water is plentiful. C4 plants grow best in warm, sunny climates where water is usually available but there is a dry season or occasional droughts when the supply is limited. C3 plants grow better than either CAM or C4 plants in temperate climates.

trees shed their leaves in winter, shutting down both photosynthesis and transpiration. Broad-leaved evergreen trees, such as holly *(Ilex)*, grow best in a warm, moist climate. Deciduous trees (which shed their leaves in winter) and conifers grow in cooler climates, where water often freezes in winter. Plants can absorb water only as a liquid, so a winter when water is frozen is equivalent to a dry season when no rain falls.

A predictable dry season, or cold winter, presents no problem for plants. They have been able to adapt to these simply because they are predictable.

It is when bad times arrive unexpectedly that plants (and animals) suffer, and droughts are always unexpected. They are periods of dry weather that occur at a time of year when there is usually rain.

Effects of drought

As the ground dries by evaporation, it is water that is lost, rather than the chemical compounds dissolved in the water. Evaporation from the surface draws water from below, through the tiny spaces between soil particles (see the section "Water below ground" on page 108). When soil water evaporates, the compounds dissolved in it are left behind and accumulate in such water as remains. This increase in concentration makes it more difficult for plant roots to absorb liquid and plants begin to suffer (see the box "Osmosis" below and the section "Desert life" on page 84).

Less water enters plants, but their rate of transpiration does not slow at once. Plants can open and close their stomata, but they do so according to their own internal clock, which opens them during the day and closes them at night. Even plants that are kept in total darkness or permanent light continue to open and close their stomata according to this rhythm, and plants that grow best in moist climates have many stomata. The average for many plants is nearly 200,000 for every square inch of leaf area (31,000 cm^{-2}). Some have more. Spanish oak, a hybrid of Turkey oak (*Quercus cerris*) and cork oak (*Q. suber*) that grows in southern Europe, has about 775,000 per square inch (120,000 cm^{-2}).

When a plant is losing more water by transpiration than it is absorbing through its roots, it is said to experience *water stress*. If this happens suddenly, the cells around the stomata may lose their rigidity, and instead of the stomata closing, they open wide. If water stress develops more slowly, the stomata will close, but they cannot be kept closed indefinitely

Osmosis

Certain membranes are partially permeable. That is to say, some molecules can pass through them, but not others. Many biological membranes are of this type, but they can also be manufactured industrially.

If a partially permeable membrane separates two solutions of different strengths, there will be a pressure across the membrane that forces *solvent* molecules (molecules of the substance, such as water, in which the *solute* is dissolved) from the weaker to the stronger solution until both are at the same strength. This is called *osmotic pressure*,

and *osmosis* is the process by which molecules cross the membrane under osmotic pressure. The most common solutions occurring naturally are of substances dissolved in water, so the movement across membranes is most commonly of water.

Cells are enclosed within partially permeable membranes and contain substances dissolved in water. If the solution outside the cell is stronger than that inside, water will pass out of the cell. If the solution inside the cell is the stronger, water will pass into the cell.

without harming the plant. These are the pores through which water evaporates, but they are also the pores through which the plant absorbs the carbon dioxide it needs for photosynthesis and excretes oxygen, the by-product of photosynthesis. A plant may survive the onset of a drought by sealing itself, but it cannot grow in this condition and, if the drought continues, eventually the plant will starve.

Crop plants need large amounts of water. About 1.5 tons of water are required to grow 1 ton of wheat and about 10,000 tons to grow a ton of cotton fiber. Even in climates where rainfall seems abundant, many crops benefit from additional watering, because there are months during which the amount of water that can evaporate from the surface is greater than the amount of rainfall.

Even if the weather is only slightly drier than usual, plant growth can be slowed and crop yields reduced. In severe drought, plants that are adapted to moist climates cannot survive. Except in regions where people can afford to import the food they need, once the stores have been eaten, drought is followed by famine.

WATER IN THE GROUND

Water below ground

Washington, D.C., receives an average of 40 inches (1,016 mm) of rain a year, distributed fairly evenly so that no single month is wetter or drier than any other. In April, for example, on average there is 3.3 inches (84 mm) of rain. This is enough rain to cover the ground to a depth of 3.3 inches (84 mm) in that one month, and over the year Washington receives enough rain to cover it to a depth of 40 inches (1,016 mm). When figures for precipitation are given as so many inches or millimeters, that is what the measures mean. It is the depth to which that much precipitation would cover the surface. Except when unusually heavy rain causes rivers to burst their banks and flood the surrounding land, however, rain and melting snow do not lie on the surface. You do not have to wade through the streets of Washington, because the water disappears as quickly as it arrives.

Most of our rain and snow comprise water that evaporated from the sea and a smaller amount is water that evaporated from wet ground and lakes, and that is transpired by plants (see the section "Why plants need water"). After it has fallen, rivers carry the water back to the sea. Obviously, rivers cannot return to the sea more water than fell as rain and snow, but if they returned less than this, most places that in fact are dry land would lie permanently beneath water. The "water budget" must balance.

Where does the rain go?

This much is obvious, but if you look at a river it is not at all obvious how it gathers the water it carries. You cannot usually see water flowing into it, even during heavy rain. The rain falls and the river flows, but although these events must be linked, the connection between them is invisible. Nor is it obvious how plants obtain the water they need. During dry weather the soil often feels very dry. Crumble it between your fingers and it turns to dust. Despite this, plants continue to grow, which means they must be able to find water somewhere.

When rain falls and snow melts, there are three ways for the water to disappear from sight. Some evaporates, returning immediately to the air as vapor. Evaporation removes a large amount of water in very hot, dry weather. Some water flows over the surface, moving downhill. Water is most likely to flow in this way after very heavy rain. Heavy rain consists of large drops that fall fast enough to batter the soil surface. Battering breaks down small, crumb-sized lumps of soil into their individual grains, then packs these tightly together, leaving almost no spaces between particles. Once this has happened, the soil is said to be *capped*. Water cannot penetrate the soil surface, so it flows across it, and as it flows, the water carries away soil particles. This can lead to serious erosion (see the section "Drought and soil erosion").

Soil consists of particles of varying sizes. Sandy soil is made up of the largest grains, silt of much finer grains, and clay of the smallest grains of all. Sand grains are from 0.02 to 0.08 inches (0.5–2.0 mm) in diameter, silt particles 0.00008 to 0.002 inches (0.002–0.05 mm), and clay particles are less than 0.00008 inches (0.002 mm) across. The smaller the particles, the more tightly they can pack together and so the more risk there is that heavy rain will produce an impermeable cap on the soil surface. This is very unlikely with sandy soils, more likely with silt soils, and a common occurrence with clay soils.

The sizes used to classify particles are difficult to visualize, but the difference between one class and another is much easier to understand if we count the number of particles in an ounce (or gram) of dry soil. One ounce of very coarse sand contains approximately 2,550 grains (90 per gram), and there are about 20 million grains in an ounce of very fine sand (722,000 per gram). One ounce of silt contains 164 million particles (5.8 million per gram), and one ounce of clay contains about 2.6 trillion (thousand billion) particles (90.3 billion per gram). Most soils consist of a mixture of sand, silt, and clay. The proportion of each type determines the texture of the soil and there is a standard diagram (see page 110) showing the way soil textures are classified by the particles in them.

Most of the water disappears downward. It drains vertically through the soil. This is the source of the water below ground on which plants depend, and it is also the source of most of the water that flows into rivers and from there to the sea.

There are small spaces between soil particles through which water can drain. The smaller the particles, the smaller are the spaces between them and the more slowly water moves downward. Spill water onto a sandy beach and it vanishes almost at once, because the spaces between sand grains are large. Spill water onto a clay soil and it soaks into the ground much more slowly. Because water spends more time near the surface of a clay soil than a sandy soil, this also means more of it evaporates.

Groundwater and the water table

The water moves downward through the soil until it reaches a layer of impermeable material. This may be hard, compacted clay, but usually it is rock. The water can sink no farther, so it starts to accumulate. In the layer closest to the impermeable layer all the spaces between soil particles fill with water. This soil is then saturated. It can hold no more water, so as more drains from the surface the layer above it becomes saturated in its turn. The result is a layer of soil lying immediately above the impermeable layer that is fully saturated with water. The water in this layer is known as *groundwater*.

The groundwater has an upper surface. This is the boundary between saturated soil below and unsaturated soil above and it is known as the *water*

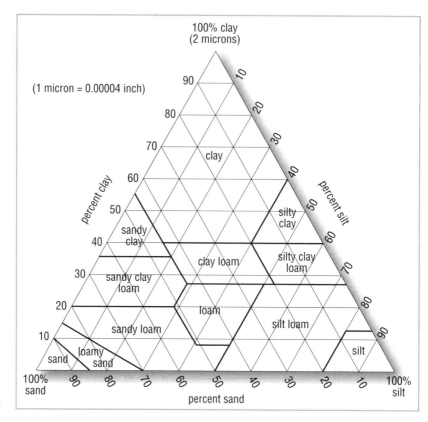

Soil textures

table. The boundary is not a sharp one, like the boundary between the surface of a lake and the air above it, because water is constantly being drawn upward from the saturated zone into the lower part of the unsaturated zone. The layer in which this happens is called the *capillary fringe*. The drawing shows how water is distributed in the layers of soil beneath the surface.

Water in the capillary fringe is flowing upward, against the pull of gravity. The mechanism is the same as when you soak up spilled water by dipping a piece of blotting paper into it. The phenomenon is called *capillarity*, and this ability to flow uphill is one more of the remarkable properties of water.

Capillarity and surface tension

Water molecules are *polar*. This means there is a positive electric charge at one end of each molecule and a negative charge at the other. In the liquid state, hydrogen bonds between the hydrogen atom in one molecule and an oxygen atom in another link water molecules together as groups. Each molecule is attracted to those around it and, except at the surface, these attractions cancel one another, so a molecule is pulled with equal force in all directions.

At the surface, however, there is no pull upward and all the attractive force is to the side and downward. This holds the molecules at the surface very firmly. It is called surface tension and is surprisingly strong. Many small insects can walk on the surface of water because the surface tension is sufficient to support their weight.

Surface tension pulls the surface molecules into the shape that requires the least amount of energy to sustain. This is the shape with the smallest surface area in relation to volume, which is a sphere. A drop of water on a greasy (water-repellent) surface will adopt a spherical shape, flattened somewhat by its own weight.

This is also the force that drives water upward through very narrow tubes or pathways. Polar molecules are attracted to opposite electric charges in the walls of the tube. This draws them a short distance up the sides of the tube and as they rise they pull behind them the molecules to which they are linked by hydrogen bonds. The water surface is now concave (sags in the center), as is shown in the diagram on page 112. Surface tension then pushes the center of the water surface upward, to restore the convex (bulges in the center) shape that is closest to a sphere. This raises the level of the water at

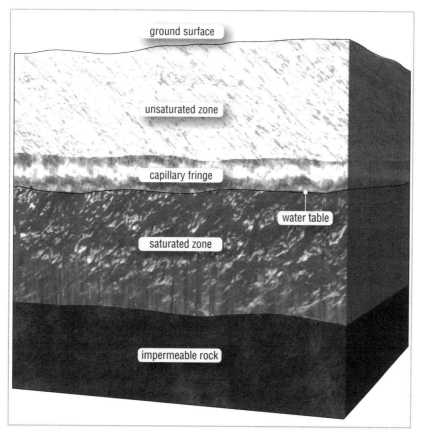

ground surface

unsaturated zone

capillary fringe

water table

saturated zone

impermeable rock

Groundwater and the water table

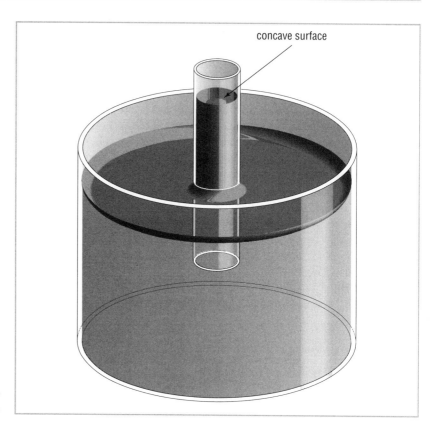

concave surface

Capillarity and surface tension

the center, exposing molecules to the side of the center to the attraction of charged molecules in the side of the tube. The water flows a little farther up the sides, surface tension seeks to restore the surface shape, and the water rises still farther. A limit is reached when the weight of the column of water in the tube is equal to the force pushing the water upward.

Capillarity occurs only in very narrow tubes, because a wide tube holds so much water that its own weight exceeds the upward force as soon as it rises at all. If you wish to test capillarity for yourself, try to find a glass tube, open at both ends, with a bore no larger than 0.04 inch (1 mm). Make sure the tube is dry on the inside. Hold the tube vertically and insert one end into a bowl of cold water (the colder the better, because surface tension decreases as temperature rises). The water is easier to see if you color it. Water should rise about 3.5 inches (90 mm) up the tube; it will rise farther if the tube is narrower and not so far if it is wider.

Soil capillarity

The spaces between soil particles link to form long, irregular channels that are narrow enough for capillarity to occur, but the channels do not rise vertically. They twist and turn this way and that. Sometimes they are vertical, sometimes horizontal, and most of the time they are at varying angles between these two extremes. Weight always acts vertically, of course, so as water rises through the channels by capillarity, much of its weight is supported by the soil particles themselves. This allows the water to move much farther than it would in a straight tube held vertically.

Suppose the soil is completely soaked after heavy rain or the melting of snow. All the capillary channels will be filled with water. Water evaporates from the surface at almost the same rate as from an open water surface, such as a lake. This reduces the weight in the water column, allowing more water to be drawn from below by capillarity to replace it.

Capillary matting, which you can buy to water plants automatically, is based on this principle. One end of the matting lies immersed in a reservoir of water and the rest of it beneath the soil or pots that contain growing plants. This soil is saturated with water and as water is lost by evaporation from the surface and by transpiration from the plant leaves, more water flows from the reservoir, through the capillary channels in the matting, and then into the soil to replace it. The matting is designed so that water will flow through it faster than it can be lost into the air from the soil and plant surfaces. As long as the reservoir contains water, the plants have as much water as they need.

Outdoors, where there is no capillary matting to help, the rate of evaporation at the wet surface eventually exceeds the rate at which capillary moisture can keep the soil saturated, and so the surface dries. Once a layer of dry soil covers the surface, evaporation almost ceases. You need not dig far below the dry surface to find moist soil. The depth at which you will find it depends partly on the number and species of plants growing in it. Plants are constantly moving water from the soil to the air, so they dry the soil. Soil with no plants is much moister than soil with plants.

Plants obtain their water from below, tapping the stream that rises by capillarity from the water table. Provided their roots extend into the capillary fringe, the plants will flourish even when the uppermost layer of soil is dry as dust. Their health and eventually their survival depend on the height of the water table, however, which depends in turn on the amount of groundwater. During prolonged drought, the groundwater is not replenished. Gradually the water table falls and, with it, the capillary fringe, and the capillary channels empty. As the water level in the soil falls, plants with shallow roots are the first to suffer, but if the drought is severe it will injure even those plants that have huge and deep root systems.

Wells and springs

Layers of rock seldom lie horizontally. Where rock is exposed at the surface you can see for yourself that it almost always slopes, even if only slightly. Pour water onto it and the water will flow downhill—and demonstrate which direction is "downhill." This is also true of rock layers below ground. Almost all of them slope, and so water that accumulates above a layer of impermeable rock will flow downhill. That is how water that falls as rain or snow over land eventually reaches the rivers that carry it to the sea.

Groundwater (see the section "Water below ground" on page 108) flows very slowly, because it moves through a fairly dense mass of sand, gravel, or soil particles. Speeds vary, from as little as one foot (30 cm) in a century to as fast as one mile per hour (1.6 km/h), depending on the material through which the water is moving. Once a molecule of water enters the groundwater it may be several centuries before it returns to the surface. For comparison, a water molecule entering the ocean may remain there for several thousands of years.

Above the impermeable layer, groundwater moves through saturated soil. In most cases, the water table marks the upper limit of saturation. Obviously, the position of the underlying layer determines that of the water table, because it is the layer that prevents water from sinking deeper. The position of the water table therefore has nothing to do with the level of the ground surface. If the soil is shallow, heavy rains may cause the water table to rise all the way to the surface, making the soil waterlogged, but if the soil were deeper the water table could rise by the same amount without causing waterlogging.

The mystery of a spring

Movements of the rocks forming the uppermost layers of Earth's crust alter the position and slope of layers of impermeable rock, and erosion by wind and water alters the shape of the surface. Over millions of years, jagged mountains are worn away into smooth hills and eventually the hills are washed and blown away until the landscape is almost level. This continuous process is known as the *cycle of erosion*. It is a cycle rather than a one-way process, because the eroded material accumulates as sediments that eventually form sedimentary rock, and later crustal movements thrust the sedimentary rock above the surface once more as mountains that begin to erode the moment they are exposed to the wind and rain. And all the time this is happening, water falling on the surface is draining downward into the groundwater and then downhill toward the sea.

Suppose these processes of Earth movement and erosion, cut through the entire system. Perhaps some upheaval below ground, mild enough in itself, strains an impermeable rock layer to its breaking point. The rock fractures as a section of it moves vertically to create a fault with one side of the fracture at a lower level than the other side. Meanwhile, erosion carries away some of the softer rock lying above the harder, impermeable layer to form a hillside. Water continues to move down the slope of the impermeable layer, but this layer now emerges at or close to the surface. Where this happens, groundwater will reach the surface. It may seep into the overlying soil in a small, waterlogged area or, with thinner soil or a faster flow, it may trickle or bubble from the ground. In either case it emerges onto the surface as a spring.

If a number of springs discharge into a natural hollow in the ground, the water may form a pool or lake. This is how desert oases form, providing evidence that even in the driest parts of the world there is often water below ground (see the section "Subtropical deserts" on page 9). Higher up a slope, springs are commonly the source of small streams that eventually grow into large rivers.

Springs are often rather mysterious. People have always had a great respect for them, because they have no obvious cause, and the water they deliver is either pure enough to drink or contains dissolved mineral salts that people believe are beneficial to health. It is as though the ground itself were spontaneously providing a reliable source of wholesome water or medicine. In a sense, of course, this is precisely what is happening, but it is mysterious only because the reasons for it are hidden below ground, and the water has usually traveled a considerable distance before it reaches the spring. As the diagram A in the drawing below suggests, the spring occurs at an accidental interruption in the long, slow journey of the groundwater.

Springs and wells.
A) spring. B) well.
C) artesian well

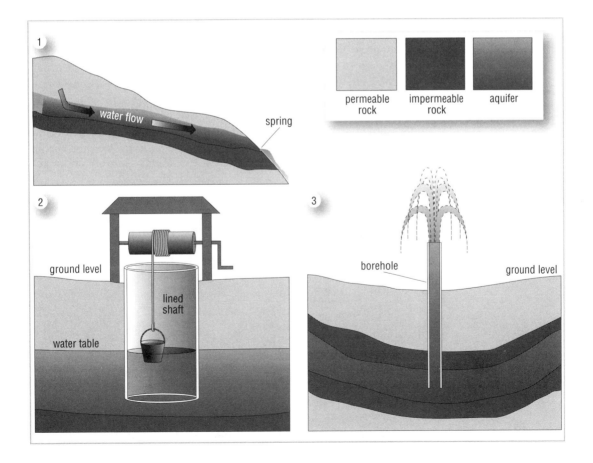

Hard water and soft water

Water never occurs naturally as pure H_2O, because it is such an efficient solvent that many naturally occurring substances dissolve in it. These change the chemical composition of the water—more correctly, the soil solution—as it moves through the ground. First the water travels downward, through the soil, reacting with some of the chemical compounds it meets and dissolving others. As its journey continues, most of these substances are removed by further chemical reactions. If the water flows over hard rock, such as granite, and through soil particles derived from it, such as sand, the emerging springwater will be fairly pure and "soft." If it flows over or through material containing large amounts of carbonates, such as calcium carbonate ($CaCO_3$) and magnesium carbonate ($MgCO_3$), some of these will react with carbonic acid (H_2CO_3) that is naturally present in the water—it is dissolved carbon dioxide (CO_2)—and the springwater will be "hard."

The reactions with water that form $CaCO_3$, $MgCO_3$, and also magnesium and calcium chloride and sulfate ($MgCl_2$, $CaCl_2$, $MgSO_4$, and $CaSO_4$), remove some of the H_2CO_3, thereby reducing the acidity of the water until, instead of being slightly acid, it is slightly alkaline. Hard water is alkaline—its pH is greater than 7. Carbonates are insoluble. They are dispersed throughout the water and can be removed from it only by filtering. The presence of carbonates causes *permanent hardness*. Carbonic acid and water can also react with calcium and magnesium to form bicarbonates ($Ca(HCO_3)_2$ and $Mg(HCO_3)_2$). These are soluble and dissolve in the water, but they are easily removed. When the water is heated the bicarbonate is converted to insoluble carbonate that is deposited as scale on the inside of pipes and kettles. This type of hardness is *temporary*. Chlorides and sulfates react with the fatty acids in soap. These reactions produce a tough, insoluble scum that is deposited on the sides of bathtubs and washbasins and on the fibers of fabrics.

Drink from a spring, especially in summer, and you are almost certain to be struck by how cold the water is. In fact, though, it is warmer than the average annual air temperature in the area around the spring. It feels cold only because it is cooler than your skin and cooler than the summer air temperature. Groundwater flows so slowly that the heat of the rocks below ground gently warm it. Most water taken from very deep wells must be cooled before it can be used.

Digging a well

Material just above an impermeable layer through which groundwater flows is called an *aquifer* and, provided it is not too deep to be reached, fresh water can be obtained from it. The simplest way to extract water from an aquifer is to dig a well. This is also the most ancient method. As diagram B in the drawing on page 115 shows, the task involves nothing more complicated than digging a hole. This determines a minimum diameter for a well, because the hole must be wide enough for the person who does the digging. Some dug wells are only three feet (91 cm) in diameter, but most are at least four to eight feet (1.2–2.4 m) wide and some are very much wider.

The hole must be lined, partly to prevent the sides falling in and filling up the hole and partly to prevent contamination of the water. Obviously, the hole must be deep enough to penetrate to below the water table. At the bottom, the sides may be perforated to allow water to enter, but just leaving them open at the bottom is usually enough. Water will fill the bottom of the well up to the level of the water table, and a bucket, lowered on a rope from a winch at the top is all that is needed in order to collect it from a dug well.

Wells vary in depth. Most are less than 100 feet (30 m) deep, but some have been dug to as much as 500 feet (152 m). Although the technology is simple, digging a well is very hard work, and it becomes even more arduous, and possibly dangerous, once it penetrates below the water table.

It is not necessary to dig such a wide hole, because with modern technology water can be pumped from the ground through a much narrower borehole. This is cut with drilling machinery and may be only 4 inches (10 cm) in diameter, or even less. The pump works by evacuating air from the upper part of a tube inserted into the borehole. Air pressure in the tube is then lower than the pressure on the water at the bottom of the borehole, and water is pushed up the tube.

Unfortunately, water can be raised no more than about 26 feet (8 m) in this way, so the technique has a serious disadvantage. If the water table is lower than this, an alternative method must be used. A much wider borehole can accommodate a pump submerged in the water at the bottom. This can lift water much higher. If the water still cannot reach the surface, additional pumps are installed at appropriate depths to raise it a stage at a time.

Alternatively, the borehole can contain a smaller internal pipe through which air is pumped from the surface under pressure. The compressed air arriving at the bottom of the well then pushes water up the main borehole. Using methods of this kind, wells can be sunk to much greater depths.

No one seems to know the depth of the deepest well in the world, but in 1999 engineers of the U.S. Air Force drilled a well more than 1,000 feet (300 m) deep to provide drinking water for the citizens of El Algodonal, in southeastern Bolivia. Some wells in Australia are up to 6,000 feet deep (1,830 m)—and water from them is so hot that it boils when it reaches the surface, where the air pressure is much lower than it is at depth.

Artesian wells

It may not be necessary to use pumps or even buckets. The water may rise to the surface of its own accord. A well of this kind is called an *artesian* or *overflowing well* and is shown in diagram C of the drawing on page 115.

An aquifer that is bounded only by impermeable material below it is said to be *unconfined*. Water drains into it freely from above, and the water table, marking its upper limit, can change in height according to the amount of water the aquifer contains. There are also *confined* aquifers. These comprise permeable material through which groundwater flows, that is bounded by two impermeable layers, one above as well as the one below. Water in a confined aquifer is trapped.

Imagine what happens where the base of an aquifer is curved to form a deep hollow. If the aquifer is unconfined, groundwater will accumulate in the hollow until the water table is at the same level above the hollow as it is to either side. If the ground surface also curves down, following the shape of the underlying rock, the water table may lie higher than ground level. In that case the depression will fill with water, forming a lake. This cannot happen to water in a confined aquifer, however. Water in a confined aquifer flows into the hollow from one side, but it is contained between two impermeable layers. Its level cannot rise and so the weight of the in-flowing water increases the pressure under which the water is held. This pressure pushes water up the other side of the dip in the aquifer and over the rim, allowing it to continue its journey, but the pressure at the center of the dip remains constant and it can be considerable.

Drill a borehole through the upper impermeable layer and the pressure will force water to rise up the pipe. How high it rises depends on the shape of the hollow, but sometimes the top of the borehole, at ground level, will be lower than the top of the confined aquifer outside the hollow. The in-flowing water will then try to behave as though it is in an unconfined aquifer. If that were so, the water would rise through the hole in the confining layer and saturate the overlying soil. It cannot do this, because the borehole has an impermeable lining. This forces the water to rise through the borehole and to flow freely from the surface. The well overflows.

An artesian well (the name is from Artois, an ancient province in what is now the Pas-de-Calais département of northern France) continues to flow because it is constantly being fed with water draining through the aquifer. Once drilled, it is very reliable.

A second aquifer can form above the confining layer, if there is sufficient depth of soil. This is a *perched aquifer* and it is often easier to tap, because it lies at a shallower depth. It can also happen that one impermeable layer is so far below the one above it that the aquifer between them never fills with water. Although it is sealed, it is unconfined. It is possible, therefore, for one unconfined aquifer to lie directly above another.

Aquifers hold vast stores of water, but they are not inexhaustible. If water is taken from them faster than precipitation can recharge them, they will be depleted. Water tables have fallen in many parts of the world because groundwater has been abstracted at a faster rate than the aquifer recharges.

WHAT DROUGHTS CAN DO

How droughts are classified

A few weeks without rain in summer and Britain suffers a drought. Officially, a British drought is a period of more than 15 consecutive days during which no rain falls, or on no day of which does more than 0.01 inch (0.25 mm) of rain fall. When water levels in reservoirs fall below a certain level, people are forbidden to use garden hoses and lawn sprinklers, and car washes close. In extreme droughts the domestic water supply may be cut off at certain times of day, and there have been droughts that were so severe that the domestic supply was shut down altogether. People had to collect water from standpipes in the streets or from water tankers.

The U.S. Weather Bureau defines a drought as a period of 21 or more days during which the rainfall is no more than 30 percent of the average for that particular place and time of year. Sometimes a drought can last much longer than this, of course. The drought that afflicted much of the United States in 2002 began in 1999, with lower than usual rainfall on the eastern side of the country. Rainfall was lower than usual throughout 2000 over much of the Midwest, and by the end of the summer the relatively dry conditions were affecting much of the country to the east of the Rocky Mountains. Average temperatures rose and the winters of both 1999–2000 and 2001–2002 were unusually warm. By the end of January 2002 drought conditions from southern Georgia to Maine were moderate to severe. In Colorado, the period from December 2001 to May 2002 was the driest in 107 years—for as long as there are records. The same period was the second driest on record in Arizona, the third driest in Utah, and the fourth driest in Wyoming. It is not to say that no rain falls during a drought. Montana experienced some of the wettest weather in more than 20 years over a few days in June 2002, and heavy summer thunderstorms brought some relief. This eased the drought, but failed to end it, and forecasters feared conditions might worsen for a time in some areas. A tropical storm or hurricane might end the drought abruptly over Florida and the Gulf Coast—at a price. Over much of the country, however, the long-term drought would end only if the winter snowfall was heavy enough to recharge the groundwater and rivers in the spring of 2003.

In parts of North Africa, a drought occurs when no rain has fallen for at least two years. In Bali, Indonesia, six days without rain constitute a drought. In Egypt, before the Aswan High Dam regulated its flow, a drought year was one in which the Nile failed to flood farmlands downstream and in the river delta. In India, there is a drought if the summer monsoon brings only half the usual amount of rain.

All of these are droughts, but they are very different and so are their consequences. In Britain a drought usually means nothing more serious to most people than brown lawns, wilting flowers, and dirty cars. It sounds trivial, but even a British drought can reduce water supplies to industry, sometimes leading to factory closures and unemployment, and it often reduces yields of most farm crops, sometimes drastically. Elsewhere in the world, drought can mean severe hardship or even starvation (see the section "The Dust Bowl" on page 136).

Clearly, defining just what we mean by "drought" is not simple. It is not enough to say it is a period without rain, or with less rain than is usual, because it may follow a period of high rainfall. Reservoirs may be full and the water table high, so the lack of rain brings no shortages and plants grow vigorously in the bright sunshine. What might have been a drought is a prolonged spell of fine weather and everyone enjoys it, including the farmers and industrialists. Perhaps, then, a drought is a period during which rainfall is insufficient to meet the needs of plants. This is better, but plants vary widely in their requirements. Cabbages need a lot more water than cacti.

The meaning of the word also depends on who is using it. To a farmer, a drought is a period of dry weather that reduces crop yields. A meteorologist thinks of it as a period of unusually low rainfall, whether this has any practical consequences or not. To a hydrologist—a scientist who studies the movement of water in rivers and through the ground—a drought is a period when water tables and river levels fall. In fact more than 150 definitions of "drought" have been published, each related to a particular activity or branch of science.

Meteorologic drought

Meteorologists define a drought as a period of unusually dry weather. This sounds straightforward, but it is not so simple. What does "unusually" mean? More than two weeks without rain is unusual in Britain and even more unusual in an equatorial rain forest, but it is not in the least unusual in New Mexico. Just to confuse matters further, a prolonged spell of dry weather would not be at all unusual during winter in Bombay, but it would be highly unusual in summer (see the section "Monsoons" on page 147).

Clearly, the dry spell must be unusual for a particular place at a particular time of year, or, in places where the climate is always dry, it must extend for an unusually long time. It must also produce some measurable consequences. In particular it must significantly reduce the amount of groundwater and therefore the level of water in rivers and lakes.

Not all droughts are equally severe. British meteorologists distinguish between *absolute drought*, *partial drought*, and a *dry spell*. An absolute drought is a period of at least 15 consecutive days without rain, or with no more than 0.01 inch (0.25 mm) of rain on any one day. A partial drought is a period of at least 29 consecutive days during which the daily average rainfall does not exceed 0.01 inch (0.25 mm). A dry spell is a period of at least 15 days during which no more than 0.04 inch (1 mm) of rain falls on any particular day.

In 1965, W. C. Palmer, a meteorologist at the U.S. Weather Bureau, tried to bring some order into the situation by devising a way to classify droughts and periods of wet weather on a scale from –4 (extremely dry) to +4 (extremely wet). He did this by measuring the amount of precipitation, the temperature, and the amount of moisture in the soil, and using these measurements to calculate a scale of severity. The result was the Palmer Drought Severity Index (PDSI), shown in the box below. The PDSI is not perfect, but it is widely used, especially in the United States.

Agricultural drought

As soon as it begins to affect farm crops, a meteorologic drought becomes an agricultural drought. This happens when the soil contains insufficient moisture for the immediate requirements of a particular farm crop.

A meteorologic drought can be measured in terms of the amount of rain that falls and the amount of moisture that is retained in the soil. It is impossible to measure an agricultural drought in such a general way. Different crops have different requirements and these change as the crop grows and ripens. Dry weather may amount to an agricultural drought while a young crop is growing, but dry weather may be desirable while grain is ripening. Consequently, whether or not a drought is agricultural depends on the time of year and the type of farming in a particular region as well as on the amount of precipitation.

PALMER DROUGHT SEVERITY INDEX

4.00 or above	extremely wet
3.00–3.99	very wet
2.00–2.99	moderately wet
1.00–1.99	slightly wet
0.50–0.99	incipient wet spell
0.49–-0.49	near normal
–0.50–-0.99	incipient dry spell
–1.00–-1.99	mild drought
–2.00–-2.99	moderate drought
–3.00–-3.99	severe drought
–4.00 or below	extreme drought

Hydrological drought

Meteorologists are the first people to report a drought, because they study detailed and accurate daily records of rainfall and can relate them to the known characteristics of the soil in a particular region. If the drought continues, farmers will be the next to observe it and the first people to experience its effects. Some time later, and on a much larger geographical scale, the drought may become a hydrological one. Hydrological droughts are usually measured on the scale of a river drainage system.

A drought becomes hydrological when the amount of water moving through the ground is significantly reduced. It takes time for this to happen. Farm crops will start to suffer when the upper layer of the soil dries and their roots are unable to absorb as much water as they need, but it will be some time after that before the water table starts to fall. Then still more time must elapse before the decrease in the flow of groundwater leads to a fall in river levels.

Rivers provide habitat for wildlife, including fish that are an important source of food in some parts of the world. They provide amenities—water for sailing and swimming, for example—and large rivers provide navigable waterways that are used for commercial transport. They may also feed storage reservoirs and supply water for generating hydroelectric power, cooling water for other types of power generation, and cooling and process water—water that is used in a manufacturing process—for industry. A drop in river levels affects society in many ways. It is serious, and can intensify competition for water resources.

Socioeconomic drought

When a drought begins to affect the supply of goods and services to a community it becomes a socioeconomic drought. That is when city-dwellers may begin to suffer more than the inconvenience of restrictions on using lawn sprinklers and car washes. It can mean water rationing, for example, when the public supply is turned on only at certain times of day, or when the supply to private homes is turned off altogether and water is delivered by road tankers. Just as the definition of an agricultural drought must take account of particular crops and their stage of development, so a socioeconomic drought depends on social and economic circumstances.

A drought may increase water pollution. This happens where the treatment of effluent relies partly on being able to discharge mildly polluting effluent into a river carrying sufficient water to dilute it to a harmless level. If the river carries less water, dilution is reduced, and the river may become polluted. A community that is highly dependent on hydroelectric power may be forced to import energy from outside the region if rivers and reservoirs have insufficient water for adequate power generation. This may be costly for industry and it may necessitate rationing of the domestic supply.

How long is a drought?

Defining a drought as meteorological, agricultural, hydrological, or socioeconomic—and a drought can be any or all of these at the same time, of course—tells us about the effects it has. That is useful, but there is another way to describe droughts.

Since cabbages and cacti grow naturally in very different climates, a useful first step in deciding whether or not a period of dry weather constitutes a drought is to consider those climates. This approach identifies four types of drought. A drought may be *permanent, seasonal, devastating,* or *invisible.*

Permanent drought and seasonal drought

A permanent drought is the drought of deserts, where farmers can grow crops only on irrigated land. Except after the very rare, but often heavy, rains there are no rivers or streams. The climate is unremittingly arid, and drought is the normal condition.

Seasonal drought, the second type, is less extreme, but no less predictable. It occurs in climates where all the rain, or almost all of it, falls during one season. Most plants native to such regions germinate and grow during the rainy season and survive the dry season as seeds or in a dormant state. San Diego, California, for example, has an average 10.2 inches (259 mm) of rain a year, but 74 percent of it falls in winter, between December and March. Bombay, India, has an average 71.3 inches (1,811 mm) of rain a year and 94 percent of it falls between June and September, during the summer monsoon. In these climates, drought is the normal condition during part of the year.

Devastating and invisible droughts

Devastating droughts are of the third type. These are the droughts that no one can predict, because they occur in places where rainfall is spread fairly evenly through the year. Some accident of nature causes the rain to fail. In middle latitudes, droughts are usually caused by blocking (see the section "Blocking highs" on page 75).

A drought of this kind can happen anywhere, at any time, without warning, and its end is no easier to predict than its start. If the drought occurs in winter most people may be hardly aware of it, because that is not the growing season for plants, but if it occurs in summer, plants wilt and die. It is then called a *contingent,* or *accidental* drought.

A drought, or a dry spell that is almost a drought, may cause water tables and the water level in streams and rivers to fall and the soil becomes very dry. The drought may seem to end with the arrival of rain showers, but this is a fourth type of drought, an *invisible* one. Rain does fall, but when the amount of water lost by evaporation and transpiration is deducted, what remains is insufficient to recharge the aquifers. River levels and water tables remain low, and plants, especially crop plants, continue to suffer. Heavy rain that fell in various parts of the United States during the summer of 2002 might have led people to suppose the devastating spring drought had ended. The ground was wet and wilting plants recovered. The recovery was not sustained, however. It could not be, because the water table was still very low and much of the rain evaporated rather than soaking into the ground.

A drought of this kind is troublesome, because many people refuse to believe it exists. They cannot see why they should economize in their use of water when rain showers are fairly frequent. Consequently, public demand, which was reduced during the "visible" drought, slowly increases as people turn on their lawn sprinklers, fill their pools, and wash their cars. Below the surface, however, the ground remains dry—and it stays dry for longer than it would if demand had remained low. There is always a risk that an invisible drought may become more severe, despite the rain.

Thornthwaite climate classification

It was the American meteorologists C. W. Thornthwaite and J. R. Mather who divided droughts into these four types in 1955, in the course of developing a system for classifying climates. There have been many attempts to classify climates and the one Thornthwaite devised in 1931 and greatly improved in 1948 is widely used.

The Thornthwaite classification is partly based on the concept of *potential evapotranspiration (PE)*. This is calculated from the average monthly temperature, corrected for day length, and it represents the amount of water that could be lost by evapotranspiration if there were no water shortage at all. It is calculated from the rate at which water evaporates from the exposed surface of a tank placed out in the open.

Once the *PE* value is known, it can be combined with the amount of annual precipitation *(r)* to calculate a *moisture index (Im)* by the equation $Im = 100(r/PE - 1)$. The moisture index allows the severity of droughts to be compared and is similar to the equation *(r/t)*, which uses average annual precipitation *(r)* and temperature *(t)* to define the aridity of climates (see the section "Subtropical deserts" on page 9).

Droughts of the past

Hurricanes, typhoons, and floods cause widespread devastation and often kill large numbers of people. Blizzards disrupt communications. All are terrible, terrifying events, but they pass and the survivors recover. Droughts are different. They can destroy empires and change the course of history. They have done so several times.

Around 2500 B.C.E. Akkad was the biggest and most powerful empire in the world. At its height, in about 2300 B.C.E. under its ruler Sargon, Akkad controlled the trade in valuable materials from Turkey to

Afghanistan and south all the way to the Gulf of Oman. In Mesopotamia, the land between the rivers Tigris and Euphrates, in territory now forming part of Syria and Iraq, fortresses were built to guard the wheat fields, and irrigation canals were dug to supply water to the crops. The Akkadian capital was a great city covering more than 200 acres (81 ha), with fine buildings, paved streets, and drains to carry away surplus water. On the Syrian plain where that fine city once stood there is now a large sand dune called Tell Leilan, burying all that remains of it.

For the Akkadians, everything started to go wrong in about 2200 B.C.E. They had captured the city at Tell Leilan and expanded it, but in less than a century they abandoned it. Between 2200 and 1900 B.C.E. people moved away from that entire region in great numbers. The rains had become irregular, and then they failed altogether. Once that happened it was not long before the wheat fields were buried beneath windblown sand. For a century or more the drought continued, and the center of the first great empire in the world turned into desert. Akkad collapsed.

The Akkadians were not the only ones to suffer, for the drought was very extensive. Between 2200 and 2100 B.C.E., towns were abandoned in Palestine, as were Mohenjo-daro and Harappa in the Indus Valley. The civilizations of Crete and Greece failed and a marked decrease in the amount of water flowing in the Nile coincided with the collapse of the Old Kingdom of ancient Egypt.

No one knows what caused the drought or why it lasted for so long, but there is strong evidence that it occurred and was widespread. In time, of course, new civilizations and empires arose to replace those that had vanished, but had drought not cleared away old empires, and perhaps old ideas, ancient history might have developed quite differently from the way it did.

Droughts in Asia

Drought has also influenced Asian history. It has always been a constant threat in Mongolia and northern China—and it still is. In the spring of 2002 the most serious drought in half a century was affecting several northern cities, including Beijing. The drought had already lasted for three years and it showed no sign of ending. Reservoir levels had fallen by 11 percent since the same time in the previous year, and water shortages in Beijing were expected to intensify.

Drought is nothing new in this part of the world. In about 300 C.E. there was severe drought in central Asia, and it recurred at intervals throughout the fourth century. Examination of sediments deposited at that time shows a fall in the water level of the Caspian Sea, and there are remains of settlements that were abandoned then in various parts of central Asia and northern China. At times, water and grazing were so scarce that it became impossible for camel caravans to travel the Great Silk Road by which exotic luxuries from China had been reaching the West since the route first opened in about 150 B.C.E.

All of this happened just as nomadic peoples were fighting the Chinese to their south, possibly because they needed pasture for their animals, their traditional grazing lands having become too parched and eroded to supply the feed they needed. The nomads invaded northern China, and the resulting conflict brought about the collapse of the Tsin dynasty. Refugees fled from the war, moving south and east, into southern China, Korea, and Japan. There they stimulated the development of culture and introduced a strong Chinese influence. It may be that the present cultures of Korea and Japan owe much to the drought that happened some 1,700 years ago.

Europe did not remain untouched. The same drought that drove the expansion of the nomadic peoples to the south may also have been what drove them westward. In about 370 B.C.E., the Hunni people, or Huns, invaded southeastern Europe, defeating every army that tried to halt them until they reached the border of the Roman Empire at the Danube. Their most famous king was Attila, known as the "Scourge of God." He was born much later, however, and ruled from 434 to 453 C.E. (his year of birth is not known). The Romans paid tribute (taxes) to him, and his ceaseless pressure on them contributed to the fall of the Roman Empire. If it was the central Asian droughts that destroyed pastures and sent these magnificent horsemen and fearsome archers westward in the fourth century, then those droughts had far-reaching consequences.

Weather in the distant past

Investigations by archaeologists, geologists, and paleoclimatologists (scientists who reconstruct what ancient climates were like) led them to realize what had happened to Akkad, but most droughts are not studied so closely. One exception is a very long drought that affected the southwestern part of what is now the United States. It began in 1246, reached its greatest severity from 1276 to 1299, and the rains did not return with any regularity until 1305. America is no stranger to droughts, of course. Since the first Europeans arrived and started recording them, they have returned to the Middle West fairly regularly at intervals of 20 to 22 years (see the section "The Dust Bowl" on page 136).

In most cases, however, what little we know of ancient droughts is pieced together from records made at the time. Harvest records are useful, because these have always been important and they often include information about the weather during the growing season. Unfortunately, they are incomplete, with long periods for which records have been lost. They do reveal that a drought in England lasted from 678 to 681 C.E. and that there was another from 1276 to 1278, but that is all they tell.

Rather more is known about two droughts that affected England in the 14th century. One that happened in 1305 was serious enough to cause the failure of the grass crop being grown for hay. This led to the starvation of many farm animals and also of humans, although the famine coincided with a smallpox epidemic. There is no way to separate famine deaths from those caused by disease, but almost certainly one would have contributed to the other, because people weakened by hunger would have had less resistance to infection. Famine returned in 1353. The drought of that year lasted from March until the end of July, and rainfall remained low and the ground dry into the following year.

The Little Ice Age

The early years of the 14th century marked the beginning of a major climatic change. During the Middle Ages until then, Europe had enjoyed a "climatic optimum," when average temperatures were relatively high. It is now called the *medieval warm period*. In England, summer temperatures were 1.25–1.8°F (0.7–1.0°C) warmer than they are today, and in central Europe the difference was even more marked. Cereal crops were grown in Norway and Iceland, and England was a major wine producer. Then, after 1300, the climate started to cool rapidly. Average temperatures continued to fall until about 1700, after which they began a slow recovery that may still be continuing. This cold period is known as the Little Ice Age. Its effects were complex, but most historians believe the disappearance of English wine production during the 14th century was at least partly due to repeated failures of the grape harvest, which made English vineyards uneconomic compared with those of the Bordeaux region.

France did not escape its share of the climatic turmoil of those centuries. In the 1650s there was drought lasting several years in the Midi, in central France. It was so serious in 1654 that in August the people of Périgueux, in the Dordogne, made a formal visit to the shrine containing the relics of St. Sabina to ask her to intervene and bring rain.

Although the Little Ice Age brought low average temperatures, it also brought extremes. There were extremely cold winters and cool summers, but also mild winters and very hot summers and the weather fluctuated very rapidly between them. In the winter of 1683–84, for example, the average temperature in central England was 37°F (2.8°C) and the following winter, of 1685–86, it was 50.5°F (10.3°C). The summers of 1665 and 1666 were very hot. The first of those two years brought the last outbreak of plague ever to affect England, and one of the most serious. It began in the winter, but by summer it was firmly established and by the end of the year nearly 69,000 people had died from it.

The following year, 1666, also brought a hot, dry summer over much of Europe. At London, the level of water in the Thames fell so low that the boatmen who earned their living ferrying goods and passengers were threatened with ruin. There was simply not enough water for them to ply their trade. Samuel Pepys, the diarist, wrote that the drought had continued so long that "even the stones were ready to burst into flames." Not that most of the buildings in London were made from stone. They were of wood, and the wood was dry as tinder.

The Great Fire of London

On the night of Saturday, September 1, King Charles II's baker, Thomas Farynor, forgot to extinguish the fire in the ovens at his shop in Pudding Lane, near London Bridge. He went to bed at around 10 P.M., and while he slept, embers falling from the fire lit a stack of firewood. By 1 A.M. on Sunday, the house and shop were fully ablaze. The baker's assistant woke up, found the house filled with smoke, and aroused everyone else. Farynor and his wife and daughter, together with the assistant, escaped through an upstairs window and across the rooftops. The Farynors' maid was too frightened to climb out the window. She stayed behind and became the fire's first victim.

The fire sent sparks into the air and some of them landed on a pile of hay and straw in the yard of the Star Inn, not far away in Fish Hill Street. The inn caught fire and then nearby St. Margaret's Church. From there the fire spread along Pudding Lane and Fish Hill Street into Thames Street, lined with warehouses and open wharves full of oil, candle fat, straw, coal, and other flammable materials. Once those were alight the fire was completely out of control.

A servant roused Samuel Pepys from his bed at about 3 A.M. to see the fire, and a while later she told him she had heard that more than 300 houses had already been destroyed. By 8 A.M. the fire was halfway across London Bridge. It never crossed the bridge—there was a gap left by an earlier fire—and so the fire was confined to the north side of the Thames River.

There it spread rapidly and blazed out of control for five days. Remarkably, only six people were reported killed, although the true figure must have been much higher, and hundreds perished during the following winter, because they had no shelter. By the time it died down, 13,200 houses, 87 churches, and many other buildings—four-fifths of the buildings in the city—had been destroyed, and so had the insanitary conditions that favored the rats that had been spreading plague.

This was the Great Fire of London. After it, the city was rebuilt, this time in brick and stone. The drought of 1666 may not have changed history on a very large scale, but it certainly altered the way London developed and it brought an end to plague in England. A tall tower, called the Monument, was erected as a memorial on the site of Thomas Farynor's house and shop. It is still there.

Hot summers returned a decade later and brought repeated droughts in France between 1676 and 1686. Springs dried as water tables fell, and in 1686 grasshoppers migrating from the south invaded the Midi. Then, some years later, it was the turn of England again. A drought began in 1730 and lasted until June of 1734.

When the desert bloomed

Much of North Africa lies within the Sahara, a name derived from the Arabic *as-Sahra*, meaning the "waste" or "wilderness." It is desert, where drought is permanent, but it was not always so.

Until about 4000 B.C.E. there were grasslands and herds of animals grazing them, and the water level in Lake Chad, which was once a large inland sea, was about 130 feet (40 m) higher than it is today. Much more recently than that, empires flourished farther south. One of these, centered on Timbuktu, was the Mandingo Empire of Mali.

Mandingo merchants traded over a wide area, spreading the religion of Islam as they did so. By the 16th century their influence was declining, however, and at the same time the climate was becoming drier. Timbuktu lies near the Niger River, where the river curves through a large bend to the north. The map shows its location. The city has been flooded many times, but it has also suffered from drought, sometimes in the same years as the floods. Between 1617 and 1743 drought repeatedly caused famine. It was the time of the Little Ice Age and the northward movement of the intertropical convergence in summer was reduced (see the box on page 60 in the section "Climate cycles and oscillations"). Until then, that northward movement had brought summer rains. Now the rains often failed. It was not the change in climate that caused the collapse of the Mali Empire in 1591, however, so much as internal dissension and a Moroccan invasion. Nevertheless, drought may have contributed to the empire's weakness and to the failure of the invaders to establish an empire to replace it.

Mali lies within the region now known as the Sahel, along the southern border of the Sahara proper. Drought in the Sahel in the late 1960s and early 1970s was one of the most serious of modern times (see the section "The Sahel" on page 141), but the Sahel was not the only region to be afflicted. By the summer of 1972, when the seasonal rains failed to materialize in the highlands of Ethiopia, it was clear that the drought had spread into East Africa. Cereal crops could not be planted in the worst affected areas the following spring and by May around 80 percent of the cattle and some camels had died in the Welo and Tigray regions and parts of the Shewa region. By September, somewhere between 100,000 and 150,000 people had died.

Realization of the extent of the catastrophe and that it was completely out of control probably contributed to the revolt against the feudal regime which began in February, with widespread strikes in the capital, Addis Ababa. Troops sided with the strikers and on September 12 the government was overthrown, but the drought continued and the revolution and civil war that followed it did little to relieve the famine. The rains started to return in June 1975, by which time Ogaden, in the south, was the most seriously stricken part of the country. There and in the neighboring part of Somalia some 40,000 people died, and suffering continued through most of 1976. A few years later, the rains failed once more. This time the effects of the drought were exacerbated by war in the Ogaden region

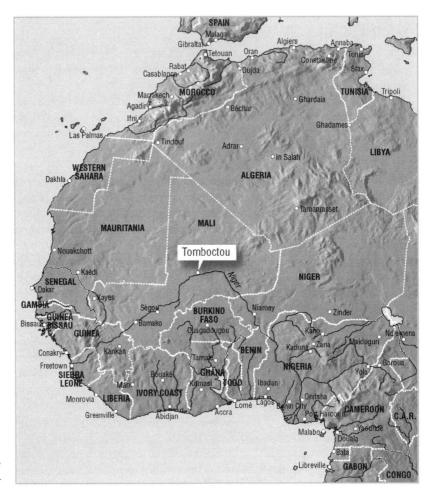

Tombouctou, Mali,
which lies close to the
Niger River

between Ethiopian and Somali guerrillas and between Ethiopian and Eritrean forces in Tigray, in the north.

Morocco also suffered from drought in 1980 and 1981, and the government was forced to import food. The cost of the imports caused serious economic difficulties, and in 1982 Morocco had to borrow $579 million for food through the International Monetary Fund.

On the other side of the world, Australia was also suffering severe drought. By September the government was having to pay huge sums to help farmers survive. Like North Africa, large parts of Australia have a dry climate. Droughts are common and must be unusually prolonged before their effects become really serious. Australians take groundwater from wells thousands of feet deep (see the section "Wells and springs" on page 113) and know how to cope.

Some parts of Indonesia receive more rainfall than others, but nowhere is the climate dry. Jakarta, the capital, has an average of 70 inches (1,778 mm) of rain a year, and it is not the wettest place in the country. People living in equatorial regions to the north, where rainfall is heavy and ordinarily reliable, do not expect drought, but in 1982, a drought in Indonesia lasted for four months. The drought did not cause famine, but water supplies were contaminated, and in October more than 150 people died from cholera (caused by bacteria and spread through infected food and water) and dengue fever (caused by a virus transmitted by mosquitoes, which breed in stagnant water). It seems likely that the 1982 Indonesian drought was linked to the ENSO event (see the section "El Niño and La Niña" on page 64) occurring at the same time. The 1997–98 El Niño, which was the severest for many years, was also linked to extensive fires, especially in Borneo. These spread a pall of smoke and smog over a large part of southern Asia.

Droughts are not like other natural disasters. Those are events that pass, allowing people to rebuild their lives and homes. Droughts do not pass so quickly. Once the aquifers dry out below ground, the flow of water to lakes and rivers slows and then ceases. The drought bites deep into the land, and there can be no full recovery from it until the aquifers have been recharged. It is not enough for rain to fall, even if it falls heavily. The rain must continue for long enough to soak the ground, so that water can drain downward and restore the lost groundwater. Then, as the aquifers resume their slow transport of water, there will be a delay before that water reaches the rivers. It is a process that cannot take less than months and often takes a year or more, even in those parts of the world that enjoy a mild, wet climate. In England, for example, the drought caused by prolonged dry, hot weather in the summer of 1995 continued through the winter. This was because winter rainfall was somewhat lower than usual. Consequently, depleted aquifers and reservoirs fed from rivers did not refill sufficiently to provide a supply adequate for the anticipated needs of the following summer, when rising temperatures would increase the rate of surface evaporation. If that is the effect in cool, damp Britain, imagine how much more serious drought can be in hot, dry Africa or Australia.

Drought and soil erosion

On a dry day in summer, the sky is often a pale shade of blue, sometimes almost white. Then there is a heavy shower and when the shower ends, the air feels fresher and the sky is a much deeper blue. Why does the sky change color after rain?

The whiteness of the sky in dry weather is due to dust particles. These are tiny, about 0.00002–0.0004 inch (0.0005–0.001 mm) in diameter, but there can be 30 or more of them in every cubic inch of clean, country air (1.8 per cm^3) and there are many more in air that is dusty enough to make the sky white.

If Earth had no atmosphere, the Sun would be very bright, but the sky would be black—as it is to an astronaut on the surface of the Moon. We see a bright sky because particles in the air scatter the sunlight, making it reach us from all directions. The way light is scattered depends on the size of the particles off which it bounces in relation to the wavelength of the light. The diameter of an air molecule is about $\frac{1}{10}$ the wavelength of light, and air molecules scatter the shorter waves more than the longer ones. Blue light is at the short-wave end of the light spectrum, so if the light is being scattered by air molecules it is predominantly blue light that reaches us from all directions. That is what makes the sky blue. Small though they are, dust particles are much bigger and scatter all wavelengths equally, so when the air is dusty the light we see is white, composed of all wavelengths.

Airborne dust

Gravity causes heavy particles to fall to the surface. This is called *fallout* and it removes some particles, regardless of the weather. *Impaction* removes other particles when they collide with solid surfaces and stick to them. Smoke and some dust are removed in this way, and impaction also occurs in both dry and wet weather.

In fact, fallout and impaction occur more in dry weather, because in wet weather rain clears the air more efficiently than either process. If the particles are very small, water vapor condenses onto them to form cloud droplets. When the cloud droplets grow big enough to fall they carry the particles with them. This process is called *rainout*. As they fall, the raindrops collide with other particles, engulf them, and carry them to the surface. This is called *washout*.

Removing particles changes the color of the sky, but during a drought there is no rain to remove them and, because fallout and impaction are slower and less efficient than rainout and washout, dust particles accumulate.

They can travel great distances in very dry air. Two or three times in most years, southerly winds carry dust from the Sahara all the way to Britain, 1,600 miles (2,575 km) away, where showers wash it to the ground. The Saharan dust is red and if there is enough of it the rain is blood-red and coats everything with a thin layer of red dust. Saharan dust can even cross the Atlantic and be washed out over the United States. During World War II, tank battles in North Africa raised so much dust that it colored clouds over the Caribbean. Scientists have calculated that a dust storm covering 5,000 square miles (12,950 km²) to a height of 10,000 feet (3,050 m) can carry up to 7 million tons (6.4 million tonnes) of dust.

Most atmospheric dust consists of soil particles. Some of these are thrown into the air by human activity. Watch a farmer plowing dry soil and you will see how much dust this raises. Driving along dirt roads raises dust. So, of course, do tank battles. Wind alone can raise dust. You can see this on any windy day in dry weather.

Erosion

No matter how it happens, once soil particles have been carried aloft they are transported from the place where they were picked up and deposited somewhere else. They are lost from their original site. The loss of soil is called *erosion* and the amount involved is considerable. The most famous example in modern times happened in the 1930s, in the area that came to be known as the Dust Bowl (see the section "The Dust Bowl," page 136), but there are others. In 1977 blowing soil caused damage and severe erosion over an area of about 750 square miles (1,900 km²) in the San Joaquin Valley, California. Within 24 hours, more than 25 million tons (22.7 million tonnes) of soil was carried away from grazing land and the same drought also caused severe erosion on the High Plains of Texas.

It is true, of course, that when soil is blown away from the surface of the land, it falls again somewhere else, but this does not necessarily mean that one farmer's loss is another's gain. Much of the blown soil may be carried over the sea and lost and even soil that does fall on farmland is not necessarily welcome there. It may bury crops that have just germinated, and it coats leaves with fine particles that damage them. It may carry with it seeds, sown by the farmer who lost the soil, that germinate as weeds in another farmer's fields. Blown soil clogs ditches and blocks roads.

In some places, however, the wind has delivered very fertile soils, called *loess*. Large areas on the northeastern and eastern banks of the Mississippi and Missouri Rivers have deep loess soils. Loess soils are also found in the Rhine basin in Europe, in the valley of the Hwang Ho (Yellow River) in China, and in various other parts of Europe, Russia, and South America. These soils were blown to their present locations when the ice sheets retreated at the end of the last ice age. Meltwaters carried away fine soil particles and deposited them as sediments. Then the climate dried and the soils blew. Unfortunately, of course, they are still capable of being blown.

Only dry soil blows

Soil particles stick together when they are wet. A film of water covers each of them and the water molecules on adjacent particles are linked by their hydrogen bonds. Even grains of beach sand will hold together in this way, if only weakly because of the large size of the particles. You can build sandcastles in damp sand, but they collapse when the sand dries. Very dry sand, on the other hand, will blow in the wind and small sandstorms are quite common on sandy coastal beaches.

Only dry soil will blow away in the wind. This means that those parts of the world where the climate is dry, with less than 12 inches (305 mm) of rain a year, are the most vulnerable to soil erosion by wind. Predictably, desert areas are most at risk, as the map on page 134 shows, but wind erosion is not confined to deserts and semi-arid regions. It can happen anywhere. If the rainfall occurs mainly at one time of year, at other times the soil surface may be very dry. Even if the rainfall is ordinarily distributed evenly through the year, a contingent drought (see the section "How droughts are classified" on page 119) can dry the soil sufficiently for a strong wind to carry it away.

Obviously, the smaller the soil particles are, the lower is the wind speed that is needed to detach them. The likelihood that a dry soil will be eroded by the wind therefore depends on the size of its particles and the strength of the wind. It also depends on the roughness of the ground surface. A rough surface, littered with large stones or clods of soil, slows the wind by friction. This reduces the amount of erosion. Vegetation also reduces wind erosion, partly by increasing the roughness of the surface and partly because plant roots tend to bind soil particles together.

Once a particle has been lifted from the ground, it will start to fall again, and the speed with which it falls is related to its diameter. The smallest particles, up to 0.0004 inch (0.01 mm) in diameter, fall so slowly that they can be caught and lifted again by eddies and remain airborne for days. These are the particles that travel long distances and cause "blood rain" in Britain and elsewhere. The particles become suspended in the air, and wind-tunnel experiments have shown that of all the particles that are moved by wind erosion, between 3 percent and 38 percent travel in this fashion.

The biggest particles are not lifted from the ground at all. They travel by what is called *creep erosion*. Too big to be lifted, they are rolled along the ground. In principle, there is no limit to how big these particles might be, but in practice most are no more than 0.08 inch (2 mm) across. Watch a light breeze blowing over the surface of dry sand and you will see grains being rolled along in this way. Between 7 percent and 25 percent of particles travel by creep.

Parts of the world where the risk of wind erosion is high

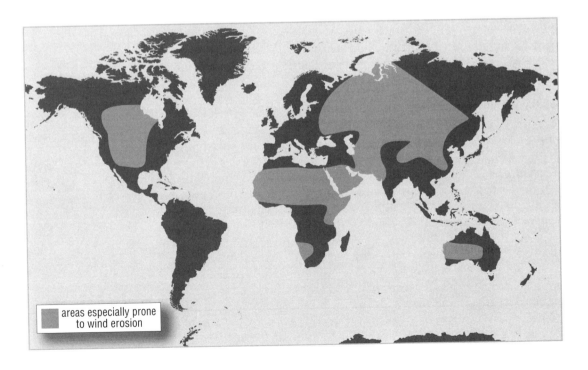

areas especially prone to wind erosion

Most, about 55–72 percent of all eroded particles, move by *saltation*— literally in leaps and bounds. The wind lifts the particle clear of the surface. It starts to fall again immediately, but the wind is still pushing it forward and accelerating it. It rises no farther than an inch or two, but travels a forward distance approximately equal to 10 times the height it reaches, and when it strikes the ground, it does so with considerable force. This knocks loose another particle, which leaps forward to dislodge a third, and so the process continues, with the dislodged particles falling, dislodging more particles, then being lifted again themselves.

Although fine particles can be carried to a great height, saltation is by far the most important factor in wind erosion, and it occurs within a few inches, or at most a few feet, of the surface. It can produce a kind of dust storm or sandstorm so shallow that people can walk through it with their heads and shoulders in clear air and the lower parts of their bodies invisible in the swirling cloud. Within a height of 3.3 feet (1 m), a wind of 18 MPH (29 km/h) can shift 490 pounds (222 kg) of sand in an hour from a strip of land one foot (30 cm) wide. A 25-MPH (40-km/h) wind can move 990 pounds (450 kg) an hour. Imagine a square plot of land with an area of one acre; a 25-MPH (40-km/h) wind can blow about 60 tons of soil out of it every hour (135 tonnes from every hectare).

Calculating vulnerability

Estimating the vulnerability of a particular area to wind erosion is complicated but possible, and obviously it is very important to farmers. Scientists measure the size of the soil particles, the roughness of the surface, and the area of land exposed, take account of the rainfall and wind, and feed the data into computers. Specialized software programs, such as the *wind erosion prediction system*, then calculate the risk of erosion from the *wind erodibility equation* devised in 1963 by two soil scientists, W. S. Chepil and N. P. Woodruff (see the box below).

Soil erodibility

The vulnerability of a particular soil to wind erosion is calculated from the wind erodibility equation, devised by W. S. Chepil and N. P. Woodruff in 1963. The equation is: $E = f(I, K, C, L, V)$, where E is the total erosion loss in tons of soil per year; I is the soil erodibility index based on particle size and the extent to which particles adhere to one another; K is surface roughness; C is the climate factor, based on wind speed and effective moisture in the soil; and L is *field length*, which is the distance across which the wind blows. The equation indicates that E is a function (f) of these factors.

The calculation is usually performed by specialized computer software. Before this was available, the complicated calculation produced an estimated value that was used to read the final value from a published graph.

This is a complicated task, but possible values for one of the factors in the equation give an idea of the scale of risk. *Erodibility* is the vulnerability of a soil to erosion when it is dry. It is calculated by sieving a measured volume of soil to determine the percentage of particles larger than 0.03 inch (0.84 mm) in diameter. Standard tables then show the erodibility of that soil in tons per acre. If 5 percent of particles are more than 0.03 inch (0.84 mm) in size, the soil can lose 180 tons per acre (404 t ha^{-1}) and if 50 percent of them are more than this size it can lose 38 tons per acre (85 t ha^{-1}).

The Dust Bowl

Inside the White House, in May 1934, dust settled on the desk of President Franklin D. Roosevelt and as fast as it was cleaned away, more collected. Outside, in New York and Baltimore as well as in Washington, the sky was so dark with clouds of dust that in some places chickens roosted, thinking it was night. Dust settled on ships, 300 miles (483 km) out at sea. Ducks and geese fell from the sky, choked to death by the dust through which they flew. People called the storms "black blizzards." At their height, a single dust cloud three miles (4.8 km) high covered 1.35 million square miles (3.5 million km^2), from Canada to Texas and from Montana to Ohio.

All the dust was soil, blown from farmlands covering 150,000 square miles (388,500 km^2) in southwestern Kansas, southeastern Colorado, northeastern and southeastern New Mexico, and the panhandles of Oklahoma and Texas. At least, those are the states that suffered most. Altogether, soil was blowing from farms covering more than three-quarters of the country, and the situation was serious in 27 states. The map on page 137 shows the size and location of the most severely affected area. This region, the source of most of the black blizzards, where soil was blown into dunes that in places were 30 feet (9 m) high, came to be known as the Dust Bowl.

Each year, the U.S. Department of Agriculture publishes a *Yearbook of Agriculture*. The *Yearbook* for 1934 recorded that: "Approximately 35 million acres of formerly cultivated land have essentially been destroyed for crop production. . . . 100 million acres now in crops have lost all or most of the topsoil; 125 million acres of land now in crops are rapidly losing topsoil."

What had gone so wrong?

Plowing the prairie

Before the first European farmers arrived, the Great Plains of North America were covered by prairie grassland. Grasses were the commonest plants, some growing as tussocks of grass three feet (90 cm) or more tall. Grasses bind soil and prevent wind erosion. The tall tussocks slow the

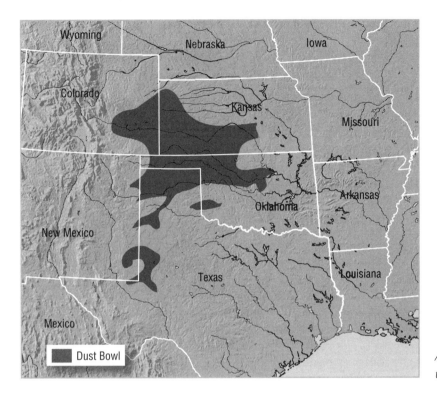

Area of the Dust Bowl in the United States

ground-level wind, and grass roots form a mat that holds soil among the fibers. Many prairie grasses have deep roots. They are not like the grasses people grow as lawns.

The climate is fairly dry and very windy. Boise City, in western Idaho, has an average annual rainfall of 16.5 inches (419 mm) and Dodge City, Kansas, 20.4 inches (518 mm). Grassland vegetation is well adapted to a fairly low annual rainfall and occasional drought.

To the settlers arriving from the East, the grasslands were deceptive. The Homestead Act of 1862 drew many families to the plains. This law offered a free plot of land to anyone willing to live on it and farm it. To the would-be farmers, the prairies looked much like eastern grasslands and to some they resembled the European grasslands they remembered from their childhood. What they failed to appreciate—and no one told them— was that the eastern and European grasslands grow in a much wetter climate (see the section "Dry-weather farming" on page 154).

The farmers cleared the natural vegetation by burning it repeatedly and plowing up the grasslands to grow wheat and other crops. When there was rain, the soil was fertile and the harvests were good. From time to time, though, drought caused the crops to fail. When that happened, farmers were ruined and were forced to abandon their land and homes. A year or two later the rains returned, the land was plowed again, and new homes were built.

So it continued until around 1915. Plowing and harrowing with horses was slow, hard work, but it was about then that the first tractors rolled onto the prairies. They made it much easier to till the land, and the farms expanded. Between 1910 and 1919 the area growing wheat in Kansas increased from less than 5 million acres (2 million ha) to more than 12 million acres (5 million ha), an increase that was achieved by plowing more of the natural prairie. Then the combine harvester was introduced, to speed harvesting.

The machines were expensive, of course, but by 1919 wheat prices were rising enough to pay for them. Farming was highly profitable and with all the newly invented machines it was becoming less arduous year by year. The pioneer farmers of the 19th century had struggled to break a land full of tough clods of soil, but eventually the battle was won and the soil had been worked into a fine, friable texture that was exactly the condition needed for sowing seeds.

The Great Depression

All went well for several years, but in 1929 the stock market crashed, leading to a huge and rapid contraction of the national economy and the Great Depression of the thirties. Prices often fall during an economic depression—deflation replaces inflation—and that is what happened then. Cereal prices fell, forcing the prairie farmers to work the land even more intensively to maintain their incomes by producing more grain. Little by little farming incomes fell, despite the farmers' working ever harder, until the poorest farmers were in a desperate plight. The weather was still favorable, however, so the farms remained productive. Between 1927 and 1933 the annual rainfall was 5 inches (127 mm) above average in Nebraska, Iowa, and Kansas.

Far away on the other side of the Atlantic, certain changes were becoming noticeable. At Spitsbergen, inside the Arctic Circle, there is a port from which coal was exported. Prior to 1920 it was free of ice for three months of the year, but each year it remained accessible for just a little longer. By 1940 it was open for more than seven months each year. Over the entire Northern Hemisphere, the climate was becoming warmer. One consequence of this climatic change was a marked increase in the number of days when westerly winds blew in middle latitudes. Lands on the eastern side of oceans received more rainfall, because they were exposed more frequently to winds carrying moisture collected at sea.

Rainfall decreasing over the prairies

That is not what happened in the prairies. There, westerly winds blowing across the Pacific lost their moisture as they crossed the Rockies, so the winds reaching the prairie farms were very dry. Rainfall that had been above average fell to 16 inches (406 mm), 7 inches (178 mm) below the average of 23 inches (584 mm) a year. Crops began to fail and the remaining natural prairie grasses began to die back. As the crops and natural vegetation both disappeared, the light, friable soil was left bare.

Rainfall had always been highly variable and in dry periods the natural grasses would disappear. This was their way of surviving. Although the leaves withered and died down, their mats of roots used to remain, binding the soil into the tough clods that had given the farmers so much trouble, and the clods would bake hard in the dry heat, forming a solid surface that was impervious to the wind. Now tilled to a fine texture by farmers and dried by the drought, the soil began to blow. The black blizzards began in 1931. In 1932 there were 14 severe dust storms and the following year there were 38. The biggest and worst dust storms were in May 1934 and the most serious of them happened on April 14, 1935, but the loss of soil was almost continuous. In December soil experts estimated that 850 million tons (772 million tonnes) of topsoil had been blown away from the southern plains during 1935. They feared that the area affected by the disaster was likely to increase from 4.35 million acres (1.76 million ha) in 1935 to 5.35 million acres (2.16 million ha) in 1936.

Already weakened economically by the depression, countless farmers were ruined and migrated with their families, most of them to California. It was the largest migration of people in the history of the nation and although the drought is usually blamed, it was the depression rather than the weather that had defeated some of the migrants—they were out of work and impoverished. A total of 2.5 million people moved, 200,000 of them to California. Around Boise City, Oklahoma, 1,642 farming families abandoned their holdings, and the population fell by 40 percent. The Dust Bowl drought continued from 1933 until the winter of 1940–41, when the rains returned and the native grasses started to recover.

Learning from the drought

The experience of the Dust Bowl led to the formation of the Soil Conservation Service in 1935, and throughout the nation the federal government started to teach and promote farming techniques that protect the soil. Even so, whenever grain prices rise, prairie lands are plowed once again.

This was neither the first severe drought to afflict the plains, nor the last. Writing in the fall of 1830, Isaac McCoy, an explorer in what is now part of Kansas, described fierce storms of dust, sand, and ash from the recently burned grasslands. The Republican River, he wrote on October 27, "runs over a bed of sand—the banks low, and all the bottom lands are a bed of sand white and fine, and now as dry as powder ought to be." On November 5 there was another storm. "It was not three minutes after I had discovered its approach, before the sun was concealed, and the darkness so great, that I could not distinguish objects more than three or four times the length of my horse."

The droughts tend to occur at intervals of 20 to 23 years, and some are more severe than others. Erosion, dust storms, and ruined crops returned to the plains in the 1950s, but the 1970s were especially harsh. Late in February 1977, a storm in eastern Colorado lasting 24 hours produced winds of 90 MPH (145 km/h). It stripped away about five tons of soil from every acre of farmland (11.2 tonnes per ha). From Nebraska to the panhandles of Oklahoma and Texas, there were dust clouds at times 12,000 feet (3,660 m) thick, and visibility was reduced almost to zero.

Then, in the 1990s, the rains failed again. In the winter of 1995–96 there were record snowfalls over the eastern states and in the Rockies, but in Kansas, Oklahoma, and Texas, the plains remained dry. Between October and May, San Antonio, Texas, ordinarily expects 15.8 inches (401 mm) of rain. In that period of 1994–95 it received 4 inches (102 mm), and in 1995–96, 3.7 inches (94 mm) fell. Winter wheat died. This is the crop that is sown in late fall to germinate just before winter sets in, then resume its growth in spring to produce a bigger harvest than spring-sown wheat. Such crops as survived yielded harvests less than half of normal. The pastures failed, and there was a shortage of cattle feed. By May 1996, 40 percent of Texas was too dry to be grazed, and farmers were selling their cattle at auctions that had to continue through the night to cope with the numbers. Shortages caused grain prices to double, and animals were selling for less than the price of one ton of feed. Four out of five of the cows were pregnant. This meant farmers could not afford even to wait until the calves were born and sell two head instead of one. The losses cost Texan farmers an estimated $2 billion, but the rainfall returned to normal in August 1996, and water levels in the reservoirs began rising again in October. The recovery continued through 1997, helped by a strong El Niño (see the section "El Niño and La Niña" on page 64) that brought heavy rains, but another drought began in 1998 and continued into 1999. This was much shorter than the 1996 drought, but at an estimated $6 billion, farm losses were higher. Another drought brought further hardship to rural communities in 2002, but the extreme conditions of the Dust Bowl years have not returned since.

Windbreaks and shelter belts have been planted since the Dust Bowl years, and grasses to bind the soil. Although droughts continue to occur, they no longer darken the noonday sky with blowing soil. Nevertheless, for rural communities each drought is a catastrophe.

Why the cycle?

No one knows why drought returns to the Great Plains at such regular intervals, but it is curious that the interval, of 20 to 23 years, coincides more or less with the solar cycle. Solar radiation varies in intensity, reaching a maximum about every 11 years, and one solar cycle includes two radiation maxima. The intensity is indicated by sunspots, visible as dark patches on the surface of the Sun.

On no account must you try to see sunspots by looking directly at the Sun, even if you are wearing sunglasses, or by looking at the Sun through binoculars; this can cause permanent damage to your eyes. Glasses with lenses made from aluminized mylar are safe to use, provided there are no flaws or scratches on them, but they are not easy to obtain. There are two ways to view the Sun safely—with a pinhole projection, or a projection using binoculars or a small refractive telescope.

To make a pinhole projection you will need two pieces of stiff card about 18 inches (45 cm) square and a pin. Make a clean (with no irregular edges) pinhole in one piece of card. Stand with your back to the Sun and arrange the two cards so that light passes through the pinhole and onto the other card. This will produce an inverted image of the Sun on the card. Don't make the pinhole too big or it won't work.

To use binoculars, keep the cover on one of the objective lenses (these are the larger lenses). Make a tube of cardboard and place it around the other objective lens to act as a shade. Prepare a telescope in the same way. Standing with your back to the Sun, point the objective lens toward the Sun so that it projects an image onto a piece of cardboard set about one foot (30 cm) from the eyepiece. Use the focusing mechanism to sharpen the image.

Solar output is greatest when there are most sunspots, and this variation may affect the climates of Earth indirectly. There are two ways this may happen. Cosmic radiation bombards air molecules, producing particles that act as condensation nuclei and encourage the formation of clouds. This increases rainfall and cools Earth's surface. When the intensity of solar radiation is high, the stream of particles leaving the Sun as the *solar wind* is also very vigorous and it deflects the cosmic radiation, reducing cloud formation and increasing the surface temperature. The difference in the radiation output between solar maxima and minima is only about 0.1 percent, but most of this variation is in ultraviolet radiation, rather than visible light or heat. Ultraviolet radiation is absorbed in the ozone layer of the stratosphere, which warms the stratosphere and slightly alters the atmospheric circulation in the troposphere. Some scientists think that between them these processes might be enough to trigger ENSO episodes (see the section "El Niño and La Niña" on page 64) and possibly the periodic droughts of the Great Plains. If they are right, it may be possible in years to come to forecast major climatic events of this kind far in advance, because the activity of the Sun can be predicted fairly accurately.

Such knowledge will not prevent drought, but if farmers are prepared at least they may escape the personal tragedies it causes.

The Sahel

In 1972, the total amount of food produced throughout the world was the second highest ever, but it fell 2 percent short of the 1971 output. World production had been rising steadily since 1945, usually by about 3 percent each year, but in 1972 it suffered its first reverse. In Russia, the grain harvest in 1972 was 13 percent below the amount that had been predicted. The Australian wheat harvest was 25 percent below the average of the previous five years. In that same year the coffee harvest failed in Ethiopia, Kenya, and Côte d'Ivoire, the peanut, sorghum, and rice crops failed in Nigeria, and an El Niño drastically reduced the Peruvian fish catch (see the section "El Niño and La Niña" on page 64). Apart from the failure of the Peruvian fisheries, the decline in crop yields was due wholly to heat and drought.

There were widespread repercussions. Countries that needed to increase their imports of food looked to the large reserves held by the United States. Russia got there first, buying up one-quarter of them and then buying still more from other countries that had surpluses. Rising demand caused wheat prices to double in a matter of months, and those countries with abundant oil but a desert climate suddenly realized that they needed to address the issue of food production, because one day their oil fields would be empty. To secure their future they raised oil prices. In 1973 and 1974 the world price of oil increased fourfold.

The meaning of poverty

When prices suddenly increase in this way, invariably it is the poor who suffer most. If they cannot afford the new price for oil, their factories may close, increasing unemployment, and there will be shortages of fuel for transport and for running essential services such as hospitals. Many countries lack sufficient reserves of foreign currencies to pay for the food imports they need and, even if they can pay, many of their people cannot afford the new, higher food prices—so they go hungry.

Of all the poor in the world, some of the very poorest live in the countries along the southern border of the Sahara, in Mauritania, Mali, Burkina Faso, Niger, Chad, Sudan, Ethiopia, and Eritrea (see the map on page 143). To give an idea of the economic situation of these countries, the following table sets out the per capita gross national product for each country in 1998 (the most recent year for which figures are available), in U.S. dollars, with that of the United States for comparison. *Gross national product*, or GNP, is the total value of all the goods and services produced in a country in that year; *per capita* means per person living in that country.

These are the countries of the Sahel region, and it was their plight that caught the attention of the world in the 1970s, as their lands were ravaged by a drought that probably began in the late 1960s and that continued until the mid 1980s. Although it was the Sahel countries that were most seriously affected, the drought extended much farther. It was severe in Angola and Mozambique, and most of East Africa was affected, as well as Senegal and Guinea Bissau in West Africa.

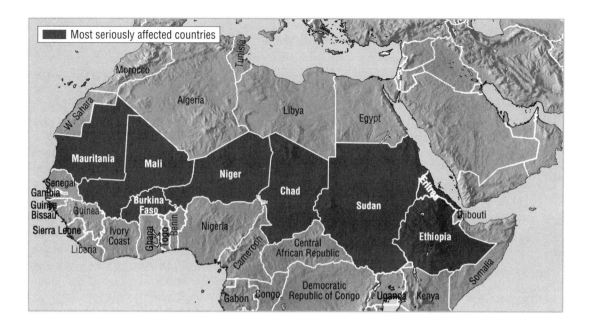

Life on the desert's edge

Countries of the Sahel region of Africa

Except in small, scattered areas, lands near the edge of a desert cannot be cultivated. Rainfall is always too sparse and too unreliable for crops to grow, and the plants adapted to this climate are mainly grasses, herbs, and small, thorny shrubs. When it does rain these plants produce leaves and flourish, and between rains they lie dormant.

The land cannot be farmed, but it is possible to earn a meager living from it as a pastoralist—a person who tends herds and flocks of animals,

Country	Per capita gross national product
	(US $)
Mauritania	410
Sudan	290
Mali	250
Burkina Faso	240
Chad	230
Niger	200
Eritrea	200
Ethiopia	100
United States	34,030

(Source: *2001 Book of the Year.* Encyclopaedia Britannica)

moving with them from one area of pasture and watering place to another. This is the seminomadic, traditional way of life for many people in the Sahel (see the section "Peoples of the desert" on page 96).

Although the people follow their livestock from one area of pasture to the next, this does not mean the land is not managed. Fire is used as a tool to remove dead grass and encourage new growth, and also to clear land for planting crops. The fires burn extensively in March and April, and lightning sparks many more fires in addition to those that are ignited deliberately. Then, when the summer rains arrive, people move north with their animals to take advantage of the improved conditions. They retreat south again at the end of the rainy season.

The inhabitants of the Sahel have pursued this way of life for centuries and are accustomed to drought. Rainfall in this area has always been erratic. In the good years, more of their domesticated animals survived and so the herds and flocks increased. The added numbers provided food and materials for the next bad year. In those few places where there was a reliable supply of water, people tilled the land and grew crops, including cotton, some of which was exported to generate a cash income.

This way of life began to change in the 1960s. As the countries of this region of Africa developed, veterinary care and medicines became available. Fewer animals died from disease and their numbers increased. In the cities, there were people rich enough to buy meat, and this market also encouraged pastoralists to increase livestock numbers. The newly independent countries needed to earn foreign currency, so the growing of crops for export was encouraged. Between them, Burkina Faso, Chad, Mali, Niger, and Senegal produced 22.7 million tons (20.6 million tonnes) of cotton in 1961–62, and in 1983–84 they produced 154 million tons (140 million tonnes).

These changes brought a little prosperity, but it was bought at the price of increased vulnerability. When the rains failed, such pasture as remained was consumed more quickly and, because more animals were now grazing it, plants that might have survived being nibbled almost to ground level were uprooted or trampled to death, leaving the ground bare. This is overgrazing. At the same time, cash crops had been grown on land that previously would have grown food, some of which would have been stored for future use. Now there were insufficient stores.

Consequences of the drought

Because they had no choice, the pastoralists began to move in search of water and better grazing. Thousands crossed from Mauritania into Mali, others from Mali into Burkina Faso and Niger. More than a million people entered Côte d'Ivoire. This mass migration increased the pressure on such little pasture as remained in the countries receiving the migrants and compelled governments to establish refugee camps. Despite all the efforts of governments within the region and those of the international

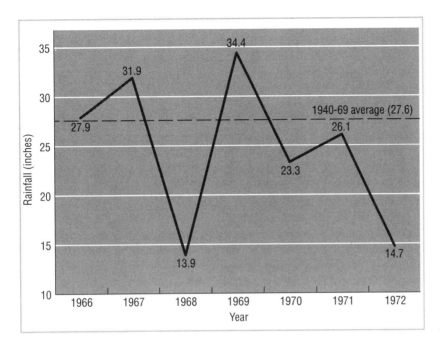

Rainfall in Diourbel,
Senegal

community, the scale of the tragedy was colossal. The United Nations Environment Program (UNEP) has suggested that between 1974 and 1984, at least 500,000 people died in Africa as a direct consequence of the drought, and that between 1970 and 1990 possibly two or three times that number perished. Since then the rains have returned.

The changes of the 1960s were helped by a series of years when rainfall was reliable and relatively high. At Diourbel, in central Senegal, for example, the average annual rainfall between 1940 and 1969 was 27.6 inches (701 mm). In 1966 it was 27.9 inches (709 mm), and in 1967 it was 31.9 inches (810 mm), but in 1968 it was only 13.9 inches (353 mm). Then it increased again, to 34.4 inches (874 mm) in 1969, only to fall to 23.3 inches (592 mm) in 1970, 26.1 inches (663 mm) in 1971, and 14.7 inches (373 mm) in 1972. The graph shows the magnitude of these changes. At Podor, in northern Senegal close to the Mauritanian border, 17 inches (432 mm) fell in 1969, compared to the 1940–69 average of 13.2 inches (335 mm), but in 1972 the rainfall amounted to only 3 inches (76 mm). In Niger, rainfall in 1970 was only one-quarter of the annual average and it was less than half the average in 1972. The graph shows changes in rainfall at one place over just a few years. Over a longer period, the records show that the rainfall has been below the average of 1890–2000 in most years since about 1968.

The drought did not start suddenly, with a single disastrous year, but gradually, with a sequence of years in which rainfall was lower than usual. It was not dry enough to cause great harm, but it was bad enough to lead to some overgrazing and the lowering of water tables. Although rainfall was much heavier in 1969, this was not enough to recharge the aquifers and bring about a recovery from the steady deterioration of the preceding years. The drought became invisible (see the section "How droughts are classified" on page 119), but it did not come to an end. By the time the drought became severe, both the groundwater and pasture were already depleted.

The monsoon and blocking

West Africa north of the Tropics relies for much of its rain on the summer monsoon. People usually think of the monsoon as a season of heavy rain in India, but other parts of the world also have them, including the United States (see the section "Monsoons" on page 147).

Over the Sahel region, between about 10° N and 20° N, warm, dry air is descending on the high-latitude side of the Hadley cell circulation (see the box on page 39, "George Hadley and Hadley cells" in the section "Air movements and the transport of heat"). Near the surface, the prevailing winds in the Tropics are the northeasterly trades, but high above the surface, at around 10,000 feet (3,000 m), and from there all the way to the stratosphere, they are westerlies (blowing from west to east). Farther north, the prevailing surface winds are also westerlies.

In some years, anticyclones become stationary for weeks on end in middle latitudes over the North Atlantic. Air masses and weather systems continue to drift from west to east, but these blocking highs (see the section "Blocking highs" on page 75) refuse to budge to make way for them. Air masses have to go around them to the north or south, taking with them the low-pressure weather systems that develop along the fronts between dissimilar masses. When blocking highs become established in winter and spring they can divert the low-pressure systems south into the Mediterranean region. This brings cold and usually dry weather to northwestern Europe, often with northerly winds. In southern Europe, the weather is cool and wet. These patterns persist until air spilling out from the blocking high weakens it and the normal movement of air establishes itself once more.

These are the conditions people experience living at ground level, but the effects extend into the upper atmosphere. The southward deflection of the low-pressure systems is also accompanied by a similar deflection of a branch of the upper westerlies. When this happens, the northward movement of the intertropical convergence zone (ITCZ) is restricted. The ITCZ is where the trade winds from either side of the equator meet. It moves north in the Northern Hemisphere spring and summer, and south in the Southern Hemisphere spring and summer (see the box on page 60, "Intertropical convergence and the equatorial trough" in the section "Climate cycles and oscillations." As it moves, it carries with it the equatorial rains, bringing them farther north or south. In the Northern Hemisphere they extend to about 20° N—the latitude that separates the Sahel in the south from the Sahara in the north.

If the seasonal migration of the convergence is checked so it does not move so far or moves more slowly, the summer rains do not extend so far as usual or they arrive late. If they arrive late, they will also be briefer than usual because at the end of summer the intertropical convergence zone begins moving toward the other hemisphere. If the rains do not last so long, there will be less time for rain to fall, and consequently the total rainfall will be less than usual. When this happens, the Sahel will experience a dry year and if it happens for several years in succession there will be drought. Scientists do not know what causes blocking highs to form over the North Atlantic, but their consequences for weather in the Sahel are clearly understood.

Blaming the victim

Back in the 1970s, some people believed that the tragedy of the Sahel was the fault of the people living there. They said that greed led the pastoral peoples to keep more livestock and that this led to overgrazing of the sparse pastures, leaving the ground exposed to the heat of the Sun and the wind. The soil dried and blew, burying adjacent land and killing the crops growing on it. In this way the Sahara was expanding to the south.

This was unfair, although it was partly true. Certainly, overgrazing damages the land, but the drought was due to the failure of the rains, not to anything local people had done, and there was nowhere else for them to take their animals. The pastures would have been overgrazed even if there had been fewer livestock, and many of these people, who are among the poorest in the world, measure their wealth and social status by the number of animals they control. It is also true that sand and dry topsoil blown from the drought areas buried crops and more fertile soil on adjacent land, but this has always happened when there was drought in the Sahel. When the rains return, the land recovers in the area bordering the Sahel as well as in the Sahel itself.

Monsoons

From November to May, Bombay, India (the Indian name is Mumbai), has a dry climate. The average total rainfall during all of those seven months, calculated from records going back 60 years, amounts to a mere 1.6 inches (41 mm). Then, in June, the rain starts. Between June and October the city receives about 70 inches (1,778 mm), July being the wettest month. The rain starts to ease in August and dies away altogether by the end of October. Meanwhile, the temperature hardly varies. It is above 80°F (27°C) throughout the year, with an average January temperature of 83°F (28°C). May is the warmest month, just before the rains begin. Then the average temperature is 91°F (33°C).

People who live in middle or high latitudes, well outside the Tropics, think of the difference between summer and winter mainly in terms of temperature. Winters are cold. We wear thicker clothes and turn on the

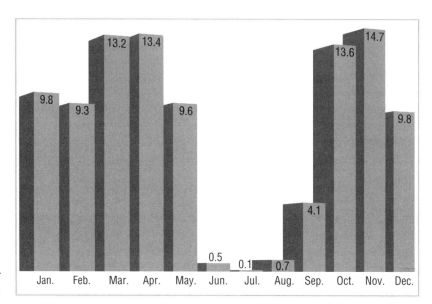

Rainfall in Libreville, Gabon (inches per month)

heating. In summer we wear lighter clothes and open the windows. Summer days are longer than winter days, and the farther you are from the equator the bigger is the difference. This can lead us to suppose that those people who live in the Tropics, and especially those who live very close to the equator, experience no seasons at all. It is true, of course, that close to the equator the day length changes very little through the year, although there is some change, and equatorial plants are quite sensitive to it. Like plants in higher latitudes, flowering is triggered in many by changes in day length, but the changes that influence them are extremely small. High-latitude plants would not respond to them. It is also true that daytime temperatures change little through the year. The difference between the daytime and nighttime temperature is greater than that between "summer" and "winter" temperatures.

Add to this the idea (which is true) that rain forest is the natural kind of vegetation throughout most of the equatorial region, and we may suppose that rainfall is as constant as temperature. Rain forests, after all, grow in wet climates, where it rains heavily every day of the year. This is wrong, however. Libreville, for example, is almost exactly on the equator (0.38° N) in Gabon, West Africa, and it has an average annual rainfall of 98.8 inches (2,510 mm), but, as the chart shows, the summers are dry, little more than 5 percent of the annual total of rain falling between June and September. This is typical of much of the equatorial and tropical regions. There are seasons, but in these parts of the world it is rainfall that marks the difference between summer and winter, not temperature. At Libreville, the average daytime temperature ranges from 83°F (28°C) in July to 89°F (32°C) in March and April. So if you move to the Tropics you will find that people talk about the weather there, too, but not about whether the day is warm or cold.

Winter and summer monsoons

The difference between the rainy and dry seasons is not usually so extreme as it is in Bombay, however. Bombay has a monsoon climate. The word *monsoon* was first used in the late 16th century by Dutch and Portuguese explorers who may have picked it up from an Arabic word, *mausim*, which means "season." Arab sailors, who traded widely around the coasts of Arabia and India, used the word *mausim* to describe the seasonal changes in the winds over the Indian Ocean and Arabian Sea. The English word has reached us from Dutch and Portuguese, but all "monsoon" really means is "season," although we apply it to a special kind of season that is very strongly marked. We usually associate the monsoon with heavy rain, but this describes only one monsoon season and in fact there are two. The winter monsoon is dry and it is the summer monsoon that is wet.

There are only those two seasons. Spring and autumn, each lasting for three months and easing the transitions between winter and summer, are seasons in their own right, but they are seasons that occur only in temperate climates. In the monsoon regions, the months that we call spring are a time of rising temperature and humidity. At Jacobabad, in Pakistan, for example, the average daytime temperature in May is 111°F (44°C) and it has been known to reach 123°F (51°C), falling at night to an average of 78°F (26°C). In Bombay the average temperature is 91°F (33°C) by day and 80°F (27°C) at night.

It is a dry heat, but in late May and early June it becomes almost unbearable. The Sun beats down mercilessly out of a sky that is pale gray or white, not blue, because of the persistent haze caused by the large amount of dust in the air. Then, around the second week of June, clouds start to appear in the sky. They develop each morning, grow larger through the day, but dissipate at dusk without bringing any rain. Meanwhile, as the humidity rises, the dry heat gives way to an oppressive, clammy heat that is even harder to endure.

Finally, the day comes when the clouds grow bigger and darker than ever, and suddenly the skies open. The change is instantaneous. They call it the *burst of monsoon*, and it clears the air, reducing the temperature and washing the airborne dust to the ground. Bombay receives an average of 0.7 inch (18 mm) of rain in May and none at all in April, but 19 inches (483 mm) fall in June. The heavy rain continues through the summer, decreasing in September to an average of 10.4 inches (264 mm) and falling to 2.5 inches (64 mm) in October. Jacobabad, much further inland than Bombay and so inevitably drier, has an average of 0.1 inch (3 mm) of rain in May and 0.3 inch (8 mm) in June, but in July and August this increases to 0.9 inch (23 mm). Cherrapunji, 4,309 feet (1,313 m) above sea level in the mountains of Assam, is one of the wettest places in the world. It receives an average of 425 inches (10,795 mm) of rain a year. Of that total, 366 inches (9,296 mm), amounting to 86 percent, falls between May and September.

Movement of the climatic equator

The seasonal change occurs as the climatic equator (where temperature is highest) moves north and south of the geographic equator. As it moves it takes with it the belt of equatorial weather and extends the tropical and subtropical climate belts into higher latitudes. This is enough to produce seasons, but not to cause monsoons. They are due to the fact that there is much more land in the Northern Hemisphere than in the Southern Hemisphere. This means that the subtropical region of high pressure and the low-pressure region, produced in higher latitudes by the general circulation of the atmosphere (see the box "General Circulation of the Atmosphere" on page 40 in the section "Air movements and the transport of heat"), are centered over land in one hemisphere and over sea in the other. This reverses the distribution of pressure from winter to summer and, with it, the direction of the prevailing wind.

It is rather like the change along the coast that, on a hot summer's day, produces a daytime sea breeze and a land breeze at night. During the day the land heats up faster than the sea. Warm air over the land expands and rises, drawing in cooler air from over the sea to replace it. That is the sea breeze. At night, the land cools faster than the sea, and the situation reverses. Air moves from the land to the sea as a land breeze.

Jet streams and the Tibetan Plateau

In winter, the interior of the Asian continent lies beneath a shallow layer of cold, subsiding air. Pressure is high at the surface, and the weather is dry. Above about 6,500 feet (1,980 m) the winds blow from west to east, reaching a maximum force in the jet stream associated with the subtropical front (see the section "Jet streams and storm tracks" on page 70). The jet stream lies over the Himalayas at about 40,000 feet (12.2 km), but it divides into two branches that reunite over northern China. The Tibetan Plateau rises to more than 13,000 feet (4 km) over a huge area, and India to the south of the Himalayas is very much warmer than Tibet, simply because of the difference in altitude. The average January daytime temperature in Lhasa, Tibet, is 44°F (7°C), while in Delhi it is 70°F (21°C). This big temperature difference between south and north, combined with the barrier formed by the mountains, holds the southerly branch of the jet stream in position across northern India.

Air subsiding beneath the upper-level westerlies spills out from the Tibetan Plateau. Over the oceans to the south, the maritime air is warmer and surface pressure lower, ensuring a "land breeze" type of wind. As the wind blows down from the mountains, at first it blows from the northwest, but by the time it reaches the Indian peninsula its direction is northeasterly.

It blows across India and out across the Arabian Sea. Because it originated in the dry interior of central Asia, the winds are also dry and bring no rain to the lands they cross. This is the dry winter monsoon.

Summer monsoon

Early in spring the upper-level westerlies move away northward, but the jet stream remains in position across northern India, although it weakens. As the Sun moves north, temperatures rise. The weather grows very hot, and this causes a large area of low pressure to develop over the land, as warmed air rises by convection. Then the intertropical convergence, where the trade winds of both hemispheres meet, starts to move north across India. The jet stream weakens further, becomes intermittent, and finally shifts to the north of the Tibetan Plateau. South of the plateau, the winds above about 20,000 feet (6 km) become easterly and the low-level winds blow from the southwest. These are the Southern Hemisphere trade winds. While they remain south of the equator they blow from the southeast, but in the Northern Hemisphere the Coriolis effect (see the box on page 53 in the section "Ocean currents and sea-surface temperature") swings them to the right. Consequently, as the intertropical convergence moves north, the winds on its southern side become southwesterly. They flow all the way across India, but are blocked when they reach the Himalayas. There they swing again until they are blowing from east to west and then north to south, carrying air back over the sea.

As trade winds over the ocean, they already held a considerable amount of moisture. Now they approach India across the Arabian Sea, which the early summer sunshine has warmed to more than 80°F (27°C), and they collect still more. As they rise over the edge of the central Indian plateau, the air cools, clouds form, and the rains begin. This is the summer monsoon, with its torrential rains. It ends with the fall, when the intertropical convergence and its winds move south again and the winter pressure and wind systems return.

Farther east, the summer monsoon affects all of southern Asia and extends eastward as far as southern Japan, although it is much less pronounced by then because the winds have lost much of their moisture over Burma, Thailand, and Vietnam. At Nagasaki (33.7° N) about 30 percent of the total annual rainfall occurs in June and July.

Monsoons in Africa and the United States

Summer and winter monsoons are caused by seasonal shifts in the distribution of pressure and winds, leading to a reversal in the direction of prevailing winds. In summer they blow one way and in winter from the opposite direction, bringing dry air from one direction and rain from the other. They are extreme in India and southern Asia, because of the size and height of the Tibetan Plateau and the huge area of the Asian continent, but seasonal shifts of this kind occur throughout the Tropics.

In winter, the northeasterly winds blowing down from the Tibetan Plateau and bringing the dry monsoon to India continue across the Arabian Sea, blowing almost parallel to the coast of East Africa. They have gathered moisture but, because they blow parallel to the coast and not across it, they bring little rain. At Addis Ababa, Ethiopia, an average of 6.2 inches (157 mm) of rain falls in the six months from October to March. Mogadishu, Somalia, receives an average of 3 inches (76 mm) of rain between October and December, and none at all from January to March. Farther north, however, the Asian northeasterlies gather no moisture. They blow across the arid Arabian Peninsula and narrow Red Sea. In spring, as the intertropical convergence moves north, the southeasterly trade winds affect regions to its south, but they bring only small amounts of rain.

It is in summer that the Asian summer monsoon exerts a strong influence. Southwesterlies then prevail and although they blow from the South Atlantic right across the African continent, they bring a pronounced rainy season. Addis Ababa receives an average of 28.3 inches (719 mm) of rain in the six months from April to September, July and August being the wettest months, and Mogadishu receives almost 14 inches (356 mm). This is the African monsoon. It affects southern Arabia and most of the eastern side

Parts of Africa and Asia affected by the monsoons

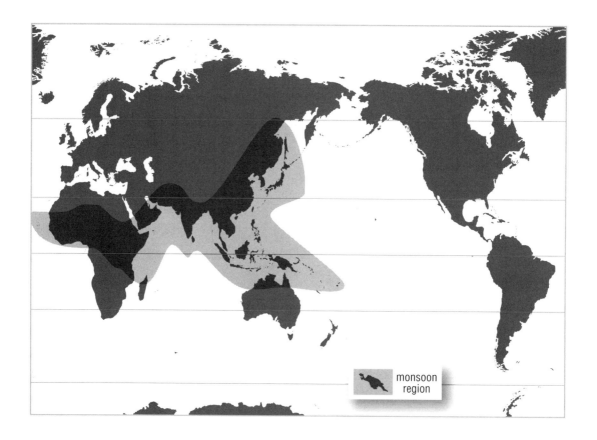

monsoon region

of Africa in both hemispheres, from Ethiopia to northern Mozambique and also a smaller region of West Africa, from the Ivory Coast to Nigeria.

A similar, but less pronounced seasonal reversal of pressure and wind direction occurs over the gulf region of the United States. The seasonal difference in rainfall is not great everywhere, but at Miami an average of 15.4 inches (391 mm) of rain falls between November and April, and 43.4 inches (1,102 mm) between May and October. This is the American monsoon.

When the monsoons fail

Monsoons matter most where the difference between the dry and wet seasons is most extreme, because it is then that farmers depend most heavily on the monsoon rains and the whole of their farming year is geared to them. Late arrival of the rains causes difficulties; if they are lighter than usual, crop yields will be reduced, and if they fail so will the harvest. Excessive monsoon rains cause difficulties that are little less serious. Then rivers burst their banks, and there is widespread flooding.

Unfortunately, the Asian monsoon, which is by far the most important, has always been somewhat unreliable. Paleoclimatologists have found evidence of major monsoon failures in about 1230, 1280, 1330, 1530, 1590, and 1640. One of the worst of all monsoon failures began in 1790 and lasted until 1796. In India alone, more than 600,000 people are believed to have died in the resulting famine—at a time when the population of the world was about one-sixth of its present size. From 1876 to 1879, between 14 million and 18 million people are estimated to have died from starvation in India and China because of famines due to the failure of the monsoon rains. The rains failed again in 1890 and that failure led the British government to ask the head of the Indian meteorological service, Sir Gilbert Walker (1868–1958), to investigate the meteorological reasons for the failure and to try to find a way of predicting future failures, so that preparations might be made and the scale of the disaster reduced. Although he was unable to achieve this, in the course of his search Walker discovered the atmospheric circulation that is now named after him and also the Southern Oscillation (see the section "El Niño and La Niña" on page 64). The monsoons failed again twice in the early 1970s. On this occasion more than 1 million people are believed to have died in India and Bangladesh. These are the most serious failures, but there are less serious ones as well, when the rains arrive, but are light. There were several such years in the 19th century, and 1918 was another. More recently, 1965 and 2000 were years of low monsoon rainfall.

It is easy for those of us who enjoy climates in which the rainfall is spread fairly evenly through the year to forget the extent to which the seasonal rains matter when almost no rain falls during the remainder of the year. People adapt to such extremely seasonal climates, but adaptation works only when the seasons are reliable. When the rains fail, there is drought, and when there is drought, there is hunger and often starvation.

COPING WITH DROUGHT

Dry-weather farming

Plants consist mostly of water, by weight. As they grow, they absorb water into their newly formed cells and they use water to transport nutrients and provide mechanical support (see the section "Why plants need water" on page 102). Some plants, such as cacti, have adapted to desert conditions by storing water in their tissues and releasing as little of it as possible. A few of these plants are edible, but in general they are not the ones that supply us with food. Our crop plants have been bred over thousands of years to produce high yields of nutritious food, and most of the breeding that led to our modern varieties took place in parts of the world where the rainfall is reliable and ample for their needs. Today if the climate does not supply enough water, the usual remedy is to provide irrigation (see the section "Irrigation" on page 158).

There is an alternative, however. It involves leaving some of the land fallow for part of the time.

Arrival of the homesteaders

In the middle of the 19th century, when the railroads were expanding westward across the United States, farmers followed. The federal government gave railroad companies grants of land extending up to 20 miles (32 km) on either side of the track. This left the companies with more land than they needed and so they sold it to settlers at about $4 an acre ($10 per hectare). The federal government, seeking to raise funds as well as to encourage the development of agriculture, also sold land to settlers and they charged only $1.25 an acre ($3 per ha). The closer their farms were to the railroad, however, the easier and cheaper it was for farmers to take their produce to market and to buy equipment and supplies and bring them home. Farmers preferred to be close to the railroad, and the companies warmly welcomed and encouraged them.

After a time, free land also became available. The Homestead Act of 1860 gave 160-acre (65-ha) plots to people who would settle, farm, and improve them for five years. After five years, the settlers owned the land.

Hundreds of thousands of people were attracted by the offer of free land and headed out to join those who had bought their farms. The homesteaders came from the eastern United States or were recent immigrants from Europe. In 1874, for example, colonies of Mennonites, a European Christian sect, in this case comprising people of German ancestry who moved to the United States from Russia, bought 60,000 acres (24,280 ha) in Kansas.

All of these immigrants had learned their farming on land that was watered by abundant rains. When they settled on their new lands they tried the farming methods that were familiar to them, but soon found them unsuccessful. The climate on the western side of the Great Plains was too dry and the crops failed (see the section "The Dust Bowl" on page 136). Recognizing the problem, the railroad companies urged the government to help the settlers, and in 1906 the Bureau of Dry Land Agriculture was established.

Dry farming

The bureau recommended a type of fallow farming. In the system it proposed, the farm is divided into two equal parts. A crop is grown on one half and, after it has been harvested, the land is left fallow for a year while the other half is cropped. While the fallow land is "resting," it is plowed and harrowed at regular intervals. This destroys weeds and plants that grow from seed left in the soil by the previous crop (known as *volunteer plants*). It also opens up spaces in the soil, allowing water to penetrate more easily, and removing all of the plants prevents the loss of water by transpiration. For a whole year the fallow land gathers such water as falls on it. Inevitably, much of the water is lost, but enough remains to increase significantly the rate of seed germination and early growth for the crop that follows. In effect, each annual crop is able to use more than one year's water.

The bureau did not devise this method by itself. Farmers in Tooele County, Utah, had been practicing it since 1877 and by the 1880s it was firmly established over much of northern Utah. A few years later a version of it was also being used in Colorado. Several varieties of corn (maize), potatoes, and onions grown by dry-farming methods won prizes at the 1906 Colorado State Fair.

In 1909 the Enlarged Homestead Act amended the original act by doubling to 320 acres (130 ha) the size of the free plots that were made available in areas where the climate was dry. Politicians recognized that only half of the land could be cultivated in any one year, and so homesteading families needed twice the area. The act stipulated that settlers would be given permanent title to their land if they farmed 80 acres (32 ha) of their homestead for five years.

This type of agriculture is called *dry farming*, and it proved highly successful throughout the drier regions of the American West. Farmers in the Palouse region, in southeastern Washington state and extending into parts of Oregon and Idaho, still grow wheat and peas in this way, although they now grow a different crop in each field every year, rather than leaving land fallow. Like the prairie grasses native to the area, wheat can send its roots six feet (1.8 m) deep in search of water. This sustains it through the dry summer months, and yields are high.

Desert farming

American farmers developed their own dry-farming methods by trial and error, but they are not unique, even in North America. While they were experimenting, the Hopi in Arizona had already been farming this way for a very long time.

They chose shallow depressions, where water is most likely to collect, and cultivated them from April to July. Hopi farmers cleared the natural vegetation to make small fields and sowed each field with melons, squash, beans, and at least 24 different varieties of corn (maize). They erected windbreaks to reduce evaporation and soil erosion. Success depended on rain at just the right time during the growing period. That was always uncertain, but when the plants received the water they needed, crop yields were adequate.

Thousands of miles away, in Sudan, people also developed a very similar type of dry farming. There the average annual rainfall varies from a mere five to eight inches (127–203 mm) and in some places it is only four inches (102 mm), so the land is desert. The rain all falls in three or four months, however, so it is concentrated.

Like the Hopi, the Sudanese farmers cultivate shallow depressions and grow sorghum (*Sorghum vulgare*), a kind of millet that looks rather like corn (maize) while it is growing and produces grain that is ground into a flour resembling corn flour, but with a higher protein content.

Versions of dry farming are also found in other parts of North Africa and in southwestern Asia. The method is obviously ancient. Southwestern Asia is where wheat and barley were first domesticated. It is one of the regions where farming began, so perhaps dry farming is the oldest of all types of agriculture.

Using water efficiently

Dry farming is not farming without any water at all. That would be impossible. It is farming in a dry climate on land that is not irrigated. This is very different. It amounts to using such water as there is in the most efficient way and reducing losses to a minimum.

In Israel there are orchards growing pomegranates in places where the annual rainfall averages six to eight inches (152–203 mm). The trees are very widely spaced, making the orchard look more like a scattering of isolated shrubs than the orchards found in Europe or the temperate regions of America.

This looks wasteful of space—although there is no shortage of space in the desert—but there is a good reason for it. Desert shrubs naturally grow far apart from one another. If they were closer together their competition for the available water in the soil would mean that none of them would obtain an adequate amount. This would kill all of them. The Israeli orchards are designed the way they are for the same reason. Each shrub, slightly taller than a man, stands at the center of a small basin dug into the desert surface. Rain and dew flow down the sides of the basin and provide the shrub with enough moisture to survive.

There are other versions of this method. On a gentle slope, level fields can be made at intervals. When it rains, water flows down the slope

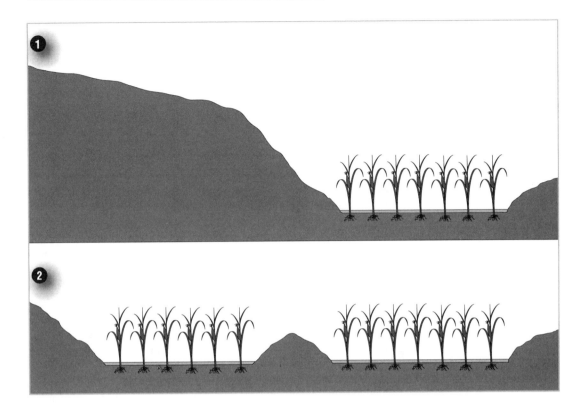

and onto the field. A ridge at the farther end prevents the water running off the field. As drawing 1 in the diagram shows, each field, made as a terrace, catches and holds all of the water flowing down the slope. If the ground is level, slopes can be made, as in drawing 2. In this case, there can be a series of sunken terraces each of which catches water flowing into it from either side.

Farming to conserve water

Mulching

Often, the retention of water is helped by working a layer of dead plant material, usually the residue of a previous crop, into the surface soil. Barley has been grown successfully in this way in California, producing 93 pounds of grain for every acre-inch of rainfall. An *acre-inch* is the amount of rainfall that would cover one acre of ground to a depth of one inch, and it is equal to 3,630 cubic feet of water (93 lb acre-inch^{-1} = 4 kg per hectare-millimeter). The system seems to work most efficiently when a crop is grown in each sunken terrace every year, but sometimes terraces are left fallow in alternate years.

Plant material worked into the surface is called a *mulch* and gardeners often use it to suppress weeds and retain water. Mulches also reduce evaporation by shading the soil, which keeps it cool. They do not have to be made from vegetation, although this is a useful way of disposing of stubble, surplus straw, chipped wood, and other wastes. Gravel and a variety of other materials are also used. Spreading mulches is not such hard work as it sounds. There are machines that scoop up soil from the surface, sieve it to collect the gravel that is present in it naturally, then spread the gravel on the surface as a mulch.

Plastic sheeting

Conventional mulches slow the rate at which water evaporates from the soil, but they do not prevent evaporation altogether. If conditions remain dry for weeks on end, both mulch and soil will dry.

Moisture can be retained much longer if the ground is covered by opaque plastic sheeting with holes punched in it through which the crop plants are sown. Plastic sheeting is widely used in growing horticultural crops, even in areas of abundant rainfall, because it is often the cheapest and most effective way to control weeds without using herbicides. Plastic sheeting is even used to collect water. Where plants are grown in shallow depressions or sunken terraces, if the whole area is covered with sheeting, dew that condenses onto the plastic at night will trickle downhill to the plants and be absorbed by them before the morning Sun evaporates it.

It is impossible to grow crops if there is no water at all, but dry-farming methods make do with surprisingly little. They have been developed wherever in the world rainfall is sparse and, although they cannot produce yields as large as those from well-watered land, throughout history they have helped make dry regions habitable.

Irrigation

Mexico City lies 7,575 feet (2,310 m) above sea level on a large plain surrounded by mountains. It receives about 30 inches (762 mm) of rain a year, but 90 percent of this falls between May and October. The rainfall between November to April amounts to only three inches (76 mm). The climate is healthy for people, but in winter it is so dry that crops can be grown only if they are supplied with water.

If you visit the city today, you will find there are many canals. These were not built for transport, however. They are what remains of one of the most remarkable agricultural systems the world has ever known.

The chinampas

When the first Europeans arrived in Mexico, in 1519, they found an empire that was ruled from the Aztec capital of Tenochtitlán–Tlatelolco, an impressive city located where Mexico City is now. At that time, a large lake covered about one-quarter of the valley in summer. In winter, as water evaporated during the dry season, this was reduced to five smaller lakes. One of these, Lake Xochimilco, to the south of the city, was fed by springs on its southern shore, where the water table was higher than the surface of the water in the lake. The ground there was swampy, and local farmers had drained the land by digging canals. This allowed clean, fresh water to flow more freely into the lake and from there into the deeper Lake Texcoco, to the north.

The canals were of various widths, but they ran more or less parallel to one another and were linked by other canals at right angles, making a grid pattern. Mud dug from the bottom of the canals was piled on the land between them, raising its level and creating a system of narrow, rectangular islands surrounded by canals and peninsulas into the lake. These islands and peninsulas were called *chinampas*. At first they were kept in place by branches and vines woven between posts around their edges. Later, willow trees replaced many of these fences.

Each chinampa is about 300 feet (92 m) long and 15 to 30 feet (4.5–9 m) wide, and the chinampas are cultivated. Farmers travel between them in flat-bottomed boats, which they also use when dredging mud from the beds of the canals. Dredging keeps the canals open and the mud provides fertilizer for their plots. Water plants grow in the canals. The farmers gather these and tow them, like huge rafts, back to their plots, where they spread them on the surface and cover them with mud. When stories of these rafts of vegetation reached 16th-century Europe they led people to believe that the Mexicans grew their food in floating gardens. Carp and other fish are also raised in the canals. In modern times, the *chinamperos* who cultivate the chinampas say that each year they can raise two crops of corn and five crops of other plants from each plot.

The area around Xochimilco became part of the Aztec state in the 15th century, and the high productivity of the chinampas probably helped sustain the Aztec Empire, but this farming system is much older. Archaeologists believe that the first chinampa canals may have been dug as much as 2,000 years ago.

It is likely that, at first, the canals were dug in order to drain the swamps. The chinampas, made from the excavated mud, were an incidental form of land reclamation, similar to the reclamation that has provided fertile farmland in the Netherlands and parts of eastern England. It went much further than these, however, because the canals also provided water for crops throughout the dry season, as well as vegetation and mud that gave each chinampa its own compost heap. Water was removed from where it was not needed and delivered to where it was needed by a very efficient system of resource management that also conserved plant nutrients.

Knowledge of the system may have spread north into what is now Arizona. *Hohokam* means "those who have gone" in the language of the present Native Americans who live in the area around Salt River, but it refers to a people who are believed to have moved there from Mexico in around 300 B.C.E. Those people were farmers who cut a total of 150 miles (241 km) of irrigation ditches, some of them 30 feet (9 m) wide and 10 feet (3 m) deep, and who grew corn (maize), beans, squashes, and cotton.

Their irrigated farming system supported a population large enough and with enough spare time to build towns and develop arts, trade, and government. Then, soon after 1400 C.E., the Hohokam people vanished and their canals were abandoned. No one knows why this happened, but it may be that their farming succumbed to the greatest danger facing any irrigation system, and the fertility of their land was destroyed.

Irrigation is as old as civilization

Where the climate is dry, the most obvious way to make farming possible is by directing such water as there is into the cultivated area. This is irrigation, and it has been practiced for thousands of years and discovered independently in many places. Today, for example, 99 percent of all the water available in Egypt is used to irrigate crops. Egyptian farmers were irrigating their land 4,000 years ago and they probably learned how to do so from the farmers of the "Fertile Crescent." That is the area between and to either side of the Tigris and Euphrates Rivers, in modern Syria and Iraq. It is where Middle Eastern civilization—from which Western civilization is descended—first developed. The earliest farms and towns were being developed in the area 8,000 years ago, and within a short time, those farms were being supplied with irrigation. You might say, therefore, that irrigation is as old as civilization itself.

Irrigation canals are often dug from the sides of rivers, to divert part of the flow around the edges of fields. Dams are often built to make artificial lakes from which water can be channeled into irrigation systems.

Where there is no suitable river, the simplest way of watering crops involves digging a well to gain access to the groundwater (see the section "Wells and springs" on page 113) and pouring water from the well into irrigation ditches. The traditional ways of doing this have been in constant use for thousands of years and are still to be seen in many parts of the world.

Possibly the most familiar device is called a *shaduf* in Egypt. In some parts of India it is called a *denkli* and in other parts a *paecottah*. It can irrigate about two acres (0.8 ha). It comprises a horizontal beam mounted eight to 10 feet (2.4–3 m) above the top of the well, supporting to one side a long, tapering, horizontal pole. A bucket is hung from the longer, thinner end of the pole, and counterweights are fixed to the shorter, thicker end. A person pulls on a rope to pull the long end of the pole downward and make the bucket descend into the well. When the bucket is full, the counterweights swing the pole to raise it and the person operating the device then tips the water into a channel feeding into the network of ditches.

Alternatively, draft animals (usually oxen) can be used to turn a vertical wheel. Buckets are attached to ropes passing over the wheel, in such a way that while half the buckets are descending, the other half are rising.

When they reach the top the buckets tip automatically, pouring their water into channels.

Digging canals and pouring water onto the land from buckets requires little technological skill, but some traditional irrigation methods are much subtler. In parts of the Sahara, for example, there are gently sloping channels that collect groundwater and direct it into oases, thus increasing the cultivable area. The channels, called *foggaras*, were covered over after they had been made, so they run below ground.

Nabatean irrigation and the Archimedes screw

Farmers in the Negev Desert, in Israel, invented a method to "harvest" water during the Israelite period, about 950–70 B.C.E. and they extended it during the Nabatean and Roman-Byzantine periods, from about 300 B.C.E. to 630 C.E. Annual rainfall in the Negev amounts to about four inches (102 mm) a year, but it falls as heavy local showers that send torrents racing down river channels and cause flash flooding.

The ancient farmers built low walls to capture this water and direct it to terraces of fields in a low-lying area. Water entered one field, was allowed to remain there long enough to soak the ground, then flowed over a spillway to the next field below, and so on until what remained drained into an underground storage tank. If this seems similar to modern methods of dry farming (see the section "Dry-weather farming" on page 154) perhaps it is because the modern methods are based on those of the ancient Nabateans. This system made it possible to supply fields with five times more water than rain could deliver by falling directly onto them. At its height, this irrigation system made it possible for the Nabateans to farm some 500,000 acres (202,350 ha) of the Negev and to support thousands of farming families and six towns.

Eventually, the channels fell into disuse and knowledge of the Nabatean farms was lost. It is only in recent times that archaeologists, working in what is now desert, have traced the lines of their walls and reconstructed the way the system worked. Israeli workers are now restoring the terraces, using concrete rather than desert stone to build the walls.

They were not the only people to harvest scarce water. Farmers in the Thar Desert, on the border between India and Pakistan, have devised a very similar method. Theirs is a monsoon climate (see the section on page 147, "Monsoons") and during the summer monsoon, up to 10 inches (250 mm) of rain falls in the space of about a week. The rainfall is so torrential it would flow away over the surface before it had time to soak into the parched ground. To prevent this, the farming communities have built walls across the valleys to dam the water, with sluice gates to allow surplus water to be removed in a controlled fashion. Water is held behind the dam, where it soaks into the ground and deposits onto the surface a layer of nutrient-rich silt, carried down from higher land. After it disappears from the surface the soil remains moist enough to grow wheat and chickpeas.

Water can be lifted by hauling on ropes to raise buckets or by turning a wheel, but there is another, altogether more ingenious method. It is called the *Archimedes screw*, suggesting that it was invented in Syracuse, Sicily, by that city's most famous son, the Greek mathematician and engineer Archimedes (ca. 287–ca. 212 B.C.E.), although some people believe the Egyptians were using it long before Archimedes was born.

As its name suggests, the screw is a cylinder, about 10–15 feet (3–4.5 m) long, with a spiral flange, like the thread on a screw, winding along its surface. The "screw" is tilted at an angle with the lower end in water. As it is turned, water is lifted up the "thread" and spills out from the top. Ancient though it is, the Archimedes screw is still used today, industrially as well as for lifting irrigation water.

On most modern farms, though, the commonest irrigation device is the sprinkler. Water is pumped to it and sprayed through rotating nozzles. When the area the spray reaches has been thoroughly soaked, the sprinkler is moved. Some farm sprinklers are self-propelled, traveling slowly in a straight line under their own power. The farm sprinkler works the same way as the garden lawn sprinkler, but is bigger.

Problems with irrigation

Unfortunately, irrigation can cause serious problems. Often, it is wasteful. Obviously, crops need irrigation most when the weather is hot and dry, but that is also when the rate of evaporation is highest. Of the clouds of spray ejected from sprinkler systems, up to 30 percent of the water may evaporate without reaching the ground, although losses can be reduced by sprinkling at night, when lower temperatures mean the evaporation rate is lower.

In many places, irrigation water is taken from the groundwater (see the section on page 108, "Water below ground"). This can remove water from an aquifer faster than it is replenished by water flowing into it. When this happens, the water table falls, so that wells and bore holes have to penetrate to a greater depth. Eventually, though, the water table may sink too deep to be reached. This is serious, but near sea coasts there is an even greater danger. If the water table falls below sea level, seawater will start flowing into the aquifer. Being salty, the seawater is denser than the freshwater and pushes beneath it, like a wedge. This displaces the freshwater, but also mixes with it to some extent, so the water being used for irrigation becomes increasingly salty. Eventually, the salt concentration can be enough to poison crop plants.

Salinization and waterlogging

Saltwater intrusion is a risk only near coasts, but salts can destroy land anywhere. *Salinization* is the accumulation of salt near the soil surface and it is closely linked to *waterlogging*. The combination of these may be what destroyed the agricultural system developed by the Hohokam. The problem is both widespread and ancient.

Some of the water falling onto the ground as rain evaporates from the surface, and the remainder drains away through the soil and eventually into rivers. This water flows constantly. Irrigation water, on the other hand, may not flow. The aim of irrigation is to wet the soil and to keep it wet, so there is a tendency to supply water faster than it can drain into the groundwater. Usually this is highly successful. Crops grow well, yields increase, and farmers are happy. So they continue with the practice. Gradually, though, the water table is steadily rising because the farmers are adding water faster than it is being removed. For a long time this may not be noticed. The water table is still well below the roots of the crop plants.

Then plant growth starts to falter. It may be that the water table has risen high enough to cover part of the root system. Roots need air for respiration. Some plants are more tolerant than others to having their roots submerged, but before long most crop plants start to suffer. Literally, some of their roots are drowning and are no longer able to absorb nutrients to sustain the plants. The soil is becoming waterlogged.

Waterlogging brings with it the risk of salinization. Irrigation water is never pure. It always contains some dissolved mineral salts. If it drains away into the groundwater, the salts it carries are removed with it, but if the water table is rising they are not, because water is accumulating below ground, rather than flowing away. Above the water table, water is drawn upward by capillarity (see the section "Water below ground" on page 108), and in the hot, dry conditions where irrigation is most useful, water evaporates from the surface.

The water that evaporates is pure H_2O vapor. At evaporation the water molecules detach from the dissolved salts. These are left behind in the topmost layer of soil, where they accumulate. Water moving upward dissolves them, and the soil water becomes increasingly saline until it alters the balance between the solution inside root cells and the solution in the soil outside them. When the soil solution becomes more concentrated than the cell solution, pure water flows out of root cells instead of into them. This kills plants by starving them of nutrients and by dehydration. By the time the crops fail, the soil has become badly poisoned.

Cure and prevention

Remedying the situation is difficult. Salts can be removed from the soil by flushing it with freshwater, so the salts dissolve and are washed away. If the soil is waterlogged, however, this will not work unless the water table is lowered first.

One method is to sink wells deep enough to penetrate to some depth below the contaminated water (which has arrived from above and does not sink very far into the groundwater) and pump freshwater from there to the surface. This can be used to flush salts from the soil, and the amount that evaporates and is lost ensures that the water table continues to fall for as long as pumping continues.

This is costly, and it is much better to foresee the danger and avoid it. If irrigation pipes are laid below the surface and deliver measured amounts of water directly to the soil around plant roots, evaporation will be minimized, the water table will not rise, and salinization will not occur. Many irrigation systems now work in this way.

Neither will soil become waterlogged or saline if drainage is installed at the same time as the irrigation system, to ensure that the water used to irrigate crops flows out of the area, rather than accumulating. Probably by accident, this is the secret of the success of the chinampas. Because the springs supplying the irrigation water are higher than the water level in the lake at the other end of the canal network, water flows from the higher to the lower level. The irrigation water flows, and the plots it irrigates lie above the water level in the canals, so they never become waterlogged. The canals are not stagnant ditches, but small streams.

Irrigation makes it possible to grow crops in dry climates. This extends greatly the area of farmland available to feed us. In the world as a whole, there is at present more than 900 million square miles (233 km^2) of irrigated farmland, and more than 60 percent of it is in regions with a dry climate. As the table below shows, approximately 48 percent of all farmland is irrigated in the Near East, and about 37 percent in Asia. Overall, about one-sixth of all cultivated land is irrigated, and this land produces about one-third of the world's food. On average, the output from irrigated land is double that from land watered only by falling rain.

Not surprisingly, the area of irrigated land has been increasing. Even where rainfall is moderate, irrigation can increase crop yields. It is an important technique and farmers have always known this. Unwise

IRRIGATED FARMLAND

Region	Area		Percent of total cultivated land
	(000 acres)	(000 ha)	
Africa	30,082	12,174	9.9
Northern	14,616	5,915	24.8
Sudan–Sahel	6,138	2,414	12.1
Gulf of Guinea	1,161	193	4.0
Central	299	121	3.9
Eastern	1,072	434	2.9
Islands	2,730	1,105	40.3
Southern	4,065	1,645	8.1

(continues)

IRRIGATED FARMLAND (continued)

Region	Area		Percent of total cultivated land
	(000 acres)	(000 ha)	
Former Soviet Union	56,315	22,790	11.0
Russian Federation	15,132	6,124	5.2
Central Asia	28,114	11,377	26.2
Eastern Europe	7,532	3,048	7.7
Caucasus	5,456	2,208	67.4
Baltic States	81	33	0.7
North America	54,658	22,120	9.9
Canada	1,779	720	1.1
Unites States	52,879	21,400	13.8
Latin America & Caribbean	45,454	18,395	13.9
Mexico	15,459	6,256	34.1
Central America	1,112	450	6.7
Greater Antilles	3,105	1,257	17.6
Lesser Antilles	13,007	5,264	not available
Guyana sub-region*	497	201	35.8
Andean sub-region	9,037	3,657	21.4
Brazil	7,092	2,870	5.8
South sub-region	9,139	3,698	11.2
Near East	117,955	47,736	48
Maghreb	6,716	2,718	16
North East. Africa	13,326	5,393	46
Arabian Peninsula	5,531	2,238	80
Middle East	22,033	8,917	30
Central Asia	70,349	28,470	75
Asia	1,646,981	666,524	37
Indian subcontinent	137,375	55,595	36
East Asia	1,370,139	554,487	55
Far East	99,129	40,117	60
Southeast Asia	24,670	9,984	25
Islands	1,567	6,341	13
Europe	64,874	26,254	not available

* Sub-regions are defined by the U.N. but do not correspond precisely with national boundaries.

(Source: Food and Agriculture Organization of the United Nations, 2002; Statistics Canada, 2002.)

irrigation can poison the land, however, and this is something farmers have not always realized. The table on the preceding page shows the area of irrigated land in each region of the world, and the area as a proportion of all the cultivated land.

Water for people

Without water to drink, we die. If you minimize the loss of water from your body, by resting in a cool place so you do not perspire, you are unlikely to survive longer than about a week if you have nothing at all to drink. In hot weather you may not live for more than two or three days. Food is a less urgent requirement. You can survive several weeks without eating.

All of the chemical reactions in our bodies take place in water. Of all the water in the body, about 60 percent is located inside cells, 30 percent in body tissues between cells, and the remainder in the blood plasma. Water accounts for about 60 percent of the weight of a human body. Hair, parts of bone, and fingernails and toenails are dry, but our muscles are 80 percent water by weight.

The total amount of water in our bodies must be maintained in order to keep constant the concentration of substances dissolved in it. If that concentration changes, the osmotic pressure on either side of cell walls will also change, causing water to flow into or out of cells, (see the box on page 106, "Osmosis," in the section "Why plants need water"). If water flows out of cells, they become dehydrated and eventually die. If water flows into them, they swell and may rupture.

Drinking too much water is bad for you

It is rare for people to drink so much water that it makes them ill, but occasionally it happens, and people have even died from water poisoning. Drinking too much can cause *water intoxication*, for which the medical term is *hyponatremia*, a word that means "shortage of sodium." This is the opposite of dehydration, and most often affects people who have taken vigorous exercise that made them perspire heavily for a long time and who failed to stop to drink small amounts of water at fairly frequent intervals. A person in this condition will be dehydrated, extremely thirsty, and may feel a strong urge to gulp down a large quantity of water as rapidly as possible. This is dangerous.

Sweat is salty, so when you sweat your body loses salt (sodium chloride). The water that you drink contains no salt, so you are replacing the water your body has lost, but not the salt. The water enters your bloodstream and dilutes it, altering the balance of concentration between the fluid inside and outside cells and causing water to enter cells—a condition known as *fluid overload*. This makes the cells swell.

Swelling can cause serious damage to the brain, which is confined inside the skull with little room to expand. It can also damage the lungs. Victims of hyponatremia become confused and disoriented, their speech becomes slurred, they may experience nausea with dry retching, they may cough up blood, and they may suffer from muscular cramps. If nothing is done to help them they can experience seizures resembling those of epilepsy and then lose consciousness. Their unconsciousness can lead to coma. In extreme cases, pressure inside the skull forces part of the base of the brain down into the spine. That prevents it from maintaining breathing. This condition is fatal.

Dying of thirst?

If your body loses more water than you drink to replace it, it will not be long before you feel ill. You may not feel thirsty. The first indication that you need more fluid may be a marked reduction in the amount of urine you pass and the unusually dark yellow color of your urine. A while later you may feel generally unwell and have trouble sleeping. Then your muscles will weaken. If your body weight falls by 2 percent due to dehydration, the working capacity of your muscles may decrease by as much as 20 percent. For an adult man of average weight (140 pounds; 63 kg) a 2-percent loss of body fluid amounts to about five pints (3 liters). If that man loses seven pints (4 liters) he will be too weak to perform even the smallest tasks. His skin will feel dry and rather stiff, and he may have hallucinations. If he loses between 14 and 18 pints (8–10 liters) he will die. In very hot weather he may rapidly succumb to *explosive heat death* (see the section "Desert life" on page 84).

Need for water

We need to drink at least 2.5 pints (1.4 liters) of water a day and more than that in hot weather or after any kind of physical exertion. Most people drink much more, not so much because they are thirsty as because they enjoy the taste of what they drink. Drink a cup of coffee or a glass of fruit juice or soda and you do not think of it as water, but remove the flavoring, coloring, sugar, and a few other minor ingredients and water is what is left. When you are very thirsty you may eat fruit instead of drinking, but it is the water in the fruit that your thirst is demanding. Even fishes drink water. Marine fishes have special ways of extracting and excreting the excess salt from the seawater they drink.

Our food also contains water. Just as the human body is about 60 percent water by weight, so is most of the food we eat. Look at the label of ingredients on a packet of food, add together the amounts, and you will find the total is far short of the weight of the food item. The difference is water, which is not listed as an ingredient (perhaps because people might object to paying so much for water). Many green vegetables are 90 percent water, meat and fish are up to 65 percent water, and even bread is about 30 percent water. If you eat a healthy, balanced diet, your food will provide you with a significant proportion of the water your body needs.

All animals need water, of course, but some are able to use it much more efficiently than humans (see the box on page 88 on the camel in the section "Desert life"). This enables them to survive in deserts, where they may find drinking water only occasionally. Some mammals never drink at all, obtaining all the water they need from the food they eat, and most reptiles obtain all their liquid from their food. We are not like that, however. Our bodies lose fluid readily, because we sweat to keep cool and maintain a constant body temperature. In hot weather, or when playing a strenuous sport, sweating to keep cool can make us lose between 0.2 and 0.5 ounces of fluid an hour for every pound of body weight (12.5–31 milliliters kg^{-1}). A man weighing 140 pounds (63 kg) can lose 28–70 ounces (0.8–2 liters) of fluid per hour in this way.

Respiration—the cellular process, not the inhalation and exhalation of air in breathing—involves the oxidation of carbon, and this also removes water. The reaction releases energy, and the carbon dioxide and water we excrete when we breathe out are the by-products. Breathe onto a mirror and the water that condenses there came originally from the water you drank or the food you ate.

Animals adapted to life in deserts can reduce their loss even of respiratory water and they produce very dry feces and very concentrated urine. An adult human body, in contrast, loses an average of about three pints (1.7 liters) of water a day in the fairly dilute urine it produces, as well about three-quarters of a pint (0.4 liter) in sweating and about one-quarter of a pint (0.1 liter) in feces. Even if you remain quite still and in a cool place, you cannot avoid losing about 2.5 pints (1.4 liters) of water a day. If the kidneys are unable to produce at least 1.3 fluid ounces (30 milliliters) of urine an hour, metabolic waste products will start to accumulate in the blood, eventually with fatal consequences. If you reduce losses to the barest minimum, but do not eat or drink to replace the fluid your body loses, it will take rather less than six days to lose 15 pints (8.6 liters) and just over seven days to lose about 18 pints (10 liters). This is how the length of time someone can survive without drinking is calculated.

Providing clean water

Not surprisingly, people have always valued sources of water that is clean enough to drink. Natural springs and wells have often been associated with benign spirits and in some countries there are many "holy wells," associated with Christian saints. The saints chose to settle close to a reliable source of safe drinking water, so the wells or springs that they found came to be associated with them. Usually there were rivers and sometimes lakes not far from such springs and wells, but these were less dependable. During droughts they dwindled and might even disappear, and their waters were not always pure. Drinking from them could cause illness and often did. In many countries, where rivers are used to supply water for drinking and cooking as well as for washing and the disposal of wastes, debilitating and sometimes fatal water-borne diseases are common.

Supplying enough water for everyone to drink safely is now a major challenge facing the world. This is mainly because of the cost of purifying it to a safe standard (see the section "Water recycling and purification" on page 171), but partly because natural sources of freshwater are not distributed evenly throughout the world. In some regions, the amount of freshwater naturally available per person per year is $\frac{1}{50}$ of that available in others, and demand for freshwater is increasing rapidly in countries that are developing their manufacturing industries. In the world as a whole, we are now using almost four times more freshwater than we were using 50 years ago (254 cubic miles in 1945 and 990 cubic miles in 1995).

The challenge is being met, but much too slowly. According to the World Health Organization of the United Nations, in 1990 a total of 4.1 billion people (79 percent of the global population) were supplied with water that had been at least partly purified. By 2000 this figure had increased to 4.9 billion (82 percent of the total population). During the same period, the number of people with access to proper facilities for disposing of their sewage increased from 2.9 billion (55 percent) to 3.6 billion (60 percent). The situation is much worse in rural areas than in towns and cities. A total of 2 billion country-dwellers—1.3 billion of them living in China and India—have no proper sanitation and almost 1 billion people have no supply of purified water.

Where does the water go?

We drink no more than a tiny fraction of all the water we use, of course. Indeed, the water that is piped into private homes accounts for only about 10 percent of the total we use and we drink an insignificant amount even of that. We drink at most a few pints of water a day, but when we take a bath the tub usually contains more than 30 gallons (136 liters). Flushing the toilet uses 5 gallons (23 liters), and if we leave the water running while we wash the dishes after a meal it is easy to use about 30 gallons (136 liters). Depending on whether it is set to a full or economy load, a washing machine uses between about 20 and 45 gallons (91–205 liters) each time it is used. All of this water can be recycled, however, and whether it is recycled or not, eventually it is returned to the sea. The total amount of water on the planet does not alter.

Much more water than this is used in factories. In North America and Europe industry uses four to five times more water than is supplied to private homes. Some of the water is incorporated into manufactured products, but most is *process water*—water that is a necessary ingredient of the manufacturing process—or used for cooling. The textile, iron and steel, and petrochemical industries use large amounts of process water. Cooling water does not come into direct contact with the product. It passes through a system of pipes, called a *heat exchanger*, that run through or around the vessel in which the process is taking place. A large amount of cooling water is used to condense water vapor into steam (liquid droplets).

Process and cooling water can be used again or cleaned and returned to the source from which it was taken, but a proportion is lost by evaporation each time it is heated. Factories in the United States use water an average of 17 times before they finally discharge it.

Where does the water come from?

Many of the great industrial cities of the world lie beside rivers or on the shores of lakes, close to a convenient source of the water they need. Obtaining this water may involve nothing more complicated than excavating a channel to divert water into a factory or installing pumps to force it into the pipes that deliver it. Where water is taken from a deep lake, however, there is a chance to match the supply to the demand more precisely. In the Great Lakes, for example, vertical towers set on the lake bed have inlets at various depths. The temperature and chemical composition of lake water vary with depth and so the different inlets are used to supply different requirements. If surface water is not available or the amount is insufficient, groundwater can be tapped (see the section "Water below ground" on page 108).

River water may be suitable for industrial use, but not fit to drink, in which case a source of clean drinking water must be found and, once obtained, the water must be moved to where it is needed, perhaps over a distance of several miles. A channel to carry water is called an *aqueduct*. The earliest aqueducts were underground pipes carrying water from a spring to a pool, but in Roman times magnificent overhead aqueducts were built to serve many towns in southern Europe. Aqua Marcia, for example, an aqueduct built in 144 B.C.E., was almost 56 miles (90 km) long and supported on tall arches for 5.9 miles (9.5 km) of its length. Like all aqueducts, it carried water downhill, from hilltop springs to people living at a lower level.

Rome lies on the Tiber River, but its waters have never been drinkable. By 97 C.E., the water supply for the city was being carried by nine aqueducts delivering a total of 38 million gallons (173 million liters) a day inside the city walls and a further 20 million gallons (91 million liters) for those living outside the city walls. The tradition continues. Today the modern Apulian aqueduct carries 132 million gallons (600 million liters) of water a day from the western side of the Appenines, through a 9.5-mile (15-km) tunnel, and then to the city of Taranto, 152 miles (244 km) away in the dry southeastern corner of Italy.

Rivers that provide water also carry away wastes and by-products. Provided the amounts are small, rivers are able to cleanse themselves.

Pollution becomes serious when contaminants are discharged into them in amounts that exceed this self-cleansing capacity. Such pollution increases the difficulty and cost of providing safe drinking water.

Water recycling and purification

Drought makes water pollution worse, and it can lead to the pollution of waters that were previously clean. This increases the cost of making water safe to drink just when people wish to use more water because of the intensely dry weather.

The link between drought and pollution is simple. Substances that enter water mix with it. Usually they become greatly diluted within a short time, especially if the water is flowing. Just how much they are diluted depends on the volume of water with which they mix. During a drought, rivers carry less water, often very much less, and the water level in lakes and ponds also falls. This means that there is less water available to receive and dilute the contaminant, and so the concentration of the pollutant increases. If the amount of a substance entering the water remains the same, but the volume of water receiving it is reduced by half, the concentration of the pollutant doubles. This could increase a level of contamination that is safe to a level that is not.

Harmful algal blooms

Even if the polluting substance is not poisonous to humans in itself, it may nevertheless lead indirectly to poisoning. Nitrates and phosphates, for example, are plant nutrients. Most nitrates and phosphates reach surface water in drainage from adjacent land, but sewage also contains them. These compounds can stimulate the growth of algae and cyanobacteria. Algae are simple aquatic plants, and cyanobacteria (formerly known as "blue-green algae") are even simpler organisms—classed as bacteria—that also grow in water. If the water is warm, the aquatic organisms will grow even faster, and during a drought the weather is likely to be hot. In these conditions the organisms multiply so rapidly that they color the water or lie like a scum over its surface. This proliferation is known as an *algal bloom*. Blooms are unsightly and often smelly, and some species of algae and cyanobacteria produce poisons in amounts that are large enough to make people swimming in the water seriously ill or even to kill them.

Algal blooms are very common. In 2001, for example, there were blooms on 15 occasions in lakes or ponds near towns in Maine. The biggest bloom of all, though, happened in November 1991 along the Bar-won and Darling Rivers in New South Wales, Australia. That bloom of cyanobacteria stretched in a continuous line for 620 miles (1,000 km).

Farm animals died from poisoning, and people living near the rivers and taking their domestic water supplies from them had to resort to stored rainwater and the use of emergency filtration equipment.

When rivers carry plant nutrients into the sea, algal blooms can develop along coasts. These blooms are often due to *dinoflagellates*. Dinoflagellates are single-celled organisms, classed as *protists*, that move around by means of two hair-like structures called *flagella*. Some dinoflagellates, including *Karenia brevis* (it used to be known as *Gymnodinium breve*), are brown or red in color and when there are enough of them, they produce "red tides" that color the water (but have nothing to do with the tides, despite the name). Red tides occur in summer in many parts of the world, and especially along parts of the Florida and Texas coasts. They can be dangerous, because *K. brevis* and certain other dinoflagellates, including another common species, *Alexandrium tamarense*, produce powerful nerve poisons. Anyone who swallows the poisoned water or even swims through it is likely to fall seriously sick. Red tides can even affect people on the shore who are exposed to particles of the poison that are thrown into the air in spray. This causes irritation to the eyes, nose, and throat, and a tingling sensation in the lips and tongue.

Affected beaches are closed to protect the public, but the danger does not end there. The poisons kill fish, but they accumulate in shellfish without harming them. Mollusks such as clams, oysters, mussels, and whelks are immune. Fish are safe to eat provided they are behaving normally at the time they are caught, but how can the customer buying them know? Eating contaminated shellfish can cause serious, even fatal, food poisoning.

Separating the water supply

Natural surface water is never pure. Rainwater is slightly acid because of the carbon dioxide, nitrogen oxides, and sulfur dioxide that dissolve into it from the air. It also contains solid particles of soil. These are chemically inert, but there are also particles of soot and dust from factories that are chemically reactive. Rivers carry silt particles and chemical compounds draining from the land to either side. Groundwater may be safe to drink, but it usually contains minerals dissolved out of the surrounding rocks, and these can be present in harmful concentrations. Water draining into wells from surrounding land can contaminate the well water, and well water often harbors bacteria that can cause illness.

Before it is piped to our homes, water must be purified. We drink only a small proportion of the water we use, of course, and so purification can seem wasteful. Why go to all the trouble of purifying water to a high standard if it will be used only for showering or laundry? From time to time this consideration leads people to suggest separating the water supply so that we have one tap to deliver drinking water and another delivering water for other uses. Duplicating all the plumbing would be very expensive and such a dual system would lead to health risks. We could label the taps, of course, so that one was clearly marked "Not For Drinking," but would this be good enough? How would we feel if a child were accidentally to drink from the wrong tap and fell ill? Then again, the taps might be confusing in other ways. Obviously we should use drinking water to wash and cook food, but which tap should we use to wash the dishes? Would it be safe to bathe or wash clothes in water that is not fit to drink?

Even with a dual system, the low-quality water would still require some purification to prevent the spread of disease. Bacteria found in polluted water include those that cause cholera, dysentery, typhoid fever, and paratyphoid fever. These are potential killers that must be controlled by some means more effective than simply labeling the tap. Poliomyelitis may be eliminated entirely from the world within the next few years, but at one time the virus that causes it was spread mainly through contaminated water.

In practice, all water is treated to make it safe to drink before it enters the domestic supply. Water for industry may not need to meet such a high standard, however. The quality a factory requires depends on how the water will be used.

Water recycling

Most factories recycle their water. American factories utilize water an average of 17 times before they finally discharge it. As the table below shows, however, the proportion of water that is recycled by American industries varies widely between industrial sectors. The most recent figures available are for the year 2000.

Even then, of course, the water must be cleaned of substances that might harm aquatic plants and animals before it can be discharged following its final use.

Water for domestic use can also be recycled. The treatment that purifies it once can purify it a second time. This happens where many communities take water and discharge waste water along the course of a long river. People in the Netherlands, for example, drink water from the Rhine. Before it reaches them it has also supplied many small towns as well as the cities of Basel in Switzerland, Strasbourg in France, and Karlsruhe, Ludwigshafen,

Industry	percentage of total water consumption that is recycled, 2000
Paper and paper products	11.8
Chemicals and chemical products	28.0
Petroleum and oil products	32.7
Metal smelting and refining	12.3
All manufacturing	17.1

Mannheim, Mainz, Koblenz, Bonn, Köln, and Düsseldorf in Germany. By the time the Rhine discharges into the North Sea, its waters have been drunk and repurified countless times.

Purification treatment

Treatment to purify water starts as soon as the water is taken from its source. It begins with screening. The water passes through a row of iron bars, about four inches (10 cm) apart, to remove bottles, tree branches, and other large objects. Then it is allowed to stand while grit and smaller particles settle to the bottom. Water that is being recycled is treated in the same way to remove solid matter. Copper sulfate is often added to prevent the growth of algae. This is known as *primary treatment*. Once the water is more or less clear it is ready to be pumped to the treatment plant for *secondary treatment*.

There it is filtered through *activated carbon*. This is charcoal that has been heated by steam or hot carbon dioxide to 1,650°F (900°C). This makes it highly porous. Activated carbon is very good at absorbing those chemicals that make water taste or smell bad. After that, chlorine is added. Chlorine dissolves in water and is then a powerful oxidizing agent that kills bacteria—and is destroyed in the process, so it does not remain in the water. Ozone is also very effective and is used in some treatment plants. At the end of this stage the water is fit to irrigate orchards, vineyards, and crops that are not intended for human consumption. It can be used industrially for cooling and can be discharged into certain aquifers and natural environments.

If it is to be used to irrigate food crops or on land where people may come into contact with it, water being recycled undergoes *tertiary treatment*. It is passed through very fine filters to remove most of the tiniest particles suspended in it. Still smaller particles cannot be removed by straining the water through filters, however. Instead, they must be made to gather into bigger lumps that settle to the bottom. This process is called *coagulation* or *flocculation*, and it involves adding a compound comprising molecules that attract and hold the particles. Aluminum sulfate ("alum") is often used, but ferric sulfate, ferric chloride, and calcium hydroxide (lime) are also suitable.

The water is then filtered again, this time by passing it through a bed of sand, sometimes comprising several layers. It may flow down through the bed under its own weight, or be forced through under pressure in a closed vessel. Both produce the same effect, but filtration under pressure is quicker. After filtration, the water is aerated by bubbling air through it. This introduces oxygen, which will oxidize any organic material that still remains unoxidized, and it also improves the flavor of the water. Finally, more chlorine is added to disinfect the water and, after disinfection, potassium permanganate or sodium thiosulfate is added to remove any remaining chlorine. In the United States, the Environmental Protection Agency permits recycled water in this condition to be used for many purposes, but does not consider it fit to enter the domestic supply directly, although it may do so if first it is mixed thoroughly with clean water in a river, lake, or reservoir.

At every stage of treatment, and especially near its completion, water samples are analyzed. Routine analysis measures the pH (acidity or alkalinity), the hardness of the water (the concentration of magnesium, iron, and calcium salts that affect the ease with which water forms a lather with soap), and detects the presence and concentration of a range of substances. These must not be present in amounts greater than certain specified limits.

The concentration of pollutants, as well as the maximum concentrations permitted, are often measured in parts per million (p.p.m.) or sometimes parts per billion (p.p.b.). It is difficult to understand what "one part per million" and "one part per billion" really mean. Suppose you had one teaspoonful of some substance that you wanted to dilute in water to a concentration of one part per million. You would need to mix your teaspoonful thoroughly in 1,100 gallons (5,000 liters) of water. That is about enough water to fill a tank five feet square and six feet deep (1.5 × 1.8 m). One teaspoonful diluted to one part per billion would require enough water to fill a pool about 50 yards long, 33 yards wide, and 10 feet deep (45.75 × 30 × 3 m). That permitted limits are set in parts per million or parts per billion demonstrates the sensitivity of modern scientific instruments used for analysis and also the care that is taken to protect public health.

When it goes wrong

Accidents can and do happen, of course. Occasionally an unusual contaminant finds its way into water unnoticed, passes through the treatment process, and remains undetected. Treatment is not designed to neutralize or remove it and no test is applied to look for it, because no one has any idea it is present until it makes someone ill.

It can also happen that a pollutant enters water and escapes into the supply before it can be stopped. That is what happened in July 1988 at Camelford, a small town in Cornwall, in southwest England. A load of about 22 tons (20 tonnes) of aluminum sulfate intended for flocculation was delivered to an unmanned water treatment plant. The chemical was to be poured into a storage tank, but the tanks were unmarked and the driver, unfamiliar with the site, mistakenly poured the chemical into the wrong one, where it mixed with water that was about to be released into the supply. Before anyone knew what was happening, water containing up to 4,000 times the permitted amount of aluminum was sent into the pipes serving 22,000 people. The water was fairly acid (pH 4.2). It curdled milk, stung the lips and mouths of people who tried to drink it, and reacted with lead, zinc, copper, and other metals in the pipes, adding to the contamination. To clean out the pipes, officials flushed them with clean water and poured everything into local rivers, killing between 43,000 and 61,000 salmon and trout as well as countless other fish. Fortunately, such incidents are rare.

Testing for bacteria

Some of the bacteria and viruses present in sewage transmit diseases. All of these organisms should have been killed by chlorine during the treatment process, and when water is tested for quality, there is one test that looks for them. They are present in organic matter, which is broken down by bacteria (not all of which cause disease). The process consumes oxygen dissolved in the water. The test measures *biological oxygen demand* (or BOD).

The first step is to measure the amount of dissolved oxygen that is present in a 1.75-pint (one-liter) sample of water. The sample is stored for five days in darkness at a constant temperature of 68°F (20°C), and the amount of oxygen is measured again. The two measurements are then compared, and the difference between them indicates the degree of bacterial activity. Clean river water should have a BOD of approximately 0.0004 ounces per gallon (0.0025 milligrams per liter). The BOD of raw sewage is about 100,000 times greater than that (4 oz gal^{-1}; 25 mg l^{-1}).

BOD refers to oxygen that is dissolved in water (not the oxygen in the water molecule itself). This is the oxygen the bacteria use, and in doing so they reduce the concentration in the water. Fish and other aquatic animals also depend on dissolved oxygen, so they can die from asphyxiation if the water is contaminated with raw sewage. That is why raw sewage is considered to be strongly polluting, even in water that is not intended for human use.

Wastewater should be treated to remove most pollutants before it is discharged into rivers, lakes, or coastal waters. It is this treatment that removes sewage as well as industrial chemicals.

In most countries great care is taken to ensure that the public water supply is safe. Treatment is costly, however, and in poor countries where cities are rapidly expanding, it is not available everywhere. Drought adds to the dangers by increasing the concentration of pollutants just when demand for water is at its highest.

Desalination

Earth is a watery planet. Water covers more than two-thirds of its surface and this vast store of water is inexhaustible. No matter how it is used or how often, all of the water eventually returns to the oceans—the store. Some evaporates and falls into the store as rain. Rivers return the rest. It is recycled constantly. If you were an alien approaching the solar system from your distant world, the first thing to strike you about our planet would be its abundant supply of water. If your advance party of explorers then returned to your ship and told you that the beings living in some parts of this world were desperately short of water you would find it very hard to believe. It would seem utterly implausible.

Location	percentage of total freshwater
icecaps and glaciers	75
groundwater	22
soil	1.75
lakes and inland seas	0.6
rivers	0.003

(Numbers do not add to exactly 100 because of rounding.)

Closer examination would soon reveal the reason. Although Earth has so much water, almost all of it is seawater, and poisonous to those plants and animals that live on dry land. They have to manage with the meager 3 percent of the total that is not poisonous to them and even then more than half of that 3 percent is frozen in polar icecaps and glaciers and some of it is in aquifers that are too deep to be reached. The table below shows where the freshwater is located. The planet may be wet, but water remains a scarce commodity. We rely on the slightly more than 22 percent of the total freshwater that we obtain from groundwater, lakes, inland seas, and rivers.

Even so, you might still find the situation puzzling, because its solution is so obvious. The poisonous water contains dissolved salts, so why not remove them? These salts, mainly sodium chloride (common salt), are present at an average concentration of about 3.4 percent (there are 3.4 parts of salt to 100 parts of water).

The table below lists the ions (atoms or groups of atoms that carry charge) that are dissolved in seawater and their average amounts and

	COMPOSITION OF SEAWATER	
Ion	Parts per thousand by weight	percentage of dissolved material
chloride (Cl^-)	18.980	55.05
sodium (Na^+)	10.556	30.61
sulfate (SO_4^{2-})	2.649	7.68
magnesium (Mg^{2+})	1.272	3.69
calcium (Ca^{2+})	0.400	1.16
potassium (K^+)	0.380	1.10
bicarbonate (HCO_3^-)	0.140	0.41
bromide (Br^-)	0.065	0.19
borate ($H_3BO_3^-$)	0.026	0.07
strontium (Sr^{2+})	0.008	0.03
fluoride (F^-)	0.001	0.00

proportions of the whole. The amounts are expressed in parts per thousand (*per mil*, symbol ‰), which is the way the composition of seawater is usually measured, rather than in percentages (to convert ‰ to %, divide by 100). Common salt (sodium chloride) is the most abundant substance, present at 29.5‰ and accounting for 85 percent of the total 34.5‰ of dissolved salts. This is stronger than the solutions inside cells, so if cells are bathed in seawater, water flows out of them by osmosis (see the box in the section "Why plants need water" on page 102). Saltwater dehydrates cells, and this can be fatal. The remedy, therefore, is to remove the dissolved salts. Purify the water and it will no longer be poisonous. Then there will be more than enough water for every conceivable need.

Removing the salt

Separating water from the salts dissolved in it is not difficult. It is called *desalination* (or *desalinization*), and there are many ways to do it.

Supply the water molecules with enough energy to break the hydrogen bonds linking them to each other and they will escape from the liquid, leaving all the dissolved ions behind. This is evaporation, of course, and it is the way freshwater is made naturally.

Or you could do the opposite. Take energy away from the water until enough new hydrogen bonds have formed to change it into ice, a solid. Again, the freezing process expels ions and leaves only water molecules. That is why icebergs consist of freshwater. In this case, though, freezing seawater in some kind of giant freezer may not be necessary, because ice already occurs naturally on a huge scale. All you need do is attach cables to a suitable iceberg and tow it to where it is needed. It would start to melt as it entered warmer regions, of course, but there would still be plenty of it left by the time it reached, say, the deserts of the Middle East. Icebergs could provide a great deal of water. A big one may comprise several cubic miles of ice.

Then again, it is possible to make osmosis work in reverse. Ordinarily, when a semipermeable membrane separates two solutions of different concentrations, an osmotic pressure is exerted that pushes water molecules through the pores in the membrane from the weaker to the stronger solution. Apply enough pressure on the other side of the membrane, however, and water will flow in the opposite direction—from the stronger to the weaker solution. If the weaker solution is pure water, reverse osmosis will add to it water that is removed from the saltwater on the other side of the membrane. This process is called *reverse osmosis*.

Or electrodialysis will do the trick. Pour saltwater into a vessel containing two electrodes. When a current flows through the water from one electrode to the other, the ions in the saltwater separate according to the positive or negative charge they carry. Place a set of semipermeable membranes in the vessel, arranged so that half of them allow positively charged ions to pass and half allow negatively charged ions to pass. The positive ions (such as sodium) will then move toward the negative electrode (the cathode), the negative ions (such as chloride) toward the positive electrode (the anode), and pure water will be left in the middle of the vessel.

But what does it cost?

Sitting in your starship, somewhere out near Pluto, by this time you may well be scratching your head (if you have one). Water shortage on Earth is a mystery. All of these methods work, and many more are technically feasible, so why is there a problem? The trouble is that you have failed to spot two difficulties common to all of them.

The first is that they are expensive. In order to evaporate water you must heat it. That uses energy, which costs money to generate. Freezing also uses energy and if you plan to tow icebergs thousands of miles you will need ships with powerful engines. Engines burn fuel and someone has to pay for it. Reverse osmosis is an excellent technique, but to make it work you need to increase the pressure on the semipermeable membrane to 25 times the surface atmospheric pressure. This takes a great deal of energy. The electric current for electrodialysis has to be generated in some way and it is never free. All the methods work, but all of them produce water that costs much more than water you simply take from a river, lake, or borehole.

At present, in the United States, desalination plants with a capacity to produce 1–10 million gallons (3.8–38 million liters) of freshwater per day can do so for $1–2.40 per 1,000 gallons (26–63 cents per thousand liters). For smaller plants yielding up to 5 million gallons (19 million liters) a day the cost is $4–16 per 1,000 gallons ($1–4 per 1,000 l). It does not sound very expensive until you compare it with the 30 cents per 1,000 gallons (8 cents per 1,000 l) it costs to supply clean water from a river, lake, or borehole. Prices are falling, but desalination is still expensive.

Suppose, nevertheless, that there are people living far from the nearest natural source of cheap freshwater who are prepared to pay whatever it costs to have taps in their homes that deliver drinkable water. You can produce it for them, but now you face the other problem. What can you do with the residue that remains after you have separated the water from the salt? This residue will be a very strong brine. It is very poisonous and corrodes most metals. You cannot just pour it back into the sea. You could process it further to separate the salts, hoping to find industrial markets for them. For every thousand tons of freshwater, you would be left with about 34 tons of salts. Unfortunately, there is no shortage of these commodities and you would find it difficult to sell them for what it cost you to obtain them.

Nevertheless, desalination is widely used

Despite the difficulties, however, freshwater is produced in many countries by the desalination of seawater. Desalination is widely used in Israel,

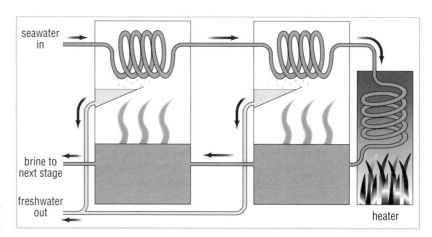

Multistage flash evaporation

Kuwait, and Saudi Arabia, for example, as well as in Arizona, at the Yuma Desalting Plant, and at coastal towns in California. Key West, Florida, became the first U.S. city to obtain water by desalination when its multistage flash evaporation plant opened in 1967. The Bureau of Reclamation of the Department of the Interior is the agency that directs research into desalination technologies in the United States. The cost continues to fall, and the concentrated brine can be stored and then diluted until it is suitable for release.

Reverse osmosis often produces freshwater more cheaply than other methods, but its rivals have been available for longer and are well established. Multistage flash evaporation, illustrated in the diagram above, is probably the most widely used. Seawater is heated under pressure, which prevents it from boiling. It is then fed into a series of chambers, each at a slightly lower pressure. As it enters, some of the seawater boils instantly (it "flashes") and the remainder passes to the next chamber where more of it flashes. The vapor condenses onto pipes that pass through all the chambers. The condensed vapor is freshwater that is collected and removed. Latent heat released by the condensation of the vapor warms the pipes carrying incoming seawater toward the start of the process, so the incoming water is fairly warm by the time it has to be heated. This saves fuel.

Vacuum freezing is also used and it, too, exploits latent heat. In this process, seawater is cooled almost to its freezing point (seawater freezes at 28.6°F; –1.91°C), then fed into a chamber where the pressure is very low. Some of the water vaporizes instantly, taking latent heat from the water around it. This lowers the temperature of the water further, and some of it freezes. The (freshwater) ice crystals are separated from the brine and washed in freshwater, then the pressure in the chamber is increased. This makes the vapor condense onto the ice crystals, releasing latent heat that melts the ice. The condensed vapor and melted ice are piped away as freshwater.

Solar ponds

Dry regions often have hot climates, so there should be a way of harnessing energy from the Sun to separate salt and water. In fact there are several, but one is particularly ingenious. Lucien Bronicki, an Israeli engineer, invented it and it uses a *salt-gradient solar pond* to generate electricity.

As its name suggests, there is a very large pond at the center of the plant. The first one to be built, near Ein Bokek, Israel, has a surface area of nearly 8,000 square yards (6,690 m²). At the bottom of the pond, there is a layer of very salt water and there is a layer of almost freshwater at the surface. Sandwiched between these layers there is a third layer of intermediately saline water.

The Sun shines on the pond, its heat penetrating the upper layers and raising the temperature of the bottom layer. This is heated to 160–185°F (70–85°C) or more, but the hot water cannot rise by convection because its high salt content makes it much denser than the water above it. Very hot brine from the bottom of the pond is then piped through a tank containing a fluid with a low boiling point. This fluid vaporizes, expands, and is fed under pressure past a turbine. The spinning turbine drives a generator producing electricity, and the vapor enters a second tank, where it is cooled by pipes carrying water from the surface of the pond and back to it. The vapor condenses and is fed back into the first tank to be vaporized again, while the hot brine is fed back to the bottom of the pond.

If the electricity is used to separate salt water from freshwater, some of the salt that is produced can be used to replenish losses from the bottom of the pond. There are many sites suitable for salt-gradient solar ponds in most dry-climate countries. There is one in Texas, built by the Army Corps of Engineers, although the power it produces is used to pump brine into a storage lake, preventing it from flowing into the Red River, rather than for desalination. The biggest one in commercial operation is at Bhuj, in the Indian state of Gujarat. Its pond is 328 feet (100 m) long, 197 feet (60 m) wide, and 11.5 feet (3.5 m) deep. It is not used to desalinate water, however, but to supply hot water to the nearby Kutch Dairy.

Not far from the coast in many desert countries, there are shallow lakes or marshes lying at or just below sea level. Water evaporates rapidly from them and in many cases they are dry for at least part of the year. If seawater were pumped into them and then left to stand, evaporation would concentrate the salt to produce the dense bottom layer for a salt-gradient solar pond, onto which less salty water could be poured. This technology could supply fairly cheaply the energy needed to desalinate very large amounts of seawater.

For most of our history, removing the salt to make seawater drinkable was not practicable on a scale that is large enough to provide useful amounts of water. People had to make do with the freshwater that fell as rain, and if they lived in a dry climate, they learned to value water highly and use it sparingly. Now that is changing. Already desalination is supplying affordable drinking water to coastal communities in many countries. In years to come it may satisfy the needs of many more, and visiting aliens will no longer be puzzled at widespread scarcities of water on such a watery planet.

Water storage

Long ago, almost at the dawn of history, the people living close to the Tigris River constructed a huge dam of earth to control the flow of the river. A little while later another dam was built across the Nile, this time from rock. The Romans built many dams in North Africa and Italy and dams were also built in India and Sri Lanka. For people living in a climate with a dry season, during which little or no rain falls, or in places where the rainfall is always unreliable, building a dam is an obvious way to store water. In other places, heavy seasonal rains or the melting of snow near the source of a river can cause sudden floods that destroy crops and wash away homes. Again, a dam can hold back the floodwaters and release them a little at a time, so there is water for irrigation and other uses, and no flooding. Modern dams also generate electrical power.

People have always built dams and they build them still. Only archaeological traces remain of the most ancient dams, and the average age of the dams in use today is 35 years. In 2001 there were more than 45,000 functioning dams in more than 150 countries, and this figure counts only the larger examples, more than 50 feet (15.25 m) high. Together, these dams hold back about 1,500 cubic miles (6,248 km^3) of water. Every year, an average of 160–320 new large dams are completed. Half of all dams are built to supply water for irrigation. In the world as a whole, dam water irrigates approximately 200–268 million acres (81–108 million hectares) of land—between 30 and 40 percent of all the irrigated land in the world. One-third of all countries obtain more than half of their electricity supply from hydroelectric plants supplied by dams, and dams produce about 19 percent of all the world's electricity.

How big is a large dam?

Technically, a "large" dam is defined as one that is more than 492 feet (150 m) high, or that holds back more than 19.6 million cubic yards (15 million m^3) of water, or that forms a reservoir capable of containing 12 million acre-feet of water. This is enough water to cover 12 million acres (4.9 million ha) to a depth of one foot (30 cm). It is equal to 3,910 billion gallons (14,802 billion liters).

Some of the dams that are being built now or that were recently completed are very large indeed. When it is completed, the highest dam in the world will be the Rogun Dam, on the Vakhsh River, Tajikistan. It will measure 1,099 feet (335 m) from base to top. It is due to be completed in 2003 and it will have a generating capacity of 3.6 GW (gigawatts; 1 GW = 10^9 watts). The distance along the crest of the Yacyretá-Apipe Dam, on the Paraná River near the border between Argentina and Paraguay, is a little more than 43 miles (69 km). That dam was completed in 1998 and has a generating capacity of 12.6 GW. The crest of the Birecik Dam, on the Euphrates River in Turkey, is 1.56 miles (2.5 km) long.

New dams have also been constructed in the United States. In California, the Seven Oaks Dam on the Santa Ana River, completed in 1999, is nearly 1,000 yards (305 m) long, and Los Angeles and San Diego now receive some of their water from the reservoir behind the Domenigoni Valley Dam, completed in 1999. It can store 1.321 billion cubic yards (1.01 billion m³) of water, equal to 26.7 billion gallons (101 billion liters).

These are big, but they are small compared with the real giants. Lake Oahe, behind the Oahe Dam in South Dakota, holds 7,694 billion gallons (29,123 billion liters), and Lake Mead, behind the Hoover Dam in Nevada, holds 10,121 billion gallons (38,312 billion liters). Even this seems small beside the Volgograd Dam on the Volga River, in Russia. Its lake holds 15,328 billion gallons (58,023 billion liters), and the lake behind the Kariba Dam, on the Zambesi River between Zambia and Zimbabwe, holds 42,380,000 billion gallons (160,425,670 billion liters).

Historically, most dams have been built to make artificial lakes to store water, mainly for irrigation, but nowadays most double as hydro-electric power plants. Some water flows continuously from the reservoir and past turbines inside the dam itself, generating electricity and then entering the river downstream of the dam. The power output of such schemes can be very large. The Manwan Dam, for example, on the Lancang River (also called the Mekong) in China, generates 1.5 GW of power, an output comparable to the largest of modern nuclear or fossil-fuel plants.

How dams are made

The earliest dams were made from earth, a material that is readily available in the large quantities needed and that is also easy to move, because it can be carried in small loads. A valley would be sealed at the downstream end to make it fill with water. Many dams must have failed, sending huge volumes of water cascading across the lower ground downstream. Earth is still used and, although failure is still a risk with any dam, modern earth dams are safer than those built in the distant past, because engineers have learned a number of rules that must be observed if the dam is not to fail.

If water flows through or beneath the dam wall it will wash away enough material to make the entire structure collapse, so the dam must be watertight. If the earth cannot be packed tightly enough to achieve this, a modern earth dam has an impervious foundation and a waterproof internal core.

Water must not flow over the top of the dam. That, too, will wash away material and destroy the structure. Achieving this means studying the behavior of the river over several years. It is essential to know how much water the river carries at different times of year and the greatest volume of flow that is likely to be experienced. Then the dam can be built high enough to prevent waves ever washing over it, with a margin for safety between the top of the dam and the highest level the water is predicted to reach. This distance, between the highest water level and the top of the dam, is called the *freeboard*. Spillways, made on one or both sides of the dam, provide further protection by allowing surplus water to escape rather than overflowing the dam.

The shape of the dam is also important. As the diagram below shows, the walls should have a shallow slope. On the upstream side this spreads the force of the water over a larger surface area, thus protecting the structure from being battered until it fails. This strengthening is often increased by covering the surface with a layer of large, loose rocks, called *riprap*, to absorb some of the energy of the moving water. On the downstream side, the surface must be protected from rain. If not, in time the rain can wash away enough material to cause failure. The downstream surface can be protected by growing grass or other plants on it and these are most easily planted and managed if the slope is not too steep.

Eventually, the pressure of water on the upstream side will cause the earth of the dam to become saturated. Water will then begin to flow through the dam below a *seepage line*. Unless the rate of seepage is controlled, eventually the dam will be weakened and will fail in a catastrophic mudslide. Similarly, if the water level on the upstream side falls suddenly, water may not have time to drain from the saturated earth. Instead it will flow out rapidly, carrying earth with it, and cause a mudslide on the upstream side. Again, having a shallow slope helps, by reducing the risk of material slumping to the bottom. Some dams also have a drain, made from a layer of sand and gravel set into the impervious foundation beneath the

Earth dam

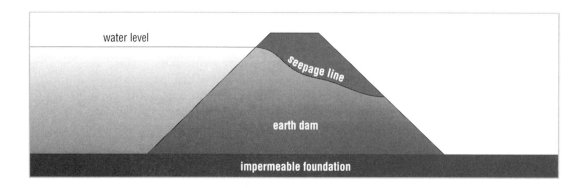

water level

seepage line

earth dam

impermeable foundation

dam near the downstream face. The drain carries away water seeping from the dam and the effect is to draw the seepage line back into the center of the dam, away from the downstream surface.

As dam construction developed, many earth dams came to be partly, and eventually completely, filled with rock and sealed by an outer skin of masonry. Other techniques were introduced and today there are many different ways to construct a dam. Engineers choose the one best suited to the site or design a dam incorporating elements from two or more basic types.

Damming a river is the most obvious way to make a large reservoir, but there is an alternative. Part of the river can be diverted along channels or pipes and taken into storage. The store can be outside the river valley through which the water was flowing before it was diverted, in a natural hollow or one excavated for the purpose.

At first, reservoirs were made to supply drinking water for humans and livestock. That is why the village ponds of Europe were dug. The provision of a reliable water supply to factories and homes is still important, but today most dam water is used to irrigate farm crops and generate electricity, and on some rivers, reservoirs are used to hold excess water that would otherwise cause flooding.

Drawbacks of dams

Reservoirs behind dams suffer from two serious drawbacks. Especially in low latitudes, they lose a substantial amount of water by evaporation from their huge surface. This can amount to several feet of water a year and, of course, the rate of loss is greatest during drought, when the air is dry and hot. Over much of Australia, the potential evaporation rate (see the section "Where the deserts are" on page 1) is greater than the annual rainfall and in some places it is very much greater. At Broken Hill, for example, the average annual rainfall is seven inches (178 mm), and the potential evaporation is 96 inches (2,438 mm). Evaporation losses are reduced in some reservoirs by pouring enough oil into the water for it to form a continuous layer one molecule thick over the entire surface, sealing the water from the air.

Sedimentation is the other problem. It shortens the life of all reservoirs, and some are built larger than would otherwise be necessary simply to allow for sedimentation.

All rivers carry soil particles of various sizes suspended in their water. The amount the river carries depends on its energy, which is determined by its rate of flow. A dam brings the water to a standstill. As it loses energy, the water also loses its capacity to carry silt and, small though they are, the particles sink to the bottom. There they accumulate as a layer of sediment that grows steadily thicker, raising the bottom of the reservoir and reducing the amount of water it can hold. The sediment can be removed by dredging, but this is usually too expensive and we have to accept that the capacity of any reservoir will decrease gradually until eventually the lake is too shallow to be much use.

Loss of land, homes, and antiquities

A reservoir is a lake, but a reservoir that is made by damming a river is not a natural lake. It occupies what was formerly dry land and most dry land is inhabited, or was inhabited in the past and contains important historic or archaeological sites. For this reason, the construction of dams and their associated reservoirs often causes serious social disruption and scientific concern.

The New China Dam in the Three Gorges region of the Chang Jiang (Yangtze River) in China, is due for final completion in 2009. When completed, the dam will be about 1.2 miles (1.9 km) long and the reservoir behind it will be 1,200 yards (1,098 m) wide and 370 miles (595 km) long. The project is meant to prevent the floods that have occurred throughout history and that kill untold numbers of people, to provide water where none was available previously, to increase the size of the local fishing industry, and to allow the expansion of industries that will provide much-needed employment. The valley is home to 750,000 people, however, and they are being relocated, most of them against their will. This is an extreme case, but most large reservoir projects cause similar problems. Even if no people live in the area to be flooded, it may nevertheless be of great importance to wildlife conservation.

It is never easy to balance the benefits a dam may bring against the adverse effects its construction will have. The World Commission on Dams (WCD), an international body supported by the United Nations Environment Program, has estimated that in the world as a whole, the construction of large dams that are planned or currently being built may displace between 40 million and 80 million people. Between 1950 and 1990, the dams that were built in India and China alone displaced some 26 million to 58 million people. People are not always consulted before work commences. The WCD found that of the 34 dams it studied in detail, local people participated in the decision making of only seven. It also found that the people whose lives are most severely disrupted are country-dwellers, many of whom are small farmers, members of ethnic minorities, and women.

The construction of the Aswân High Dam, completed in 1970 and said to have been the greatest building project in Egypt since the Pyramids, allowed water to fill Buheiret Nâsir (Lake Nasser), 310 miles (499 km) long and an average of six miles (9.6 km) wide. The lake inundated land where the pharaoh Ramses II (c. 1279–1213 B.C.E.) ordered the building of the temple of Abu Simbel, with four statues of him, each 65 feet (20 m) tall, flanking the entrance. Below the feet of one of the statues, there is a relief carving showing two images of the god Hapy, symbol of the annual Nile flood. The temple itself is carved into the sandstone cliff. Despite the lake, the temple and its statues were saved. They were cut from the cliff and moved to another site above the river, where they can still be seen. By regulating the flow of water and trapping silt, however, the dam has greatly reduced the flow of nutrients into the eastern

Mediterranean Sea. This has reduced fish catches to less than one-quarter of those before the dam was built.

The lake behind the Birecik Dam on the Euphrates was filled in June 2000, inundating the ancient Roman and Hellenistic twin cities of Seleucia and Apamea, together known as Zeugma—a Greek word that means "yoke." Zeugma bridged the river and was where the East and West Hemispheres met. It was of great historic importance—some scholars compare it with Pompeii—and archaeologists recovered as much as they could from the site before it disappeared, but it is now hidden. The cities are not necessarily destroyed, because many artifacts can survive beneath water and may even be protected by it. The proposed Ilisu Dam on the Tigris River threatens even more ancient sites, including Çatal Höyük, possibly the world's most ancient city, and Hasankeyf, believed to have been the home of one of the most important Kurdish dynastic families in medieval western Asia. So great has been the outcry over the effects of the Ilisu Dam—because of the number of people it would displace as well as the threat to antiquities—that the project may not proceed.

The issues are never simple. Water is essential for irrigation and for industrial use, and modern dams generate huge amounts of electricity. Together, these benefits allow agriculture and industry to expand, creating employment and raising standards of living. These benefits—more and better schools and hospitals, better homes, better nutrition—are shared by everyone, but the costs are not. The people forced to leave their homes and farms are often among the poorest and most disadvantaged in the region and dam construction marginalizes them still further. Years ago, large dams seemed entirely beneficial. Today the problems associated with them are recognized. This does not mean that no more dams will be built, for they bring genuine benefits. It does mean that in future much greater care must be taken to minimize the harmful consequences and to ensure that the people who will be affected are given a voice in planning their own futures.

Saving water

Most reservoirs provide a range of recreational facilities. Visitors can walk around them, picnic on their shores, and use the water itself for sailing and fishing. They become popular attractions. When a new reservoir is proposed, however, there is usually strong resistance to the scheme. People do not like to see familiar valleys flooded, and the construction itself causes considerable annoyance to people living in the area.

The immediate response is to propose that everyone economize. It is suggested that with a little care, we could manage perfectly well with the amount of water already available. More reservoirs are not really needed.

Showers, baths, leaking taps, and toilets

While this is an overstatement, and new reservoirs are certainly needed in some places, conserving water makes good sense. (The websites listed under Further Reading provide tips on ways to save water.) When you take a bath, for example, you probably use more than 30 gallons (136 liters) of water. Take a shower instead and you use much less water. With a regular showerhead, you will use about three to 10 gallons (14–45 liters) of water a minute. Of course, if your shower lasts more than three to 10 minutes, depending on the design of the showerhead, it will use more water than a bath in which you can soak for as long as you wish. If you like to spend longer in the shower you could use an economy head. Then you will really save water. It uses only two to 2.5 gallons (9–11 liters) a minute, giving you 12 to 15 minutes before the shower becomes less economical than the tub. If there are four people in a household and they each take one bath a day, in a week they will use a total of 840 gallons (3,819 liters) of water. If, instead, they take a five-minute shower using an economy showerhead, they will use 280–350 gallons (1,273–1,591 liters) a week. This is a considerable saving and, if the water supply is metered so you pay for the water you use, it also saves money.

Leaking taps are easy to fix and they can waste a surprisingly large amount of water. A constant drip seems small, but if a tap leaks one drop per second, in the course of a year it will drip away 2,500 gallons (11,365 liters).

Depending on how long ago it was made, a conventional toilet uses 3.5 to six gallons (16–27 liters) of water each time it is flushed. Again, savings are possible. A low-flow toilet, of the type available since 1994, uses 1.6 gallons (7.3 liters). Between them, a family of four flush the toilet an average of 20 times a day, so with a conventional toilet they use about 490–840 gallons (2,227–3,819 liters) of water a week. With a low-flow toilet this amount falls to about 224 gallons (1,018 liters).

Garden watering uses even larger amounts of water. Family households use an average of 100 gallons (455 liters) a day to water the garden. This demand can be reduced by collecting rainwater for garden watering, but during a drought the supply is soon exhausted. Some people use bathwater to water the garden. This also helps. With some ingenious plumbing, bathwater or water used to wash the dishes could be used to flush the toilet.

National consumption

The amount of water used varies from place to place. In New York City, each person uses about 220 gallons (1,000 liters) a day for all domestic purposes, the people of Phoenix each use about 260 gallons (1,182 liters) a day, but in Tucson they use only 160 gallons (727 liters). The demand in Tucson is lower than in other cities because its citizens are actively encouraged to save water by a range of measures, including the growing of native desert plants, which do not need watering, instead of lawn grasses, which do. There can be wide variations in consumption within a region. In 1985, consumption in Ancho, New Mexico, was about 54 gallons (245 liters) per person per day, but in Tyrone, New Mexico, it was 423 gallons (1,923 liters).

In the United States as a whole, each person uses an average of 183 gallons (832 liters) of water a day. Clearly, we could make do with less water and still have ample for drinking, preparing food, and cooking. These require no more than about 2 gallons (9 liters) a day for each person.

Water can be recycled, of course. After it has been used, it can be collected, purified, and returned to the supply (see the section "Water recycling and purification" on page 171). Even if the water is not considered safe for drinking, it can be made suitable for industrial use or crop irrigation.

Where the water goes

There is a big disparity between the 2,000 gallons (9,000 liters) a day required for all purposes—industrial and commercial as well as domestic—and the 183 or so used per person domestically. Most of this difference is accounted for by crop irrigation. Farms use about 81 percent of all the freshwater supplied in the United States, nearly all of it in the West, where water is most scarce. That is why many western cities now find themselves competing with farmers for water.

Industry uses about 8 percent of the freshwater supply. It takes about 400 gallons of water to extract and refine 1 gallon of gasoline (400 liters of water per liter of gasoline) and more than 50,000 gallons (227,300 liters) to make the automobile that burns it. Even making one soft drink can uses about one-third of a pint (0.2 liter) of water when the amount needed for mining and refining the metal are included, although almost all of this water is used for cooling and washing, so it can be recycled many times.

Despite its economical use, water is still being extracted in Tucson several times faster than the sources of that water are being recharged. The problem has been eased, but not solved. Using less water is not merely a good idea. It is essential. Unless we learn to irrigate crops more efficiently, increase the number of times industrial water is recycled, and use less at home, eventually shortages will become acute and water rationing, for at least part of most years, will be inevitable.

Will climate change bring more droughts?

Climates are changing constantly, and at various times in the past they have been very different from those we experience today. During the most recent ice age, a thick ice sheet covered much of the land north of about latitude 50° N and the climate around what is now Chicago was much like the present climate of central Greenland. That ice age ended about 10,000 years ago, but there were many earlier ones. In medieval times, northern Europe and North America were warmer than they had been before or than they were later. That was called the medieval warm period. It was the time when Scandinavian settlers colonized Greenland and grew crops there. Then, after 1300, the weather became colder during a period called the "Little Ice Age." Temperatures did not start to rise again until the 18th century and the warming continued through the 19th century and until early in the 20th century. Today scientists believe the average air temperature over the whole world is rising. Since about 1880 it is believed to have increased by about 1°F (0.6°C).

It has not been a steady warming. Temperatures rose quite rapidly from the 1920s until about 1940, then fell from about 1940 until around 1980. The fall was slight, and smaller than the amount by which they had risen before 1940. Many climatologists believe they have risen sharply since 1980, making climates today warmer than those of the 18th and 19th centuries and possibly warmer than they have been at any time during the preceding thousand years.

Temperature records

Temperatures are recorded from measurements made at selected surface weather stations. Temperatures are also measured directly by instruments carried aloft by weather balloons (called *radiosondes*), and since 1979 orbiting satellites have also monitored temperatures. Temperatures are measured indirectly by radiosonde pressure measurements made at particular altitudes. If scientists know the atmospheric pressure at a particular altitude, they can calculate the temperature at that altitude very accurately. The three sets of balloon and satellite measurements show no significant temperature change and neither do the records from some surface stations. This does not necessarily mean that air near the surface is not warming, but it does suggest that the warming affects only the lowest part of the atmosphere and, perhaps, that the warming indicated by surface measurements may be a little too high. It seems likely that some warming has occurred—although some climate scientists dispute that there has been any overall increase in temperature since 1980, except for the remarkably warm year of 1998 that was caused by an unusually strong El Niño (see the section "El Niño and La Niña" on page 64).

The warming is not spread evenly, but this is not to be expected with a system as complex as the global climate. Arctic regions, north of 70° latitude, were colder from 1960 to 1986 than they had been between 1931 and 1960. The Antarctic Peninsula has warmed much more than most other parts of the world, but the interior of Antarctica has been growing colder for several decades. Glaciers are retreating in many places, but those in New Zealand and southern Scandinavia are advancing. Arctic sea ice has grown thinner, but this is probably due to an acceleration of the warm ocean current flowing beneath the ice rather than to a rise in air temperature. There have been mild winters in Europe during the 1990s, but these are probably due to a cyclical change in the distribution of pressure, called the *North Atlantic Oscillation*, that affects the vigor of weather systems crossing the ocean—and also accelerates the currents flowing into the Arctic. Sea levels are rising by an average 0.06 inch (1.5 mm) a year, but the rise is not happening everywhere and in any case its measurement in complicated. This is because in some places the height of the land is rising or falling due to movements of Earth's crust. Scandinavia and Scotland are rising, for example, as they rebound following the removal of the weight of the ice sheets that pressed them down during the ice age.

Blackbody radiation

Climate scientists believe that there is a link between average temperatures and the atmospheric concentration of certain gases and particles. Incoming solar radiation is predominantly at short wavelengths (see the box on page 192). The atmosphere is transparent to short-wave radiation. This passes through the air like light through a window. The radiation warms the surface.

When a body is warmer than its surroundings—in the case of a star or planet, warmer than its region of space—it emits radiation at a wavelength that is inversely proportional to its temperature. That is to say, the hotter the body the shorter the wavelength of its radiation. A body that absorbs all the radiation falling on it and then re-radiates all of that energy but at a longer wavelength is called a *blackbody*, and the radiation it emits is *blackbody radiation*. There is no such thing as a perfect blackbody, but Earth is close to being one.

Blackbody radiation emitted by Earth radiates back into space. The radiation from the surface is at long wavelengths.

The enhanced greenhouse effect

Air is not completely transparent to long-wave radiation. Molecules of certain gases absorb it. They then radiate it, but in all directions, and some of the radiation warms other gas molecules. This warms the atmosphere itself. It is rather like a greenhouse, which allows (short-wave) light to enter, but prevents (long-wave) radiant heat from leaving, so the air inside the greenhouse is warmer than the air outside. (In fact, this is slightly misleading. The interior of a greenhouse is warm mainly because the building prevents air inside from mixing with air outside.)

This is often called the *greenhouse effect*, but is more properly known as the *enhanced greenhouse effect*. This is because the gases, especially carbon

The solar spectrum

Light, radiant heat, gamma rays, X rays, and radio waves are all forms of electromagnetic radiation. This radiation travels as waves at the speed of light. The various forms differ in their wavelengths, which is the distance between one wave crest and the next. The shorter the wavelength, the more energy the radiation has. A range of wavelengths is called a *spectrum*. The Sun emits electromagnetic radiation at all wavelengths, so its spectrum is wide. The diagram shows how solar radiation is divided into the types of radiation forming the solar spectrum.

Gamma rays are the most energetic form of radiation, with wavelengths of 10^{-10}–10^{-14} μm (a micron, μm, is one-millionth of a meter, or about 0.00004 inch; 10^{-10} is 0.0000000001). Next come X rays, with wavelengths of 10^{-5}–10^{-3} μm. The Sun emits gamma and X radiation, but all of it is absorbed high in Earth's atmosphere and none reaches the surface. Ultraviolet (UV) radiation is at wavelengths of 0.004-4 μm; the shorter wavelengths, below 0.2 μm, are absorbed in the atmosphere but longer wavelengths reach the surface.

Visible light has wavelengths of 0.4-0.7 μm, infrared radiation 0.8 μm–1 mm, microwaves 1 mm–30 cm, and radio waves have wavelengths up to 100 km (62 miles).

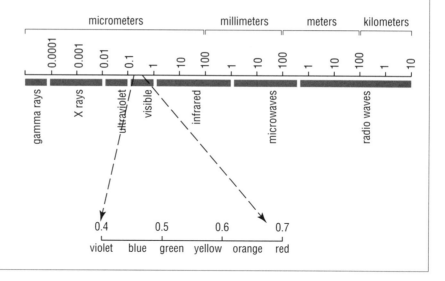

The solar spectrum

dioxide but also methane, nitrous oxide, and ozone, are present naturally in the air and they, together with water vapor, the most powerful *greenhouse gas* of all, exert a natural warming, or greenhouse, effect. If there were no natural greenhouse effect, the global average surface temperature would be –4°F (–20°C), rather than the actual average temperature of 59°F (15°C).

The present concern is that the burning of coal, oil, and gas, the clearing of forests, and certain farming practices add to the concentration of these greenhouse gases. Our activities may therefore enhance the natural greenhouse effect. CFCs (chlorofluorocarbons) also have a warming effect, and certain particles, including soot, also absorb long-wave radiation and warm the air. Other particles, especially of sulfur dioxide, reflect incoming short-wave radiation. That has a cooling effect.

Scientists of the Intergovernmental Panel on Climate Change (IPCC) have calculated that if the concentration of these greenhouse gases were to double, then average temperatures would rise between 2.5°F and 10.4°F (1.4–5.8°C) in the period from 1990 to 2100. The computer models used to reach this conclusion are extremely complicated, but the very wide range in the figures—a difference of 7.9°F (4.4°C) between the high and low temperatures—indicates the extent of the scientific uncertainty. This arises from the need to include many assumptions about future economic and technological development, population growth, and human behavior, as well as about the extent of the cooling effect of particles. In years to come the computer models will improve, but at present the projections should be treated with considerable caution.

What would the effects be?

A general warming over the entire world might be expected to result in a shift of the present climate belts. The equatorial and tropical belts would expand and the temperate regions would be pushed into higher latitudes. Tundra and polar climates would cover a smaller area.

The reality is much more complicated, however. Warmer air would mean an increase in the evaporation of water. That would cool the water surface, by removing from it the latent heat of evaporation (see the box on page 44, "Latent heat and dew point" in the section "Precipitation, evaporation, sublimation, deposition, and ablation"), but water vapor is a powerful greenhouse gas, accounting for almost all of the natural greenhouse effect. More atmospheric water vapor would have a warming effect. Rising air cools, however, so more clouds would form, especially in the Tropics where the oceans cover a larger proportion of the surface than they do in temperate latitudes. This would also have a warming effect, because of the release of latent heat as the vapor condensed, but at the same time a cooling effect, because low-level clouds reflect incoming sunlight. If cloud cover increases—and cloudiness has increased over recent decades—precipitation would increase, carrying cold air downward. High-level clouds, made from ice crystals, reflect much less sunlight, however, because they are so thin, but they do absorb long-wave radiation. Consequently, clouds such as cirrus and cirrostratus warm the atmosphere. What is more, different regions would experience different kinds of change.

Clearly it is very difficult to calculate the effects of warming, but it seems likely that air temperatures would increase more over land than over the oceans. Precipitation would increase in high latitudes and in the areas affected by the Asian monsoons (see the section "Monsoons" on page 147). Winter precipitation would increase in middle latitudes, but summers would be drier in some parts of the interior of continents.

Warming would occur mainly in high latitudes. This is because of the balance between water vapor and carbon dioxide. Air over the Tropics is always moist, so there the greenhouse effect is already strong. Adding more carbon dioxide will have a smaller effect than it would in drier air, and much of the tropical greenhouse effect is lost, because tropical air rises by convection to form big clouds that reflect radiation. More carbon dioxide will have the biggest greenhouse effect in the coldest, driest air. This is the air that contains the least water vapor and therefore experiences the smallest natural greenhouse effect. The coldest, driest air is found in winter over northwestern North America and northern Siberia. That is where the greatest warming should occur, and, indeed, that is what has been observed.

With increased precipitation, falling there as snow, the ice sheets might thicken rather than melt as some people have feared. The West Antarctic ice sheet and parts (but not all) of the Greenland ice sheet appear to be thickening. Sea levels are already rising, because the oceans are expanding as they warm, but a sustained thickening of the ice sheets would prevent them from rising very far.

More droughts or fewer?

Higher temperatures mean that more water vapor will evaporate; if the air contains more water vapor, then there will be more cloud; and if there is more cloud, then there will be more rain and snow. It appears that droughts should become less frequent.

Unfortunately, it is not so simple. Precipitation increased during the 20th century between 30° N and 85° N, and by a smaller amount between the equator and 55° S. The increase was most marked in Europe and Scandinavia—during the latter part of the century, due to the North Atlantic Oscillation—and in Australia. Since the late 1960s, however, conditions have been drier than average over all of Africa south of the Sahara. There has been no overall change in the monsoon rains.

What matters, though, is not precipitation alone, but the ratio of precipitation to evaporation. If the potential evaporation—the amount of water that would evaporate from an open water surface—exceeds the amount of precipitation, then soils will become drier. All of the precipitation will evaporate rapidly, and droughts will become more common. Potential evaporation depends on the temperature, and so the extent of any temperature rise becomes critical, but so does the pattern. If the air grows warmer during the day, then the temperature rise will affect air that is already warm and there will be a large increase in potential evaporation. If the rise in temperature occurs during the night, on the other hand, it will affect relatively cool air and so there will be less evaporation. Two-thirds of the observed warming has occurred at night and is due mainly to increased cloudiness. Clouds reduce the amount of heat radiated from the surface at night—so the warming is, in fact, a reduction in the amount of night-time cooling. This means that the warming results more from raising minimum temperatures than from raising maximum temperatures, and that the temperature difference has decreased between day and night and summer and winter. If this trend continues, combined with the fact that warming occurs mainly in high latitudes in winter, droughts are likely to become less frequent in most places.

How reliable are the predictions?

The predictions are much less certain than they may seem. Although climate scientists are convinced that the addition of greenhouse gases to the atmosphere must have a warming effect, there is considerable doubt about the extent of that effect. Climates change naturally, and if the reported warming has actually occurred, then part of it is likely to be entirely natural and nothing to do with our activities. Part of it is certainly because the Sun has been very active in recent years, so it has been emitting more radiation. There might be other explanations for the rise in temperature and, despite the care with which they have been made, the measurements on which the observed changes are based might be inaccurate. It is extremely difficult to measure temperature changes accurately to fractions of a degree over the whole world and to compare these with long-term averages. The measurements must allow a margin for error, and if the temperature rise is genuine, it could be part of a natural variation operating over decades.

The influence of the oceans in transporting heat away from the equator is not completely understood, and the computer models scientists use to study the global climate are unable to include details about the formation of clouds and local weather systems.

As a further complication, the fate of some 20 percent of the carbon dioxide being released into the air is unknown. It neither accumulates in the air nor dissolves in the oceans. No one knows what happens to it, although plants are probably absorbing some of it, and growing faster as a result, because it acts like a fertilizer. The area of forest has been increasing rapidly in most temperate regions. That will absorb some of the carbon, and the growing season has become a few days longer—due to shorter winters—so there is more plant growth overall. But the mystery of the missing carbon is not fully explained.

There are other uncertainties. From the 1940s to the 1970s carbon dioxide was accumulating in the atmosphere faster than at any time before, yet temperatures were falling. Perhaps the fall was due to a time lag in the atmospheric response, or to the even faster accumulation of atmospheric particles from factories that had not then installed equipment to reduce the pollution they caused, but no one can be sure. Nor can we realistically compare changes being observed now with changes that took place in the past, because we do not have enough reliable records. It is known, however, not only that climate does change, but that the amount by which it changes also varies.

There is a reliable record of one warm period. During the 1530s, the summers were unusually warm and dry. People might well have thought the climate was growing steadily warmer. From 1536 to 1539 the English harvests were so good that grain prices fell, and in 1540 there was drought from February until the middle of September. Cherries ripened by the end of May, and the cereal harvest was early as well as abundant, although cattle died from thirst when streams and wells ran dry. Then the weather changed. There was severely cold weather early in 1541 and, 20 years later, the winter of 1564–65 was the harshest for centuries. People played football on the frozen Thames in London. The severe 1564–65 winter heralded the onset of the coldest part of the Little Ice Age.

Doubts are justified, but they do not provide grounds for complacency. Climate change and the enhanced greenhouse effect are the subjects of intense scientific research and although much remains to be learned, so far the results support the idea that by releasing greenhouse gases, we may trigger a general climatic warming.

Clearly we should take the calculations seriously, and if there are practicable ways to reduce the amounts of greenhouse gases that we release into the air, we should pursue them. If we really are changing the climates of the world, it would be unwise to continue doing so, because the outcome might be disruptive in ways that at present we cannot foresee.

Even if the average temperature does not change, or changes only very slightly, droughts might nevertheless become more frequent. We have reliable records of climate for little more than 100 years, but scientists are able to study past climates, using information they obtain from tree rings and cores of ice drilled from the Greenland and Antarctic ice sheets. These show that the droughts of recent times have been neither so severe nor so prolonged as some droughts in the past. There was a "megadrought" in the United States in the 13th century, for example, and there were two more between the 13th and 16th centuries. All of these were much worse than the Dust Bowl drought. Droughts of this kind could happen again. It would be well to plan now for how we might survive them.

Bibliography and Further Reading

"Abu Simbel." Available on-line. URL: www.memphis.edu/egypt/abusimbe.htm. Last modified January 23, 1996. Downloaded October 25, 2002.

Allaby, Michael. *Deserts*. New York: Facts On File, 2000.

———. *Encyclopedia of Weather and Climate*. 2 vols. New York: Facts On File, 2001.

———. *Basics of Environmental Science*, 2d ed. New York: Routledge, 2000.

———. *Elements: Water*. New York: Facts On File, 1992.

"Alternative Wastewater Treatment Overview." Available on-line. URL: www.waterrecycling.com/philosophy.htm. Downloaded October 25, 2002.

American Institute of Preventive Medicine. "First Aid for Heat Exhaustion and Heat Stroke." Available on-line. URL: www.healthy.net/asp/templates/article.asp?PageType=article&ID=1291. Downloaded October 23, 2002.

American Water and Energy Savers. "Save Water 49 Ways." Available on-line. URL: www.americanwater.com/49ways.htm. Last modified April 3, 2002.

American Water Works Association. "Stats On Tap." Available on-line. URL: 12.151.62.61/Advocacy/pressroom/statswp5.cfm. Downloaded October 25, 2002.

"Ancient Pueblo Peoples Page." El Centro College History Department. Available on-line. URL: pw1.net.com/~wandaron/pueblos.html. Downloaded October 23, 2002.

Anderson, Donald M. "The Harmful Algae." Available on-line. URL: www.redtide.whoi.edu/hab/. Revised July 17, 2002.

Asmal, Kader. "Notes from the Chair." *United Nations Chronicle*, 2001. Available on-line. URL: www.un.org/Pubs/chronicle/2001/issue3/0103p50.html. Downloaded October 25, 2002.

"Aztec Floating Gardens." Bradley Hydroponics. Available on-line. URL: www.hydrogarden.com/class1/aztec.htm. Updated November 14, 1998.

Barry, Roger G. and Richard J. Chorley. *Atmosphere, Weather & Climate*, 7th ed. New York: Routledge, 1998.

Baumann, Paul. *Flood Analysis*. Available on-line. URL: www.oneonta.edu/faculty/baumannpr/geosat2/Flood_Management/FLOOD_MANAGEMENT.htm.

Baur, Jörg, and Jochen Rudolph. "Water Facts and Findings on Large Dams as Pulled from the Report of the World Commission on Dams." *D+C Development and Cooperation*, no. 2 (March/April 2001). Deutsche Stiftung Für internationale Entwicklung. Available on-line. URL: www.dse.de/zeitschr/de201-4.htm. Downloaded October 25, 2002.

"The Bedouin: Culture in Transition." Geographia, 1998. Available on-line. URL: www.geographia.com/egypt/sinai/bedouin.htm. Downloaded October 23, 2002.

"Bhuj Solar Pond." Available on-line. URL: www.terin.org/case/bhuj.htm. Updated July 2000.

Boeckner, Linda, and Kay McKinzie. "Water:The Nutrient." NebGuide. Lincoln: Institute of Agriculture and Natural Resources, University of Nebraska. Available online. URL: www.ianr.unl.edu/pubs/foods/g918.htm. February 1997.

Brewer, Richard. *The Science of Ecology*, 2d ed. Ft. Worth; Tex.: Saunders College Publishing and Harcourt Brace College Publishers, 1994.

Campbell, Neil A. *Biology*, 3d ed. Redwood City, Calif.: The Benjamin/Cummings Publishing Co., Inc., 1993.

Cane, Mark A. "ENSO and Its Prediction: How Well Can We Forecast It?" Available on-line. URL: www.brad.ac.uk/research/ijas/ijasno2/cane.html. Downloaded October 23, 2002.

"Capillarity of Soil." Available on-line. URL: www.geocities.com/CapeCanaveral/Hall/1410/lab-Soil-0.5.html. Downloaded October 24, 2002.

Climate Prediction Center/NCEP. "El Niño/Southern Oscillation (ENSO) Diagnostic Discussion." Available on-line. URL: www.cpc.ncep.noaa.gov/products/analysis_monitoring/enso_advisory/. Downloaded October 10, 2002.

Crossley, Phill. "Xochimilco: Don't Float by the Gardens." Available on-line. URL: www.planeta.com/planeta/95/0895chinampa.html. August 1995.

"Desalination—Producing Potable Water." Available on-line URL: resources.ca. gov/ocean/97Agenda/Chap5Desal.htm. Downloaded October 25, 2002.

Dollar, Tom. "The Sonoran Desert Heart." In *Wilderness Areas*. Available on-line. URL: www.oneworldjourneys.com/sonoran/natural_essay.html. Downloaded October 23, 2002.

"Dry Farming." Available on-line. URL: www.rootsweb.com/~coyuma/data/souvenir/farm.htm. Downloaded October 24, 2002.

"The Dust Bowl." Available on-line. URL: www.usd.edu/anth/epa/dust.html. Downloaded October 24, 2002.

Ellis, Terry. "Dry Farming in Utah." Available on-line. URL: www.media.utah.edu/UHE/d/DRYFARM.html. Downloaded October 24, 2002.

El-Sayed, Sayed, and Gert L. van Dijken. "The southeastern Mediterranean ecosystem revisited: Thirty years after the construction of the Aswam High Dam." *Quarterdeck*, 3.1. Available on-line. URL: www-ocean.tamu.edu/Quarterdeck/QD3.1/Elsayed.html. Updated July 24, 1995.

"Engineers dig deepest well in Air Force history." Available on-line. URL: www.af.mil/news/Jul1999/n19990712_991331.html. July 12, 1999.

"The ENSO Signal." Available on-line. URL: www.esig.ucar.edu/signal/17/articles.html. Issue 17, May 2001.

"Facts about Antarctica." Available on-line. URL: ast.leeds.ac.uk/haverah/spaseman/faq.shtml. Downloaded October 23, 2002.

Food and Agriculture Organization of the United Nations. Available on-line. URL: www.fao.org/. Downloaded October 24, 2002.

———. "Sahel Weather and Crop Situation." Available on-line. URL: www.fao.org/WAICENT/faoinfo/economic/giews/english/esahel/sahtoc.htm. Downloaded October 24, 2002.

Foth, H.D. *Fundamentals of Soil Science*, 8th ed. New York: John Wiley, 1991.

Geerts, B., and M. Wheeler. "The Madden-Julian Oscillation." Available on-line. URL: www-das.uwyo.edu/~geerts/cwx/notes/chap12/mjo.html. May 1998.

"Harmful Algal Bloom Forecasting Project." Available on-line. URL: www.csc.noaa.gov/crs/habf/. Updated August 28, 2002.

Hayes, William A., and Fenster, C. R. "Understanding Wind Erosion And Its Control." Lincoln: Cooperative Extension, Institute of Agriculture and Natural Resources, University of Nebraska. Available on-line. URL: www.ianr.unl.edu/pubs/soil/g474.htm. August 1996.

Henderson-Sellers, Ann, and Peter J. Robinson, *Contemporary Climatology*, Harlow, U.K., Longman, 1986.

Henry, Michael. "About Red Tide . . ." Mote Marine Laboratory. Available on-line. URL: www.marinelab.sarasota.fl.us/~mhenry/WREDTIDE.phtml. Updated July 3, 2001.

"Himalayan Ice Reveals Climate Warming, Catastrophic Drought." Columbus: Ohio State University. Available on-line. URL: www.acs.ohio-state.edu/units/research/archive/monsoon.htm. Downloaded October 24, 2002.

"The History of Dry-Farming". Available on-line. URL: www.soilandhealth.org/01aglibrary/010102/01010217.html. A brief account of historical examples of dry farming from around the world.

"History of the Dustbowl." Available on-line. URL: www.ultranet.com/~gregjonz/dust/dustbowl.htm. Downloaded October 24, 2002.

"History of Rogun Dam." CISRG Database. Available on-line. URL: www.cadvision.com/retom/rogun.htm. Downloaded October 25, 2002.

"Home Water Saving Tips." Available on-line. URL: www.mwra.state.ma.us/water/html/watsav.htm. Downloaded October 25, 2002.

Hope, Nicholas. "Should the World Bank Fund Large Dams?" Available on-line. URL: www.stanford.edu/~armin/hb145/may7.html. May 7, 2001.

Houghton, J.T., Y. Ding, D. J. Griggs, M. Noguer, P. J. van der Linden, X. Dai, K. Maskell, and C. A. Johnson. *Climate Change 2001: The Scientific Basis.* Cambridge; U.K.: Cambridge University Press for the Intergovernmental Panel on Climate Change, 2001.

"Hyponatremia Information." Reprinted from *Runner's World Daily.* Available on-line. URL: www.detnow.com/healthyliving/reference/hyponatremia.html. Downloaded October 24, 2002.

Idso, Graig D. and Keith E. Idso. "There Has Been No Global Warming for the Past 70 Years", *World Climate Report,* 13, July 2000. www.co2science.org/edit/v3_edit/v3n13edit.htm.

"The Indian Monsoon." Available on-line. URL: yang.gmu.edu/~yang/nasacd/www/indian_monsoon.html. Updated October 1, 1997.

"In the Beginning . . . The Great Fire of London—1666." London Fire and Civil Defence Authority in association with AngliaCampus. Available on-line. URL: www.angliacampus.com/education/fire/london/history/greatfir.htm. Downloaded October 24, 2002.

"Introduction to the Dinoflagellata." Available on-line. URL: www.ucmp.berkeley.edu/protista/dinoflagellata.html. Downloaded October 25, 2002.

"Inuit/Eskimo." Available on-line. URL: www.arts.uwaterloo.ca/ANTHRO/rwpark/ArcticArchStuff/Inuit.html. Updated March 1999.

"Inuit Tapiriit Kanatami." Available on-line. URL: www.tapirisat.ca/. Downloaded October 23, 2002.

"ITAIPU Binacional." International Research Institute for Climate Prediction. Available on-line. URL: iri.columbia.edu/application/sector/water/BRAZIL/itaipu.html. Downloaded October 25, 2002.

"ITAIPU Binacional: A Binational Hydroelectric Power Plant." Available on-line. URL: www.sovereign-publications.com/itaipu.htm. Last modified November 14, 2000.

"Jet Stream Analyses and Forecasts at 300 mb." Available on-line. URL: squall.sfsu.edu/crws/jetstream.html. Downloaded October 23, 2002.

Kitchen, Willy and Maggie Ronayne. "The Ilisu Dam in Southeast Turkey: archaeology at risk". *Antiquity,* vol. 75 (2001), 37–8. Available on-line. URL: intarch.ac.uk/antiquity/kitchen.html. Downloaded October 25, 2002.

Knauss, John A. *Introduction to Physical Oceanography,* 2d ed. Upper Saddle River, N.J.: Prentice Hall, 1997.

Lamb, H.H. *Climate, History and the Modern World,* 2d ed. New York: Routledge, 1995.

"Landscape Watering Advice." Metropolitan Domestic Water Improvement District, Tucson, Arizona. Available on-line. URL: www.metrowater.com/wateradvice.htm. Downloaded October 25, 2002.

"Land Use History of the Colorado Plateau—The Anasazi or 'Ancient Pueblo'." Available on-line. URL: www.cpluhna.nau.edu/People/anasazi.htm. Downloaded October 23, 2002.

Lomborg, Bjørn. *The Skeptical Environmentalist.* Cambridge, U.K.: Cambridge University Press, 2001.

McCall, Jim. "The Great Fire of London." Available on-line. URL: www.jmccall.demon.co.uk/history/page2.htm. Downloaded October 24, 2002.

McIlveen, Robin. *Fundamentals of Weather and Climate.* London: Chapman & Hall, 1992.

Maryland Department of the Environment. "Water Conservation: Maryland." Available on-line. URL: www.mde.state.md.us/Programs/WaterPrograms/Water_Conservation/index.asp. Downloaded October 25, 2002.

"Mass Exodus from the Plains." Available on-line. URL: www.pbs.org/wgbh/amex/dustbowl/peopleevents/pandeAMEX08.html. Downloaded October 24, 2002.

Michaels, Patrick J., and Robert C. Balling, Jr. *The Satanic Gases: Clearing the Air about Global Warming.* Washington, D.C.: Cato Institute, 2000.

The Missing Carbon Sink. Woods Hole Research Institute. Available on-line. www.whrc.org/science/carbon/missingc.htm.

Moore, David M., ed. *Green Planet.* Cambridge, U.K.: Cambridge University Press, 1982.

Morrison, David. "Canadian Inuit History." Canadian Museum of Civilization Corporation. Available on-line. URL: www.civilization.ca/educat/oracle/modules/dmorrison/page01_e.html. September 27, 2001.

National Atmospheric and Oceanic Administration. "Impacts of El Niño and Benefits of El Niño Prediction." Available on-line. URL: www.pmel.noaa.gov/tao/elnino/impacts.html. Spring 1994.

National Drought Mitigation Center, University of Nebraska—Lincoln. Available on-line. URL: drought.unl.edu/. Downloaded October 24, 2002.

National Science Foundation, Office of Polar Programs. "Amundsen—Scott South Pole Station." Available on-line. URL: www.nsf.gov/od/opp/support/southp.htm.

National Tourist Board of Greenland. "Greenland Tourism." Available on-line. URL: www.greenland-guide.dk/gt/default.htm. Downloaded October 23, 2002.

Oliver, John E., and John J. Hidore. *Climatology: An Atmospheric Science,* 2d ed. Upper Saddle River, N.J.: Prentice Hall, 2002.

Phillips, G., E. Makaudze, Leonard Unganai, J. Makadho, and M. A. Cane. "Current and Potential Use of Climate Forecasts for Farm Management in Zimbabwe." Available on-line. URL: www.ogp.noaa.gov/mpe/csi/econhd/fy99/phillips99.htm. Downloaded October 23, 2002.

"Qaanaaq." Available on-line. URL: www.greenland-guide.dk/reg-qaanaaq.htm and www.geocities.com/TheTropics/Resort/9292/uspage2.html. Both downloaded October 23, 2002.

"Reports of Algal Blooms." Available on-line. URL: www.state.me.us/dep/blwq/doclake/repbloom.htm. Updated September 12, 2002.

Royal Embassy of Saudi Arabia, Washington, D.C. "Makkah and the Holy Mosque." Available on-line. URL: www.saudiembassy.net/profile/islam/islam_makkah.html. Downloaded October 23, 2002.

Ruddiman, William F. *Earth's Climate, Past and Future.* New York: W. H. Freeman and Co., 2001.

"Sahel." Available on-line. URL: www.pbs.org/wnet/africa/explore/sahel/sahel_overview_lo.html. Downloaded October 24, 2002.

"Sahel Regional Program." East Lansing: Michigan State University. Available on-line. URL: www.aec.msu.edu/agecon/fs2/sahel/. Downloaded October 24, 2002.

"Salt and the Ultraendurance Athlete." Available on-line. URL: www.rice.edu/~jenky/sports/salt.html. Downloaded October 24, 2002.

Schneider, Stephen H., ed. *Encyclopedia of Climate and Weather.* 2 vols. New York: Oxford University Press, 1996.

"Seven Oaks Dam Project." Available on-line. URL: www.co.san-bernadino.ca.us/flood/dampage.htm. Downloaded October 25, 2002.

Smith, Frank E."Africa, to 1500." Available on-line. URL: www.fsmitha.com/h3/h15-af.htm. Downloaded October 24, 2002.

"Solar Ponds for Trapping Solar Energy." Available on-line. URL: edugreen.teri.res.in/explore/renew/pond.htm. Downloaded October 25, 2002.

"State of the Coastal Environment: Harmful Algal Blooms." Available on-line. URL: state-of-coast.noaa.gov/bulletins/html/hab_14/case.html. Downloaded October 25, 2002.

"Summary of the Discussion on Desalination." Available on-line. URL: www.commonwealthknowledge.net/Desalntn/sumdsion.htm. Downloaded October 25, 2002.

Taylor, George H., and Chad Southards. "Long-term Climate Trends and Salmon Population." Available on-line. URL:www.ocs.orst.edu/reports/climate_fish.html. April 1997.

Texas Water Development Board. "The Drought in Perspective 1996–1998." Available on-line. URL: http://www.twdb.state.tx.us/data/drought/DroughtinPerspective.htm. Updated August 8, 2002.

"Three Gorges Dam Project." ChinaOnline. Available on-line. URL: www.chinaonline.com/refer/ministry_profiles/threegorgesdam.asp. Updated October 3, 2000.

Timeline of The Dust Bowl. Available on-line. URL: www.pbs.org/wgbh/amex/dustbowl/timeline/.

"Tips to Prevent Heat Exhaustion." *Apples For Health*, vol. 1, #12, August 20, 1999. Available on-line. URL: www.applesforhealth.com/heatexhaust1.html.

Todd, Mitchell. "Sahel standardized rainfall index (20-8N, 20W-10E) 1898–June 2001." Available on-line. URL: tao.atmos.washington.edu/data_sets/sahel/. May 2002.

"Toxic Algal Blooms—A Sign of Rivers Under Stress." Available on-line. URL: www.science.org.au/nova/017/017key.htm. Posted August 1997.

"The Tundra." Available on-line. URL: www.runet.edu/~swoodwar/CLASSES/GEOG235/biomes/tundra/tundra.html. September 30, 1996.

"Tundra: The Not-So Barren Land." Available on-line. URL: www.ucmp.berkeley.edu/glossary/gloss5/biome/tundra.html.

United Nations Food and Agriculture Organization. "Yemen." Available on-line. URL: www.fao.org/ag/ag1/aglw/aquastat/countries/yemen.index.stm. Downloaded October 23, 2002.

United States Dept. of Agriculture Forest Service. "American Semidesert and Desert Province." Available on-line. URL: www.fs.fed.us/colorimagemap/images/322.html. Downloaded October 23, 2002.

United States Environmental Protection Agency. "How We Use Water In These United States." Available on-line. URL: www.epa.gov/OW/you/chap1.html. Updated June 7, 2002.

———. "Water Efficiency Measures for Industry." Office of Wastewater Management. Available on-line. URL: www.epa.gov/owm/water-efficiency/industip.htm. Updated June 28, 2002.

———. "Water Recycling and Reuse: The Environmental Benefits." Available on-line URL: www.epa.gov/region9/water/recycling/. Downloaded October 25, 2002.

United States Geological Survey. "Drought Watch: Definitions of Drought." Available on-line. URL: md.water.usgs.gov/drought/define.html. Updated June 17, 2000.

Visbeck, Martin. "North Atlantic Oscillation." Available on-line. URL: www.1deo.columbia.edu/~visbeck/nao/presentation/html/img0.htm.

"Vostok Station." Available on-line. URL: www.newzeal.com/theme/bases/Russia/Vostok.htm. Downloaded October 23, 2002.

"Water Dynamics," in *Ecosystem Function: Water.* Available on-line. URL: www.stanford.edu/~dmenge/dirt/ecofunctions/water.html. Downloaded October 24, 2002.

Weier, John. "El Niño's Extended Family." Available on-line. URL: earthobservatory.nasa.gov/Study/Oscillations/.November 1999.

"What Is Drought? Understanding and Defining Drought." National Drought Mitigation Center. Available on-line. URL: drought.unl.edu/whatis/concept.htm. Downloaded October 24, 2002.

Williams, Sara. "Soil Texture: From Sand to Clay." Available on-line. URL: www.ag.usask.ca/cofa/departments/hort/hortinfo/misc/soil.html. Downloaded October 24, 2002.

"Wind Erosion Simulation Models." Available on-line. URL: www.weru.ksu.edu/weps.html. Downloaded October 24, 2002.

"World Bank Lending for Large Dams: A Preliminary Review of Impacts." World Bank, Operations Evaluation Department, September 1, 1996. Available on-line. URL: wbln0018.worldbank.org/oed/oeddoclib.nsf/3ff836dc39b23cef85256885007b956bb68e3aeed5d12a4852567f5005d8d95?OpenDocument. Downloaded October 25, 2002.

World Health Organization."The Global Water Supply and Sanitation Assessment 2000 Report." Available on-line. URL: www.who.int/water_sanitation_health/Globassessment/Global1.htm. Downloaded October 24, 2002.

SI UNITS AND CONVERSIONS

Unit	Quantity	Symbol	Conversion
Base units			
meter	length	m	1 m = 3.2808 inches
kilogram	mass	kg	1 kg = 2.205 pounds
second	time	s	
ampere	electric current	A	
kelvin	thermodynamic temperature	K	1 K = 1°C = 1.8°F
candela	luminous intensity	cd	
mole	amount of substance	mol	
Supplementary units			
radian	plane angle	rad	p/2 rad = 90°
steradian	solid angle	sr	
Derived units			
coulomb	quantity of electricity	C	
cubic meter	volume	m^3	1 m^3 = 1.308 $yards^3$
farad	capacitance	F	
henry	inductance	H	
hertz	frequency	H_z	
joule	energy	J	1 J = 0.2389 calories
kilogram per cubic meter	density	$kg\ m^{-3}$	1 $kg\ m^{-3}$ = 0.0624 lb. $ft.^{-3}$
lumen	luminous flux	lm	
lux	illuminance	lx	
meter per second	speed	$m\ s^{-1}$	1 $m\ s^{-1}$ = 3.281 ft. s^{-1}
meter per second squared	acceleration	$m\ s^{-2}$	
mole per cubic meter	concentration	$mol\ m^{-3}$	
newton	force	N	1 N = 7.218 lb. force
ohm	electric resistance	Ω	

(continues)

SI UNITS AND CONVERSIONS (continued)

Unit	Quantity	Symbol	Conversion
Derived units			
pascal	pressure	Pa	1 Pa = 0.145 lb. in.$^{-2}$
radian per second	angular velocity	rad s^{-1}	
radian per second squared	angular acceleration	rad s^{-2}	
square meter	area	m^2	1 m^2 = 1.196 yards^2
tesla	magnetic flux density	T	
volt	electromotive force	V	
watt	power	W	1 W = 3.412 Btu h^{-1}
weber	magnetic flux	Wb	

PREFIXES USED WITH SI UNITS

Prefixes attached to SI units alter their value.

Prefix	Symbol	Value
atto	a	$\times 10^{-18}$
femto	f	$\times 10^{-15}$
pico	p	$\times 10^{-12}$
nano	n	$\times 10^{-9}$
micro	μ	$\times 10^{-6}$
milli	m	$\times 10^{-3}$
centi	c	$\times 10^{-2}$
deci	d	$\times 10^{-1}$
deca	da	$\times 10$
hecto	h	$\times 10^{2}$
kilo	k	$\times 10^{3}$
mega	M	$\times 10^{6}$
giga	G	$\times 10^{9}$
tera	T	$\times 10^{12}$

Index

Page numbers in *italic* refer to illustrations.

DATE			